The Beckoning Sea

The Beckoning Sea

Stories from my life at sea and elsewhere

Bernhard Abrahamsson

The Beckoning Sea
Stories from my life at sea and elsewhere

Copyright © 2008 by Bernhard Abrahamsson

iUniverse books may be ordered through booksellers or by contacting:

iUniverse
1663 Liberty Drive
Bloomington, IN 47403
www.iuniverse.com
1-800-Authors (1-800-288-4677)

ISBN: 978-1-4401-0265-3 (sc)
ISBN: 978-1-4401-0266-0 (e)

Print information available on the last page.

iUniverse rev. date: 03/25/2015

For

Alby, Leah and Maya

so they may know about their grandfather and his times

Table of Contents

BOOK ONE
THE BECKONING SEA

Introduction

Much has happened to ships and the people who man them since I went to sea in 1944 at age fourteen. The seafaring life of my youth does not exist anymore. Soon, descriptions of it may only be those of inventive writers' imaginations, the subject of fictitious adventures. But I want my grandchildren, Alby, Maya, and Leah to know some of the long ago reality as I experienced it as a child, seaman, and ship's officer; about the beckoning sea.

A dilemma presents itself immediately: How do I tell them? And what shall I tell? Shall I tell of particular events as I recall them? Or shall I merely relate, in a chronological order, how my life progressed? I will follow the former approach because I believe the sum of these events will give the flow of time and context of my life.

What to tell is more difficult. My wife has a book about memoir writing titled *Inventing the Truth*. I have not read it because I want my writings to be as much as possible unaffected by others' perceptions about how to present memories. Nevertheless, the title is evocative and does carry a certain weight. I am keenly aware that time affects memory and some of my stories may have gained or lost details as, over the years, my telling was often prompted by the setting in which they were told. Even so, they are true. Although people who have been part of my life may recall events differently, these are my memories as I recall them.

Many events are not recorded here. Among these are things better forgotten but still remembered, just as there are those worthy of remembrance but now forgotten. And, of course, there are things that are not to be told because they are hurtful, shameful, embarrassing, or intimately private.

And now to the task.

Seduced by the sea

The Story begins
in Stockholm, Sweden, where I was born in 1930. My first memory is of Bjurholmsplan 28-B. It is a small, dark apartment on the ground floor with a kitchen, living-cum-bedroom plus an alcove. Windows, facing the back-yard, rarely opened because the alley cats could come in and my mother was afraid of them. She often told a story from her childhood village in Latvia. A cat had come in through a window and killed a baby. People claimed that it had seen the pulse in the baby's throat and, trying to catch the "mouse", ripped it apart. As a child I also feared cats and, even today, I have no affection for them.

My three sisters sleep in the living room, my parents in the kitchen, I and my two brothers in the alcove where there are two beds – basically the apartment is a wall-to-wall bed. The bathroom has a toilet and a cold-water tap.

I love it because, as the youngest, at 4 or 5 years, I bathe in the warmth and concerns of the older siblings and my parents. My favorite, much longed for, event is when someone is using the communal warm-water bathtub in the hallway outside the apartment. Lying in my bed in the alcove I am lulled to sleep by the soothing monotony of the running water which drowns out every other sound – my parents' talking in the kitchen, my sisters' bickering, and my brothers' wrestling match.

I have read recently that the sound of running water brings memories of the womb and its safety to a small child. Even today I can feel and remember the tranquility that the murmuring water brought me. Perhaps that's the reason I today have a machine with a brook's purling sound next to my bed.

This was home until age five.

The apartment house was located in one of the poorest areas of south Stockholm; poor, but by no means a slum. There were several connected houses set in such a way that they formed a square with three entries, or exits. One entry was at a corner; another was mid-block, almost diagonally across from the first, while the third was a covered passage, mid-way between the two, providing a walk-way through the complex. The square was large, at least from a 4-year old's perspective. A couple of saplings, no flowers, a sandy hill and a few benches completed the environment, the park. To me it was a good, joyous and safe place. Only many years later could I see its essential dreariness and potential danger as it may have been perceived by my parents.

The "great" economic depression was at its peak if, indeed, depressions do peak. Many of the tenants around the square were Jewish and, with anti-Semitism rampant and strong, the difficulty of escaping, should it be necessary, through any of the narrow, and easily blocked, exits was clear to everyone. In 1935, before I started first grade, we, as did many of the others, moved elsewhere into a bigger apartment.

Traditionally, in those years leases started and ended on October first known as "moving day". Those who moved brought all their belongings out onto the pavement. To have a work crew do it was too expensive so friends and family usually helped out. Next came the long wait for the movers to arrive. The sidewalks were filled with household goods, the streets with already loaded trucks and horse drawn carriages. I still remember sitting atop our belongings waiting for the big adventure. My next memory is waking up in unfamiliar surroundings, our new apartment at Vetegatan 8.

It would be home until my mother moved away after father died in 1962. By that time all the children were long gone into their own apartments, and I had not been in Sweden for many years. Nevertheless, I took the "loss" of the old apartment very hard. While mother and my siblings continued to be my focal points and anchors in Stockholm, my home was gone. I sensed that loss as if a big part of my childhood had come to an end, an end that would be final and total when mother died fourteen years later, in 1976.

The new neighborhood was very different from the old one. It was entirely open, not hemmed in by fences or buildings. Our apartment was in a free standing three story rectangular building with five entrances each of which was independent of the others, yet connected to them through a continuous basement. There were ten buildings, similar, but not identical, to ours standing side-by-side. Streets separated the buildings into pairs with an open landscaped area between them. We called it "the yard". In addition to the front entrance, each building could be entered from the yard, so, all in all, there were ten independent entrances, a set-up that gave a sense of security. Indeed, my father cautioned me to be alert to signs of danger and not always use the same entrance. I would often circle the house, then use different doors from the back or front and reach our entrance through the basement.

One important feature of the basement was the row of communal baths to which each tenant was assigned a weekly time slot. Since these were the only hot water facilities in the building, they were busy. The bathers would leave and return to their apartments in various stages of undress. Hoping to catch titillating sights, many young people would walk back and forth in the passageway; at times it was rewarding.

Having no hot water in the apartment, my mother would boil water on the stove for her laundry, then rinse it in the, almost always, ice cold water. Over the long run this affected her hands and, particularly, fingers. She suffered much pain in her older age. The gas stove worked on a "pay as you go" basis. To get a certain volume of gas one inserted store-bought tokens into the meter located in the kitchen. Given the cost of gas, my mother had hard choices to make: laundry or food? That she managed so well has always been a wonder to me. After the war, things changed. Gas became cheaper and ultimately the token system disappeared.

Added to her workload was the tenants' obligation to keep clean the common area outside the apartment. On each floor there were five apartments sharing that obligation. It was hard work to sweep and mop the floor of the outside landing and stairs. She and my sisters took on that duty. They never asked me or my brothers to do it. We had no sympathy for such chores clearly reserved by nature for women. The sea taught me otherwise and, whenever I was home, I became the cleaner of our apartment, both inside and out.

Entering the world

At age seven I started school. I looked forward to it. I knew the way; it was within easy walking distance, and my brother, Herman, went there. It was a complex of friendly looking, new and modern buildings with grassy playgrounds, near a large park. My expectations were high, but for naught. There were too many children for the school to accommodate. The overflow, including me, was assigned to a very old school built in the early 1800s. It was far away, forty-five minutes by foot. No such thing as school buses. One possibility was the electric street-car, but that was a luxury not available to me.

My best friend was Sigvard, the only other Jewish boy living on our street. We would meet every morning to have company on the long walk to school. Sometimes we walked together talking about whatever came to mind. Often, as time passed, we would walk separately in the sense that, while we were still together, we were yet apart, as each of us receded into his own world of fantasy and day-dreaming. These forays into our inner worlds became often the topics of conversation on our walks. Our fantasies ranged everywhere. Imagine if we had the power to change our world. What would we do? Suppose we were in charge of the radio station? Or the newspapers? What if we had a magic wand? Could we then finish the war? Could we end anti-Semitism? How could we get back at our tormentors in school? And so on. Pure day dreaming. These escapes from reality made our, basically humdrum, lives bearable and hopeful.

Sigvard was a short, somewhat pudgy boy, characteristics that followed him into adulthood. They belied his innate abilities that lead to the high governmental office he eventually reached. After a short period at sea as a cabin boy, he became a waiter at Stockholm's Grand Hotel, an achievement in itself. He became active in the labor union, advanced to its chairmanship and, after a long career in labor politics, was appointed by the King to be the governor of one of the twenty-four administrative districts of Sweden; a very high position, indeed. We remained in touch throughout the years.

The school was big, and not at all inviting. That Greta Garbo had once attended it did not change anything; we did not know who she was. The classrooms were in one single, huge building made of grey granite blocks. It was surrounded by a large, bare, asphalted yard, our playground. No play equipment, not even a simple swing. At the end of the yard was another, more recent, but equally uninviting, structure. It was the gym. In its basement was the workshop where we learned simple wood working. There was also a large music room for the school band and the teaching of various wind and brass instruments.

I wanted very much to learn the trumpet and to join the school band. The teacher was nice and encouraging. He took his time to evaluate my potential. My lips, he said, were perfect for the trumpet; I beamed. But, much to his regrets, I was musically limited to the snare drum; I did not beam. However, he comforted me, I should know that the drum was the most important instrument in a marching band; I beamed again. And so I learned to drum. I joined the band for a few events, but, mostly, was held in "reserve" because of my, as they said, "odd sense of rhythm."

Just beyond one side of the yard, and below it, was another asphalt patch surrounding a smaller, very old building, the first school in the area. It now housed the school's nurse and dentist. It was a horrible place. All students had free, mandated dental care. It was usually a brutal affair. No pain killing medication, no high-speed drill. The motor that drove the drill was located in the waiting room. It's loud whirring, screeching sound announced what was going on in the dental chair and sent most of those awaiting their turns into paralyzing fear and prolonged crying. My memory of the place is of being held down in the chair by the nurse while the dentist did his work. We visited the clinic a couple of times each year. With hindsight it was good care; I have had few dental problems in adult life. But my lasting memory is of the waiting room where I joined the crying crowd trying to drown out the horrible noise of the drill announcing what was in store for us.

The classrooms were large and located off long, wide, high-ceilinged corridors. The spaces seemed enormous, we were, after all, rather small, seven-year olds and, whether intended or not, they intimidated us. We were unhappy most of the time. Seating was in alphabetical order, so I was in the very first seat. The room was neither cheerful nor drab; it was just big and took time getting used to. I have no really clear memories of the teachers, except that I was afraid of the gym instructor, liked the music teacher, loved the one in carpentry, and tried to stay out of the way of the home room teacher.

I was not the only one in fear of the gym teacher. He had a military background and was always addressed as "lieutenant". He was not ill-tempered or mean, but his method of punishing disciplinary infractions was unusual. The offending student had to bend down so that his behind protruded well in the air. Depending on the severity of the offense, the shorts remained in place or had to be pulled down. Gripping a gym shoe by the heel and holding it like a sword, he turned it so the sole faced the offender's buttocks. Wielding the shoe like an axe he then hit the behind with a downward stroke so the ridges of the sole tore at the skin. Very painful, and more so if the skin was bared.

One day I overheard a girl being excused from gym because of bad migraine. I had no idea what migraine might be, but if it worked for her, why not for me? Limping I approached the lieutenant, and pitifully asked to be excused because of my migraine. He looked at me suspiciously and asked, "Where does it hurt?" "My right knee; I can barely walk", I responded. This earned me his "bared skin" treatment.

The carpentry teacher was also a disciplinarian, but a kind one. The only punishment he meted out was to put the offender in charge of the glue pot where the smell was rather odious. I learned a great deal about tools, wood and wood working. However, this teacher had also taught my older brother, Lennart, and he could not understand why two brothers would have such vastly different abilities. But he did not hold my inferior skills against me. I, like the other students, simply loved him.

The home room teacher was, basically, a good man, I think. He was studying for an advanced education degree at the university and was probably the victim of many, seemingly conflicting, theories that affected his running of the class. Essentially the rules changed weekly, or monthly.

We never really knew what he wanted of us, except that, for him, recess was a relief from students, and no one, no matter what, could stay inside at that time. I have no recollection of his being either mean or kind. He was just there.

One feature of the curriculum was noteworthy. It mandated religious instruction. The course, "Knowledge of Christianity", was taught throughout the eight years of primary school. I, however, participated only until the Old Testament had been covered which happened, I believe, at the end of third grade. Thereafter I had a choice: continue with the study of the New Testament, including the official Hymnal and attending regular church services, or I could attend Hebrew School for an equal amount of time. With hindsight I am impressed that, given the times, the educational system gave the Jewish community such opportunities to maintain and strengthen its cultural and religious identity.

The students showed the innate meanness of their age in a school atmosphere tinged with a strong element of anti-Semitism. One boy had a picture of Hitler on the inside of his desk cover. This student was good at sports, particularly gymnastics, and taunted me for my ineptitude in that area. One day he decided to show everyone, once and for all, how superior he was to me. He challenged me to do several continuous cartwheels on the asphalt surface. I did not accept because I had never managed to do even one cartwheel. Triumphantly he began on his own in front of the admiring crowd. I looked at the spectacle, and felt only ill will toward him. I wished him, fervently, bad luck. And that he had. He slipped, broke his wrist, a finger or two, and scratched his face. That day I was grateful for the hard surface of the playground.

The few Jews in the school were spread thinly among the general student body and had little support from each other. But I and Sigvard were lucky; we were in the same class. We did not like to go outside during recess because most new students, but also old ones, tried to prove themselves by beating up the "dirty Jews." But we were not allowed to stay indoors. The home-room teacher needed his break, so we had to face the social environment of the playground.

One day, a tall, strong, burly boy showed up in our class. Sigvard and I dreaded the first recess. Surely, this fellow would claim his place in the game of popularity by giving us a sound beating. How could we possibly defend ourselves against a giant like this?

Outside we were surrounded by a number of teasing and taunting students. They expected the new boy to join in but, when he showed no signs of doing so, some decided not to wait and began pushing us. As usual, we defended ourselves as best we could, but not expecting much success. But this time we managed to hold them off; some even left in haste. How could that be? It had never happened before. As the crowd thinned, we saw that the new boy had joined the fray. On our side! He was the cause of our success, and the end of the fight.

The class, including the Hitler-adoring gymnast, tried to befriend him. He was open and pleasant to anyone who approached him. But it was Sigvard and I who became his particular friends; and we kept company both in and out of school. I lost contact with him in the late 1960s. Carl-Axel Lunding, or "Lunkan" as he was called, became a well known sculptor extensively exhibited in Sweden and elsewhere. Several of his pieces are in the permanent collection of Stockholm's Museum of Modern Art. He died in 2006.

His talents were recognized early. The carpentry teacher taught him rudimentary wood carving skills, and Calle made a number of wooden figures of seamen and fishermen, much like those that today can be found in many gift stores. He gave me several of these, but, over the years, they have disappeared. Last time we met, in 1964, I received two small, preliminary models of works he contemplated for submission to a contest. These I still have.

The Jewish community had a welfare center where children could go after school.

Its name was *Arbetsstugan*, literally translated as *The Work Cottage*. We referred to it as "the Cottage." It was located on top of a steep hill another half hour's walk from the school in a direction away from our apartment. Walking home in the evening took well over one hour. We did our home work at the Cottage, were served dinner, and, very importantly, had some instruction in book binding, broom making, carpentry, and sewing and crocheting. I am not sure if the first two activities were intended to merely keep us busy, or to give us employable skills. Sewing and crocheting, on the other hand, were very useful for mending clothes and darning socks; I certainly used these skills at sea.

From fifth grade I was accepted to *Sodra Kommunala Mellanskolan*, that is, *The South Communal Middle School*. It was also far from my home, and, since it was in a direction opposite from the old school, I stopped attending the Cottage.

I have no particular memories of that school, its teachers or curriculum. I did enjoy the studying, but, even so, quit after two years when the mandatory school requirements were fulfilled. With hindsight that was a mistake because graduation from the Middle School, two years further on, would have been a first step toward higher education. In later years I would consider it a lost opportunity. However, I received a good grounding in German and some basics of English; both stood me in good stead in my later seafaring.

Why Does the Sea Beckon?

Given my ordinary childhood, why did I choose a seafaring life? Not an easy question to answer and I have not, in the past, given it much thought. As I think of it now, I believe the choice was less the result of deliberate design and pursuit than of circumstances that led me in that direction. Also, whether she intended it or not, my mother influenced my choice.

My childhood was lonely even though the area where we lived teemed with children and young adults because the apartment houses were reserved for, what was then called, "child rich" families. The friends I did have were few and, like myself, at odds with the pervasive moods, fads and interests of the youth in the neighborhood all of which centered on sports, mainly soccer, ice hockey, and "bandy". The latter was similar to hockey. Played on ice skates, a hard ball was used instead of a puck, and the stick, used to hit the ball, was curved at the end.

I had difficulty relating to these, or any other, team sports. Not that I didn't try. But always being the last to be chosen for a team, and often not chosen at all, made me a fugitive into the world of vicarious adventures and achievements, into the world of books, into the world of reading and day-dreaming. Many of the books were romantic stories from the sea – I remember, in particular, a children's book, *Captain Grant's Children*, by Jules Verne. Other books were by Frederick Marryat, and by a Swedish seaman, Forsell, who had become a fur trapper in the Northwest Territories of Canada. His descriptions of the wild, the trapper's life and his previous adventures at sea, made strong impressions on me. I saw glimpses of a world totally outside the one I knew. I day-dreamed of the kind of life I read about. I became an incurable romantic; I wanted to see the world.

But these were dreams. Reality was starkly different. What occupations were, realistically, available to me? At that time there were no school counselors to advise and help. The various fields available, to aspire to, were those I saw around me in the neighborhood. Doctors, lawyers, or other professionals did not live there. We had a police officer who regularly walked his German shepherd in the evenings. That was an elevated and somewhat abstract status, certainly beyond my hopes. Same with the taxi driver who wore a uniform and had a car of his own. Sigvard's father was a typewriter repairman, but that, too, seemed outside the realm of possibilities. Others, more within my reach because they were concrete and visible, were the barber, the baker, and the shoemaker who had their stores along our street. Less visible, but well noted, were the longshoremen, and, importantly, the seamen, most of whom were not expected home until the war ended. Their very absence was mysterious and alluring but, with the war on, it seemed futile to consider such a future. Nevertheless, it had a hold on me, and it steered my thoughts to another, almost sea faring occupation, lighthouse keeping. The lighthouse was on a small island outside the immediate neighborhood and appealed very much to my romantic mind. But the sea and lighthouse keeping were just that, romantic dreams not to be pursued seriously.

And, of course, there were construction workers, carpenters and painters, like my father. These various occupations set the limits of my ambitions, and, within these, I was drawn to the trade of the baker and, particularly, to that of the shoemaker.

The bakery exuded wonderful aromas and displayed tempting stuff in the windows; but no outsider was allowed into the work area so I had no real perception, at that time, of what the work entailed. The shoemaker, on the other hand, was very welcoming. His youngest daughter and I were good friends and we visited him often in his workshop. I simply loved the intriguing display of tools and materials, the smell of shoe polish, glue and leather. In that trade I could see myself, and, indeed, throughout my life I have hankered to learn it. A bosun (boatswain) on one of my ships taught me some rudimentary skills of the trade and that is the extent to which I pursued that ambition.

Like most young boys I had several jobs as "errand boy" during school vacations and afternoons. These jobs were desirable because a good performance might lead to an apprenticeship and a "career". At the age of eleven, or twelve, I worked as such for the major evening paper in Stockholm. Each day, just after noon, I had to pick up a list of the day's final quotations from the stock exchange to be included in that evening's paper. One day my return with the list took me into the path of the changing of the guard at the royal palace. It was the ceremonial parade of the horse mounted guard, an infrequent event. Needless to say, I stopped to watch the spectacle. My delayed return forced my boss to obtain the stock quotations by phone in order to meet the paper's deadline. This worked so well that using the telephone for this purpose became the future norm. He received much praise for his innovative initiative. I, having been the agent for the implementation of that procedure, received nothing but rebuke for tardiness. But the job had its rewards, at least in retrospect.

Once I had to deliver a small package to a Swedish composer named Moses Pergament. The significance of this delivery did not occur to me until many years later. Moses Pergament was born in Finland but had settled in Sweden some years before Finland obtained its independence from Russia. I had heard his name mentioned in some context of no interest to me, and I knew he was Jewish. My instructions were to deliver the package to him personally and to receive a properly signed receipt. I made the delivery to his apartment located in the fanciest part of town. The house was very impressive and so was the apartment. The housekeeper let me into the living room where Moses Pergament was in the company of an older gentleman. I handed him the package, he gave it to the other gentleman who signed the receipt. But I had strict instructions and asked for Moses Pergament's signature. With the twice signed receipt in hand, I turned to leave. A call from the older man stopped me. He came up to me, patted me on the shoulder, thanked for the delivery and gave me a tip. This kind man was Jean Sibelius, a close friend of Moses Pergament.

Shortly thereafter I applied for a new position as delivery boy, this time with a small factory producing rain gear. The interview went splendidly. The interviewer, who was the owner, was very pleased with me and outlined in great detail my expected illustrious career pattern with the company. I would start doing deliveries and running general errands under the supervision of the Junior Stock Clerk. A couple of years in that work would bring me to his position, that is, I would then be doing everything the Assistant Stock Clerk demanded, and I would be delegating work to the delivery boy. A couple of years further on I would be a full-fledged stock clerk; that is, I would be the boss of the Junior Clerk. Together we would bring goods from the factory floor into the stock room and retrieve them when needed for delivery to customers, not very different from the previous work. A large number of years later I would become the Chief Stock Clerk, and that would essentially be the end of my career with them. He estimated that path would take a bit in excess of forty years.

But there were other tantalizing features. I would have paid vacation each year. Not many days during my first terms of employment, but towards the end I would get the maximum: two whole weeks at full pay. "AND", he stressed, "by age sixty, or so, you will get a pension. You'll get paid without having to work for it. We will take care of that. Where else can you find such an opportunity?"

I was overwhelmed by his kindness and generosity. I was stunned at my prospects. How had I come into such an incredible situation? I had a job. I would have a career. I would have paid vacations, and a pension. My father certainly had none of these things. I, the youngest in the family, faced a life beyond compare.

I could not wait to get home to tell my mother of my exceptionally good fortune. Running breathlessly into the apartment I told her everything expecting her to be as pleased as was I. But she looked at me somewhat bemused by my enthusiasm. Then, bemusement was replaced by concern. Her eyes left my face and she looked at something far away, then returned her gaze to me. "Is this what you want to do?" she asked, "working with rain coats? In the stock room? How will that let you see the world?" I did not understand her and did not know how to respond. She did not wait for my silence to end but simply took off her apron, put on her coat and asked me to take her to my would-be place of opportunity.

The owner greeted us cordially. He probably expected to receive my mother's gratitude for having offered her son such a desirable way out of poverty and social inferiority. He was wrong. My mother told him, in essence, to "take his job and shove it". "You've not offered him a future", she said, "You are trying to rob him of it". What he was offering was to stifle, not to say kill, a young boy's hopes and dreams for the future, to smother any ambition to realize them, and to replace them all with the most hum-drum, pedestrian life she could imagine. "Never", she said, "will my boy set foot in this place". And we left.

The further we left the factory behind, the angrier she seemed to get. I had never seen her so agitated. At home, she related the story to my father, sisters and brothers and anyone who cared to listen. They seemed to understand her, but I did not. I had seen many other instances that, in my mind, warranted more ire than this one. What I did understand, however, was that my mother wanted me to dream, wanted me to hope, and wanted me to pursue and act accordingly. I sensed my romantic ideas had her approval. And so, as my options had narrowed, my choice focused on the sea.

At this time, when I was eleven or twelve, I made friends, in school, with a boy whose father was a sea captain sailing outside the blockade. The stories my friend told about his father and grandfather were spellbinding. They were stories about the majesty of sailing ships, the heroic battles against the sea and adversaries in port. About strange lands, peoples and customs, of dangers at sea and ashore, all part of a seaman's life. The grandfather had been a gold prospector in Alaska in the late 1800s and was said to still have a legal claim there. He also had a large property on Runmaro, a big island outside Stockholm, where the grandmother still lived.

As our friendship deepened, I was often invited to the island. We spent much of the summer sailing a small boat around the archipelago. What stays in my mind is a trip we took to meet the father when his ship finally reached Swedish waters. We caught up with the ship as it reached the pilot station. Just a few words, and a couple of packages, were exchanged between father and son and we parted our ways. The encounter was unsentimental, but warmth, love, and respect were palpable.

By age thirteen I was, essentially, obsessed with dreams of seafaring. By fourteen the dreams began to be realized. Again I was an errand boy, this time with a firm located at Jarntorget (the Iron Square) in the Old City. The store, Grolls, is long since gone. Last time I visited the area in 2002 there was a coffee shop in its place. Grolls specialized in work clothes of all kinds including seamen's gear and I had a busy time delivering to homes, construction sites and ships. Of course, the ships sparked my imagination and I often thought about asking for a job. But I was intimidated by both the ships and their crews. How could I, a boy with a bicycle and no skills whatsoever, enter their exalted world?

One day there was a delivery to a small ship loading bricks at a leisurely pace. The ship was not intimidating and the work did not seem to require much skill. I mustered all my courage and asked the seaman to whom I had just given the package if there was a job for me on that ship. He, the owner-captain, told me yes, but I needed my parents' permission. I don't recall their reactions, but they did sign the paper. My future lay at sea.

There were probably many reasons for my parents' permission. Work was scarce, income needed. I don't think "a mouth less to feed" played a role. A bigger consideration was probably that the ship would mostly stay at the pier allowing me to come home in the evenings. And the ship's infrequent trips would only take us to some close-by islands, so working on the ship would not take me far away; it would not be much different from what I was already doing. And, who knows, maybe I would get the sea out of my mind.

There may have been other reasons as well. To my father it was clear that none of his sons would follow his preferred path. I was merely the last in line. He did not understand why, but, with the outcome of the war certain, he did sense new opportunities for us and he would not stand in the way. While he and I got along well, we were not close. We had few truly meaningful conversations; his was a passive role in my life.

It was different with my mother. We were very close. She was a crucial and active presence in my life, particularly when I got older. I do know she wanted me to break away from the neighborhood that molded our life. She may have seen the brick schooner as the first step in that process.

Father
My father's presence in my life was mainly felt by his absence. I really did not know him well. He was a house painter by trade and a peddler by choice, hence long absences from home. In stature he was fairly short but

very strong both physically and mentally. He was born in 1889 in Potel, a small town outside Kovno in Lithuania. At the age of seven, in 1896, he arrived in Sweden with his parents.

Notwithstanding his young age at arrival and getting his formal education by attending the mandatory eight grades of school in Stockholm, he was essentially a product of the shtetl of his birth. Religion was to him a set of unending, unbending rules. He considered himself religious because he adhered to, what was to him, the most important Jewish precepts of behavior, that is, the daily activities of prayer and "legen tefillin" which is the Yiddish expression for putting on the phylacteries, a set of ritual straps and capsules containing the Ten Commandments. Also, he frequently attended services, and kept a kosher home. To follow these precepts and to make his children, particularly the boys, do so constituted his educational and fatherly mission. The mission was not successful. None of the children followed his path.

He had a very traditional Jewish approach to education and personal freedom. His unyielding lack of understanding of the times led to lasting friction and dissent with his sons. For my sisters it was different. Few, if any, religious demands were imposed on them. He compensated for this "leniency" by being adamantly strict in his refusal to support any education whatsoever for them. To him work did not require education, only adaptation and commitment.

Lilly, the oldest, fourteen years my senior, trained as a Hollerith operator, an early data management system, and worked all her life for the Swedish State Monopoly for Spirits and Wines. Maj, the youngest of the girls, was six years older than I. She worked in various offices but, after marriage, stayed home most of the time. Nanny, the second oldest, was twelve years older than I and the only one in the family to strive for, and get, what was at that time a "higher" education. She graduated with a total of ten years of schooling, from the Middle School I attended at a later stage. Hers was a great achievement since most people stopped after the eighth grade.

However, Nanny met much opposition from our father. With a large family in close quarters, the only privacy to be had was in the bathroom. There is where Nanny spent much of her study time, mostly at night. Father, trying to save electricity, and to thwart her, removed the lightbulb. She countered by sitting in the kitchen window where the streetlight was strong. In the face of such determination, he gave in and the final outcome was Nanny's graduation. All in all, I believe there was genuine and strong affection between my father and his daughters.

Also, he did not believe in education for his sons. My brothers did not go beyond eighth grade. He reluctantly accepted my attending the Ships' Officers' School in Stockholm, and that was only after my aunt pointed out that a ship captain's 50th birthday was always noted in the society pages of the major newspapers. When I later pursued studies in the US, he was very disappointed. Work, not study, was life's essence. To him, I was wasting precious time.

Since I left home at an early age, I was not affected by long-term exposure to his demands, and I had a basically positive image of him, an image that in later years became somewhat static: a man sitting in his chair in a corner of the living room, incessantly smoking and with a cup, no, a glass, of coffee at his side. He only moved when he had to, that is, to take care of bodily needs and to prepare his coffee. The coffee was known to the family as "Yankel-coffee", Yankel being the Yiddish variant of his name Jacob. The coffee was fairly good in the morning when fresh, but weakened progressively during the course of the day as he kept on adding hot water to the pot on the stove. We jokingly said that, more often than not, one could see the bottom of the glass through the coffee even though he used cream in it. He was a heavy smoker and early development of emphysema did not affect this habit; he smoked several packs a day until his very end.

He had a robust sense of humor. As he had arrived in Sweden at the age of seven, he went to school, as did everyone else, until eighth grade, so, in essence, making Swedish his mother tongue. But people usually assumed he had just arrived in Sweden because he looked very "foreign". They were surprised by his good command of the Swedish language and often asked how long he had been in the country. His answer was, truthfully, "more than three years." He never contradicted the admiring comments about his extraordinary linguistic feat in such a short time.

One of his favorite stories was about a job he had to paint the fence around one of Stockholm's largest mental institutions. Salient to the story is that he had a cousin whom he resembled. They also had the same family name. The cousin had a high psychiatric position at the hospital and was well recognized by both patients and staff. As my father was painting the fence from the outside, one of the patients on the inside observed him with great interest. Finally he asked, "Are you Dr. Abrahamsson?" My father could not resist the temptation to joke and answered "Yes". Next question from the patient: "How much do you get paid for that job?" Again father said, jokingly, "I don't get paid, but I don't have to pay very much for doing it." After some silence, the man on the inside said, "I think you are on the wrong side of the fence!" That was a retort my father relished and he told it again and again.

I knew that he had never understood my choice of work, nor did he grasp the nature of it. But I was totally unprepared for his first attempt to offer me sage advice. In 1957, as a 27-year old ship's officer, I was offered a job with the major Israeli shipping company, the ZIM Line. Shortly before my departure for Marseilles where I was to board the ship, my father engaged me in a serious discussion about, of all things, women. In essence, was I aware of the "dangers" that awaited me in the far-away places I was about to see? He urged me strongly to bring a supply of condoms and, if I was too embarrassed to purchase them at the pharmacy, he would be happy to do so.

This, his main piece of advice, reached me, as I said, at the age of 27 when I had been at sea for 13 years. I did not have the heart to set him straight and thanked him for his advice and concern. As a farewell and bon-voyage gift he gave me a "six-pack" of the essential commodity.

I always wondered how he could sit every day in his cigarette and coffee infested corner brooding on something without any apparent interest in anything around him. Once I persuaded him to read a book, a popular mystery. He devoured it, said it was very good and went back into his own world. He never took the trouble to find another book.

He would often have conversations, evolving into debates, with himself. What they were all about is impossible to say, but he would move his lips, smile or frown, shake his head and shrug his shoulders from time to time as if he felt the debate, however one-sided, was silly at best, futile at worst.

What could possibly have gone through his mind? I believe he was brooding on his past, revisiting it and trying to make sense of it. Don't we all do that at times? I certainly do; but his dream world was different, it had become his life. I have the feeling that he got stuck in his past and, realizing that it was, indeed, irrevocably past and that his future was behind him, he may have preferred to stay in his inner world where he could still live a "what if" life in which the past could be changed and the future was still bright.

Part of that "what if" world may have included his dream of becoming a successful antique dealer. To find those ultimate treasures that he always thought would be the pay-off of his peddling trips. After all, that had happened to his brother to whom he had not spoken for most of his life. Why I don't know.

He always came back from his peddling trips with paintings of uneven quality. Usually they were not signed and for good reason. However, if the artist was ashamed of his work, father decided to assume the burden and sign for him. Problem was he did not know for whom to sign. And he faced a dilemma: while he wanted a signature, he also wanted to be scrupulously honest. He solved it by signing in block letters "D. RECK", *dreck* being Yiddish for shit. It certainly did not enhance the intrinsic quality of the works, but father felt good about his ethical solution to the dilemma.

My father was a skilled house painter. In his time there were only oil based paints and no colors were pre-mixed. It was the skill of the painter that determined the quality of the paint, its color and applications. Mostly he worked on construction projects, but, with the depression in full swing, there was not much lasting employment. His commuting by bicycle made him a strong, not to say a virtuoso, pedal pusher, and this skill prepared him well for the peddling circuit which became, increasingly, his main occupation. He merely needed to add a package holder to the bike and the perfect peddling vehicle was born.

I don't know what hours he kept during his forays into the country side, but construction work required him to be "early to bed, and early to rise", but it did not make him particularly healthy, certainly not wealthy, and not suitably wise. His relations with my older brothers, Lennart and Herman, were not good; he simply could not relax his demands and expectations that they follow his path.

His handling of an incident with Lennart, ten years my senior, was particularly unkind and unwise. When he was sixteen (this was in 1936), my brother rebelled against the daily ritual of "legen tefillin". He flung them on the floor, uttered some deprecatory remarks and refused to make amends. To my father this was heresy and desecration of the gravest kind. He threw Lennart out of the house and the very mentioning of his name was forbidden. My mother kept in touch with Lennart, but I was only peripherally aware of him until, when I was eighteen, he visited me aboard my ship in Goteborg. After that we grew increasingly closer over the years.

My father's irreconcilable, perhaps strong, but unwise, nature struck me very forcefully when Lennart told a story of his working on the same site as father during the war years. At lunch time father opened his food package but, before starting to eat, he noticed Lennart nearby smoking a cigarette with no food in sight. He asked, "Where is your lunch?" to which Lennart answered, "Don't have any." Father shrugged his shoulders, "Too bad!"

End of conversation, end of father-son encounter.

In later years my father softened, became more reflective and tolerant. Grandchildren were arriving and he felt a sense of completion; the family was beyond his molding powers and doing well. He spoke often about, and to, Lennart. They reconciled, agreed to let the past rest and, while never warm, a certain degree of affection developed. The whole family grew closer during those years.

Herman and I never had the same run-ins with father. Perhaps his disappointment with his first-born son lowered his expectations for the younger ones. Perhaps Herman's volunteering for the army of the fledgling State of Israel in 1947 gave him both pride and satisfaction. Perhaps it also told him that Herman's actions, and my earlier choice of seafaring, reflected changes he could not control or resist. Perhaps his brooding gave him some reflective background to further develop his "what if" world. Perhaps the "what if" was getting closer to his "what is" and he found peace of mind.

In his later years he developed an intense fear of losing his independence. The looming possibility of some form of nursing care frightened him. I believe this was also part of his brooding "what if" world. He knew he was not able to read, or understand, the fine legal print on whatever papers may have needed his signature, and he was distrustful of everyone, even his own family.

His solution was to simply refuse to sign anything at all. He did not lose his independence. He did not need nursing care. He died in 1962.

Holidays

Yesterday was Yom Kippur; the year 2007. As I sat in the sanctuary, long ago memories from my youth in Stockholm came forward. I saw my father who thought of himself as a religious man but, in reality, was merely observant of all the dictates of the religion as he saw them. I saw the two synagogues in the city: the Temple located centrally in the downtown area, and the smaller Polish Synagogue in the south.

We went to the smaller one which was generally referred to, in Yiddish, as the "Peylishe Shul", meaning the "Polish Synagogue". It took me about forty-five minutes to walk there. It was not a pleasant place, inside or out. No signs identified the building as a house of worship. Indeed, the windows were boarded up from the outside. The entrance was a simple, heavy steel gate that opened to a short staircase leading to a drab wooden door beyond which was a small foyer. To the left were heavy swinging doors leading to the main sanctuary. To the right were stairs leading to the balcony where the women were seated.

The main sanctuary was nicely decorated with guilt trimmings along the walls and heavy draperies covering the windows to prevent the sound of chanting from being heard outside. The Ark was against a wall with the *bima*, the podium where the Torah was read, in front of it. The pews were placed in four sections: one on each side next to the *bima*, and one on each side in front of it. The more prominent a congregant was, the closer to the *bima* was his seat. My father's was far back, close to the entrance.

The pews were such that in front of the seat was a high reading stand so that, when standing, the book was at eye-level. The stands were connected forming a solid wooden partition between each row. That feature was the only thing that appealed to me because when sitting down I was almost invisible to most of the people in the synagogue. There I could daydream, play with some small toy or just sit.

The service procedures were simple to follow. I stood up when my father did, sat down when he did, and mumbled something I did neither understand nor could pronounce whenever he did so. Any questions I asked were answered in Yiddish: "Freg nit asay fiel"- don't ask so much. The sermons were also given in Yiddish. While I did understand most words, the moral and philosophical contents eluded me. They were not intended for my age group and mostly we spent that time in the foyer trying to relieve our boredom and incomprehension by reading comic books.

My exposure to the synagogue and, in general, Jewish holidays did not create a feeling of belonging. Passover was a long evening filled with good food. But before getting to it, there was a long, long wait; a time of sitting still, being quiet until asked to read a small passage, and listening to the Exodus story meticulously told in every detail, in Hebrew, without deviation from the prescribed format. I understood nothing. Perhaps we sang some of the traditional songs, but I have no recollection of that.

Even Simchat Torah, the joyous celebration of the receipt of the Torah, was to me no different from Tisha b'Av, the sad commemoration of the destruction of the Second Temple. Indeed, I did not know there were happy Jewish holidays. As I grew older, and particularly when at sea, I took pains not to return home at those times.

These perceptions changed only when I met Varda. She came from a home and background where holidays were happy, solemn or sad as tradition prescribed, but never dismal or dreary. This attitude she conveyed to me shortly after we met. One day, somewhere in Netanya, we passed a house from which came sounds of a happy and noisy party. A couple of men in black suits and fedoras came out and, on the spur of the moment, invited us to join. That is, they brought me inside, perched me on a high bar stool where I joined them in drinking slivovitz. There were a lot of men in the room. In the back I could see a similarly large crowd of women, Varda among them. I did not give much thought to this separation of men from women. Customs are, after all, different in different countries.

There was singing, dancing, and much commotion. The slivovitz was plentiful and strong, the toasts frequent, and I became happier by the minute. After a while, Varda signaled from the other side of the room that it was time to leave. It was difficult to descend from my perch, but with help I did so. I shook hands with my new-found friends and went to fetch Varda. My route was rather circuitous and unsteady but I did reach the beginning of the women's domain. What could be more natural than to express my appreciation also to the women although none of them had shared any drinks with me? I hobbled over to the nearest lady extending my hand in a friendly manner. I was dumbfounded when she recoiled in horror. So did one or two more before Varda rescued me from further embarrassment by explaining my ignorant ways to the ladies and leading me away.

Outside she explained that we had just been celebrating Simchat Torah with an ultra-orthodox group. Although I did not understand their separation of the sexes, I had for the first time seen a truly joyful celebration of a Jewish holiday. That would be the norm for our future life.

My bar-mitzvah was not a memorable event. My father felt I needed private instruction. And so I went once a week for over a year to a man named Wolbe; his first names were August Wilhelm, but no one used them. He was an interesting and kind man from Germany and a convert to Judaism. He was not only observant, he was truly religious, he believed with all his heart.

My arrival at his apartment, at the same time each week, coincided with his reciting the Schemone-esre, the Silent Prayer, which is surrounded by its own ritual. It is read while standing in an immobile position and one may not disturb, in any way, the one reciting it. So I had strict instructions not to disturb Wolbe while he prayed, but actually recite it myself.

I did so and it created a problem. My reading was slow and halting; his fluent and rapid. Hence, by the time he finished, I was still at the very beginning. Now he could not disturb my devotion and so left me alone to pray, and that took a long time. When I finally finished, the allocated lesson time was long over and he released me from further study. This was repeated every week. My father was very happy. He thought I was immersed in my studies and made great progress. How else could he explain my staying beyond the agreed lesson time, and Wolbe's not asking for extra pay? Wolbe was happy that I prayed; that was the answer to everything. I was happy for the few demands put on me, for the easy time of preparation.

However, without study, there was no knowledge. I did not know anything applicable to my bar-mitzvah. I did not know my Torah portion, and, when in time, it was put before me, I could not read it. How I got through that day is still a mystery. Mother had prepared a big celebration. I received the customary accolades and gifts, but father was not as happy after the ceremony as he was before when I had not yet demonstrated my ignorance.

In essence, I became a bar-mitzvah by virtue of reaching thirteen, not because of knowledge. Today I think that is truly what it means: to be of the age when a boy becomes morally responsible for his deeds whether or not he knows the accepted rituals of the Torah readings. Nevertheless, I wish that Wolbe had demanded more of me than merely praying. He emigrated to Israel in 1948. I never saw him again, but my sister, Nanny, met him once in 1985 in Jerusalem. To her he appeared totally unchanged: kind, considerate, devout. I liked him very much; he was a truly good man.

The Wisest Woman in the World
was born in 1894 in a small town, Rezekne, in Latvia. She, my mother, arrived on her own in Stockholm at the age of eighteen. There were eight children in her family, an equal number of girls and boys. Three brothers and two sisters were already in Stockholm when she arrived.

As was usual at that time, she had no formal education, although she knew how to read and write in Yiddish. She spoke often, longingly, about her home in Rezekne; about the small, but beautiful garden around the simple and cozy house of her parents. My sister's impressions, when she visited Rezekne after the war, were quite different. She saw a very small hut with earthen floor, an old outhouse at the end of a path through a non-existent garden. The whole area reeked of the poverty that had clung to it, permeated it, for decades. Although many years had passed since my mother left, it could not have been much different when she was young. Even so, she loved it and it took much courage to leave, to emigrate to a new culture with a new language and new social settings.

While not devoid of hardships, life was certainly better in Sweden. She married my father in 1915, three years after arriving in Stockholm. Her six children were spread out over fourteen years. I was the youngest. Her speaking and reading skills in Swedish were self taught, but she never mastered writing. While she had a slight accent, her vocabulary was rich and nuanced.

I remember her face with the delicate, straight nose and the brightest, largest light blue eyes imaginable. Her, previously dark brown, now mostly grey, hair was usually tied in a bun at the nape of her neck. All this on a heavy body shaped by her many and frequent pregnancies. To me, she was beautiful.

I began reading at about the age of eight, in second grade. At that time reading was the only road to the world and life outside our confined space. Most of my reading was beyond my comprehension and I constantly asked my mother about the meaning of words and sayings. It was a rare occasion when she could not set me straight. Later on, when my reading was more fluent, she would ask me to read passages or stories aloud. A favorite of mine, and to be hers, was a children's edition of Greek myths. This book gave me the opportunity to explain a totally new world to her, a world we explored together. This way she had a good view of what prompted my thoughts and dreams, and she encouraged me.

Like any child I took my mother's presence for granted. It was only in 1950 when I returned to live at home while attending the Ship Officers' School that she became the central part of my life. No more was she merely background in the picture I sketched of my future. She became my confidant, adviser, supporter and best friend. The wisdom she conveyed to me came in stories or brief statements, almost aphorisms, prompted by events in my life. When I first went to sea and was frightened by the unknown, she encouraged me saying that this was the time in my life to take chances. As long as I had my family and was young with no responsibilities and obligations, I had a safety net against too dreadful consequences of my decisions. "Take a chance now; the time will come when you may have no options."

When I complained of being disliked by somebody, she did not commiserate with me. She simply asked, "Do you like everyone you meet?" My answer, "No", elicited the response, "If you don't like everybody, why do you expect everybody to like you?" "Also", she said, "it is amazing how well we treat those who dislike us. We often bend over backwards to make them like us. Don't fall into that trap; be yourself."

Similarly, when I was troubled by loneliness during the course of intense study, her brief comment was, "Have you thought of going out some time?"

No matter how unschooled, she had a deep understanding of people, particularly her youngest son. Cramming for the entrance exams to the Ship Officers' School, I, like so many others, "burnt out". Worried and sleepless I did not know how to cope with the stress. My mother suggested leaving everything behind me for a few days. "Go", she said, "to a place where you have not been before. It will do you good". She handed me an envelope with money she could ill spare, and I took off. Indeed, I had a good time. Rejuvenated, I had no difficulties passing the exams.

As had become my custom, I told my mother about my escapade away from Stockholm. Yes, I had been drinking a bit, and, yes, I had met a girl that very first day. Yes, I had met her every day and I had made arrangements with her for the evening of the day when, without letting her know, I left early for home. My mother was quiet for some time; she then told me some unpleasant things about myself. There was nothing wrong, she said, in pursuing the girl, but dishonesty was something else. I had toyed with someone's feelings and trust; I had, simply, betrayed the girl's confidence in me. I had shown myself unworthy of receiving whatever she had given me, tenderness, concern, and love. More generally, could I be trusted in any context? Was my word worth anything? If I could deceive in a matter I considered small, what would I be capable of in what I considered important? My defense that this was standard behavior in seafaring life carried no weight. Only my promise to change my attitude mollified her. And she held me to the promise. She rarely took my side in matters of romance; I had to prove to her satisfaction that I had been honest. She insisted that I should answer, with scrupulous honesty, relevant questions from girls I dated. "But", she said, "Tell her not to ask, unless she can accept your honest answer". I wondered if her concern with my behavior towards girls was based on some unpleasant experience in her youth.

After admission to the school, I had another idea. I would postpone my studies for a year to travel around Europe. I had seen the ports, why not also see the inland? My mother, calmly and thoughtfully, suggested that it was better to complete one thing at a time. Interruptions and postponements could too easily become ends in themselves, the end of my actions. Why not complete what I had started? Complete my studies and then travel? I followed her advise then and since.

When my first serious relationship broke apart, I was lost, devastated, but, as behooves a hardened seaman, I was determined not to show my feelings. Yet, the event affected my everyday existence and my demeanor became unpleasant. Again, my mother helped me through and taught me a life-long lesson. "Life", she said, "is nothing but memories. Memories are made of feelings and emotions, and they are etched into us as happy or sad by our reactions to them. If you don't cry or laugh, your feelings will not create memories, and, if you have no memories, then you have not lived". She urged me to give in to my grief, to cry so that I would have a memory of the girl who had meant so much to me. It would make my life easier both in the present and the future as I might look back into the past. Today, in my old age, I see the truth of her wisdom and am grateful she taught me this at a relatively early age. I have memories; I have had a life.

Life was hard for my mother. We never had an apartment with hot water. Long exposure to ice cold water when cooking, doing dishes or laundry, ruined her hands; her fingers were painful and deformed. Nevertheless, she did her work without complaints. A strong childhood memory is of her preparing the noodles for our Sabbath chicken soup. Dough was prepared on Thursday and rolled out into thin sheets. The sheets were partially dried by spreading them out on tables, backs of chairs, beds, and anything else that could support them. Friday morning each sheet was rolled into a loaf to be cut into thin slices. Each slice became a long noodle when unrolled and cooked. The amount of work was staggering as was the strain on her already damaged hands.

Courage she had in abundance. She had recovered from a bout with stomach cancer, but had high blood pressure and the pain of her chronically infected finger nails. There lived a nature healer on our street. He was not popular with his neighbors. Too odd in dress and behavior, he was neither spoken to, nor welcomed in many homes. But my mother went her own way. She had great respect and, I believe, admiration for him because he was exactly the free and independent spirit that, I know, was her ideal. And he liked her, too. Nevertheless, it took courage to seek his help. The times were not yet ripe for nature healers.

He treated her high blood pressure with great success. To me it seemed his medication was merely a mixture of red wine, horse radish, and some unknown herbs. Whatever it was, her blood pressure fell and, with this medication, stayed good throughout her life. Bjorkander, that was his name, moved away and, apart from replenishing my mother's blood pressure concoction from time to time, he was not seen.

My mother's finger nails continued to give her trouble. They were removed, but grew back in the same condition as before. The doctors finally recommended amputation of the upper joints of all fingers. At this point Bjorkander re-appeared with an ointment that cured the long standing infection, and amputation became unnecessary.

How courageous she was became evident to me during my time in the Navy. We were on maneuver somewhere, when I received word that my mother was in the hospital and not expected to survive the night. I got permission to be at her bedside. All children were gathered around her. She spoke calmly to us as if this was the most normal of situations. A nurse came in, pinched her toes and shook her feet asking if they felt cold. My mother looked at her, smiled as if she appreciated the nurse's concern with her comfort and said, "Not yet. I will let you know when the time comes." She then continued her conversation with us saying there was no need for us to wait; she was not ready to leave us. "But" she said, "grieve for me when I leave, but not for long. Miss me a bit longer. Think of me often; and remember me, always." There was no fear. No concern except for us. And, indeed, she came home shortly thereafter.

I spoke to her often, but did not visit Stockholm, during the last three years of her life. Late 1975 my sister told me that mother's health was declining and I ought to come for a visit soon. We had financial difficulties at the time, but finally I made arrangements to go in mid-March 1976. Early February I had a strange dream about my mother's running, in an excited state, to catch my father. The scene kept repeating, over and over. They did not seem to meet; my father was nowhere to be seen, but my mother kept on running. I awoke with an uneasy feeling that soon dissipated into the normal daily routine. Then came the telephone call. My mother had died that morning, February 11. There was no more an urgent reason to visit Stockholm. Next time I went there, it was to place small stones of remembrance on the graves of my parents.

I have always believed that the ultimate, final end of my childhood would come when my parents were both gone. When, literally, the source of my life receded into the unknown. By that definition, my childhood lasted forty-six years. It ended when my mother died. Her love and support had, at all times, been a safety net under my wobbly path in life. Now it was gone; I was on my own.

Childhood was over. I was alone to live up to my mother's wise counsel. That I did not see her for such a long time before her end does perturb me although I can hear her say, as she did many times in her life, "Don't feel regret or guilt. They are useless feelings for what is past and irrevocable. Instead, think carefully and live so that you never have reasons to feel regret or guilt."

She lived to see me as an officer both in the merchant marine and the navy; as married giving her three grandchildren. She saw me obtain my doctorate, and followed my path to an academic career after service with the International Monetary Fund. From my early youth she had jokingly referred to me as "the professor because he reads all the time." I hope that her actually seeing me as a "real" professor gave her joy, and confirmed that she was right in encouraging me to dream and to pursue my dreams to completion.

I remember her, always.

Succumbing to the sea

Along the coast

Although I had worked on ships since the age of fourteen, I became a documented seaman just before my sixteenth birthday. That is, I was registered in, and hired through, the Seamen's House. I now had my Seaman's Book and was a member of the union.

My first "real" ship, *s/s Verna*, was built in a Swedish yard around 1880 making her about sixty-five years old when I signed on as an "apprentice deckhand" (*obefaren jungman*) in 1946. One year's experience would make me a "deckhand" (*befaren jungman*); one more year would qualify me as an "ordinary seaman" or OS (*lattmatros*), and yet another year would make me eligible for an "able seaman's" job, an AB (*matros*), all depending on whether these positions were available. There was a long road ahead.

The two years I had spent as undocumented had been mostly on an engine assisted sailing vessel, carrying bricks on the inside waters of the Stockholm archipelago. The main reason documentation was not needed was that we did not keep sea-going watches. Watch keeping was not allowed for anyone under the age of 16 so, at fourteen, I could safely work on this ship. When on a trip, we tied up for the nights. Cargos for the ship were sporadic, though, and I remember very little of the ship's comings and goings. But life aboard was very similar to that I would encounter in other ships. That is, hard physical work, crowded quarters, shipmates' drinking, fighting and chasing women. There was strong camaraderie among the crew, but I was too young to be included. It was a lonely life. I had a bicycle and, although the workday was long, I would go home most evenings.

The crew numbered five, including the captain who owned the ship. The rest of us were the cheapest laborers he could find. I doubled up on duties being the deck-hand and occasional cook. The captain's wife prepared most of the food. When I cooked, I followed my mother's recipes for oatmeal, potato pudding, and mashed potatoes. When there were leftover mashed potatoes, I used it for potato pancakes. They went very well with lingonberries or fried, salted herring. No one lauded my efforts. Perhaps the real function of my cooking was to make the crew truly appreciative of any other cooking, particularly that of the captain's wife. Otherwise my job was to warm up the food, set the table, serve, do the dishes, and make the coffee. It was not really coffee -- it was some substitute concoction of chicory, heavily roasted grains, and burnt strips of sugar beets; sometimes dandelion roots were included. I tried it once not to touch it again. My first cup of real coffee was at age seventeen when I first visited the USA. This, the real thing, did not taste any better than whatever I had prepared on that small schooner, and it took many years before it became indispensable in my daily routine.

After a year with the brick schooner I got a chance to sail on a slightly larger ship trading along the Swedish coast from Stockholm to the northern port of Lulea. I was excited since it would be a trip of several days, perhaps a week, and there would be some stretches of open water. Before any longer trip, however, we had several day trips much like those on the brick schooner. Again, part of my job was to take care of the food supply and make the coffee, the drink I did not touch. Water was stored in a large tank with a spigot that allowed for only a weak flow of water. That was fine if one wanted only a cup or mug of it, but to fill the large coffee pot was cumbersome and took a long time. Luck was on my side, though. I found a big water barrel on deck and there I could fill the pot by simply immersing it in the barrel; very easy and efficient.

Most days we stopped at the captain's home island so his wife would bring aboard the food basket. After a few trips the crew developed some stomach problems and the wife's food was blamed. She took extra care with her preparations, but nothing seemed to help. The crew was not in the best shape as we set out for the north. Indeed, the only one not sick was I. While I did not reflect much on that fact, the captain did. He began to check my handling of the food. One day as I fetched water from the deck barrel for the coffee, he saw me and insight came his way. It turned out that the water in that barrel was not for drinking. It was bilge water, that is, water that had been drained from all parts of the ship into its lower parts, the bilges. Why it had been pumped up and stored in the deck barrel is beyond my comprehension even today, but there was clearly the cause of the stomach problems. The captain's wife was exonerated. I was blamed. Her reputation regained. Mine destroyed.

I was ordered off the ship as soon as we reached the next port which turned out to be our final destination, Lulea, about as far north of Stockholm as one could get without leaving the country.

There I was in northern Sweden with my bike, pillow, blanket, some clothing, very little money and not certain of the road back except that it had to be to the south. I was not really frightened. To be alone and on my own was not a new experience; I felt comfortable with it. But it worried me that my seafaring career was over just when it had started with so much promise. I was also leery about anti-Semitism. What did people feel and think in the vast north? Where would I get food? Where to sleep? As it turned out, there was no need to worry. The people I met were kind, and helpful.

The trip back took maybe two weeks, perhaps more. Biking gave me strength and stamina. A few days on the road and I began to truly enjoy everything from the scenery and weather to the people and their generosity. My food rationing book had remained with the captain, but I had no problems getting what was needed. As long as I bought small quantities, the stores did not bother about coupons; but I lived essentially on bread. There was no scarcity of sheds and barns where I could sleep. The northern summer nights were light and warm; I rested without fear of the unseen and unknown. Here and there I offered to do chores for food or a place to sleep. No one took me up on it, but often treated me to a meal, but not a bed.

To keep my family informed was a problem. Long distance calls were difficult to place and expensive beyond my means. I did send postcards but they did not arrive fast enough to set my mother at ease. Only with hindsight did I understand the anxiety I caused her, and the guilt I now feel has certainly tarnished my memories of the trip.

I saw many places I had never heard of before, or since. Details escape me, but it was a happy existence free of any structure and demands and it gave me a lasting love of the north, its nature, weather, and people. The lasting impressions are of empty, unpaved, tree lined roads, widely separated farms, and the emptiness broken from time to time by small factory towns announcing their presence with the foul smells of sulfur and sulfate from the paper and pulp factories. A sharp memory is of a girl I met at a farm. She gave me a small doll to remember her by. We corresponded for a while, but soon after returning to Stockholm, I signed on the *Verna* and my life took another turn.

The Baltic coal trade

The *s/s Verna* was what Swedish seamen called "stern loaded". It meant that all the deck structures, the bridge, the officers' accommodations, the galley, the engine room and the engine crew quarters were located at the stern of the ship. In the bow, in the focsle, or forecastle, were various storage rooms, and the quarters for the deck crew. There was a fairly large crew, six on deck, the same in the engine, the captain, two mates, the chief engineer, the first engineer, the cook and the mess-boy.

I was excited and eager to get to the ship. It was docked far from my home and could best be reached by a short-cut over a mountain road. It was a steep climb and I had much to carry. I was grateful that my brother Herman helped me to get there and to settle in. He was as curious about the ship as was I. It was not a good first impression. The deck crew's living quarters consisted of three double bunk beds, an eating table secured to the deck with bolts, and two benches similarly attached. There were several buckets hanging on the wall for sanitary use, be it for washing or bodily needs.

Herman left quickly. He was clearly disgusted by the dirty old ship. So was I, but how could I admit it? After all, was this not my dream come true?

My bunk was at the top and as far forward as one could get. The hawse-pipe for the anchor chain went through one end of the bunk. It had a slanted angle that gave me a cozy little niche where I put my pillow, so showing everyone that I had no idea of what the hawse-pipe was. I became aware of that when, about a week later, we dropped anchor in Gdynia. The noise of the chain rattling through the pipe can not be described, at least not by me. My eardrums were hurt and I was deaf for several days. No permanent damage, though. From then on I did not go to bed without first finding out if there would be any need for anchoring during my free watch. Needless to say, I turned the pillow to the other end of the bed.

That first night was an eye opener. Two of the crew brought a woman aboard and had their way with her, or she with them, in full view of everyone around. But no one paid attention. Nor did they pay attention to the very public washing-up of the three partners just in back of the table. That is how I found out what the buckets were for. Thereafter the drinking started. Now, that got everyone's attention. No one wanted to miss out on the good stuff!

Clearly, one can adjust to anything. I stayed aboard the *Verna*.

When we left for Gdynia to load coal for Stockholm, seasickness entered my life. It stayed with me for about two years. I got so used to it that when, for the first time, I did not feel the effects of the ship's movements, I thought I was really sick, that there was something terribly wrong with my internal set-up. How can one describe seasickness? Common motion sickness does not do it. It can't replicate the feeling of helplessness, the utter despair, that nothing matters any more; nothing remains in one place, everything moves without pattern, all culminating in a simple death wish because that appears to be the only way to relief. Couple that with the demands that your duties be done, no matter what. An endless, and I stress endless, and very violent roller coaster might produce a somewhat similar feeling.

In due time I became less sensitive to minor movements of the ship, then to major moves, and, after a long time, I stabilized at a level of almost well-being between the bouts of retching. Ultimately I began to enjoy the rolling and swaying, and, the worse the weather, the more did the ship's battle against the elements fascinate and thrill me.

Along the way, shipmates offered many useless cures, but recommended one in particular. They suggested that I tie a salted herring to the end of a string, swallow it and then pull it up again. That procedure repeated several times was sure to end my misery. If the herring was too difficult to swallow, then a piece of suet would surely do the job. I survived the sickness and the cures, the latter by not trying them.

At the entry to the port of Gdynia a German war vessel had been sunk to prevent the port's being used after the German departure. To get into the channel to the docks it was necessary to drop the anchor so that the ship could pivot on it until being able to go straight into the port proper. When we raised the anchor, there was a body caught on it. Without ceremony it was dislodged and sank back into the water. The mate said this was not unusual.

We needed to load only six hundred tons, but even that small load was not available in Gdynia so we moved on to Gdansk, formerly Danzig, not far away up the coast. There we stayed several weeks because, again, the cargo was not available and, when it was, we had the use of only one low capacity bucket crane. Once I went into town, or, rather, to the ruins that were Gdansk. Just in time to see the workings of immediate post-war justice. Several men were hanged publicly. No one seemed to know why. From then on I stayed mostly aboard the ship.

I remained on the *Verna* for a few more trips and there were some happy moments. Not in an absolute sense of gaiety, and fulfilled well-being, but, for me, finding a bakery with delicious cream cakes broke the otherwise unmitigated dreariness of ship-board life, and it became a happy event. What stays in my memory, though, are the dark and upsetting ones and even they are brought to mind only because of the process of writing. Perhaps it would have been better if *s/s Verna* had remained hidden in my memory.

The open water passage from Stockholm to Gdynia was infested with mines. There were relatively safe lanes swept by the various navies in the area. Nevertheless, our salaries were increased by a war risk premium when we entered these waters. I don't remember how much was added to the salary, but it was in the hundreds of percent depending on the perceived risks and the length of time in the danger zone. Given that my salary was eighty-four Swedish Crowns per month, or about sixteen US$ at the going exchange rate, war risk pay was welcome.

We did not worry very much about mines. Yet the danger was real. Once, *Verna* and another ship departed Gdansk at the same time for the Swedish port of Sundsvall. While we arrived safely, the other ship was lost without a trace; a mine was presumed to be the cause.

The *Verna* did not have machine assisted steering, it was by manpower only. In calm weather there was no problem and I learned to keep a straight course guided by the magnetic compass. The captain and the mates did not believe in modern ship-board systems, mainly, I believe, because we did not have any. We steered by cardinal compass points, not degrees. I learned early, but have now mostly forgotten, to "box the compass", that is, to read off all the points in proper order starting from north going east, to south, to west, and back to north.

In calm weather, one man at the helm was sufficient for good handling. In bad weather, though, waves would break against the rudder and it took great strength to hold the helm steady. One could easily be injured by the spinning wheel. In such weather there were two helmsmen, very much like on old sailing ships.

Sea watches were new to me. On the *Verna* the deck crew was divided into two teams, or watches, three men in each. At sea, one manned the helm, one stood lookout, and the third was standing by to do the mate's bidding such as to read the (speed) log, bring coffee to the mate, wake up the next watch, and so on. Every hour we switched tasks. The length of the watches could vary among ships. We kept the 4-5-6 system as did most other ships. Under this system, the minimum time off was four hours and the maximum six. The watches started at 12 midnight: 12 pm to 4 am (the dog watch); 4 am to 8 am; 8 am to 1 pm; 1 pm to 7 pm; 7 pm to 12 midnight. Under this system the watches rotated so that no one was stuck with the same time slot all the time. Other systems were four hours on with four hours off; six on - six off; or four on - eight off. The last one required three watches and was introduced, after the war, on large ships where the number of crew members could sustain it.

The next watch was to be woken up twenty minutes before the watch change; and a second reminder was given ten minutes later. To me, it was an unnatural schedule and I had difficulties with it from the very beginning. On this, my first trip, we left port in the evening, and I stood watch until midnight when I got to bed only to be awoken at 3:40 am to "turn to" for my next four hour watch. I was not used to so little sleep, nor was I used to get dressed and ready in less than twenty minutes. That first time I took my time to get up. I yawned, stretched and stayed under my blanket to really savor my well deserved tiredness. Perhaps I dozed off. The next thing I knew was a terribly cold mass of water inundating my bed. No threats, no warning, just a pail of cold water to make the point that I had to be on time. From then on, I was.

That the water did not leak into the lower bunk must be attributed to the thrower's skill, perhaps he had done this many times. My bedding was soaking wet. To dry it had its own problems involving finding a place in the engine room that was both warm and clean enough to do the job. Also, the mattress was the property of the ship owner and I was responsible for its return in good shape. That and a privacy curtain were all that the ship owner provided. Each crew member had his own pillows, blankets and towels. We rarely used pajamas – in fact, mine was probably the only one on the ship. It was more practical, and easier, to change into clean work clothes when going to bed. That way one was already dressed to go on watch and also ready for any emergency.

Since we ate in the focsle, the youngest, that was I, had to bring the food from the galley, clean the dishes after use and bring them back. The fare was plentiful and not bad considering that food was still rationed.

Sanitary facilities were strange. There was a narrow structure extending from the railing over the water. It was enclosed except for the part facing down into the water. It could only be used in good weather. There was no danger of falling into the water, but it evoked a very unpleasant feeling of lurking hazards. The buckets hanging on the bulkhead were easily understood.

In general, it was a lonely life. I did not drink anything alcoholic, not even beer. That made me an outsider and a loner. It did not bother me. It was simply the way my life unfolded. We would go ashore in a group. Away from the docks our ways parted, I in search of cream cakes, they in search of drink and female company. The next morning it was hard to say who suffered the most, I from binge eating or they from binge drinking.

Other ships

I left the *Verna* but had two more ships in the Baltic coal trade, the *s/s Rudolf* and the *s/s Bifrost*. Both ships were fairly large for the time, about 5,000 tons carrying capacity. They were also "stern loaders", but without living quarters under the focsle. Instead, everyone lived in the aft. The captain lived above deck just under the bridge and the officers in single cabins aft of his quarters; deck officers on the starboard side and engineers on the port. For the crew members, the arrangement was similar below deck. The engine crew on the port side, the deck crew on the starboard. Each side was a mirror image of the other. There were two people in each cabin, a separate, comfortable dining room; and shower and washing facilities up on deck. The kitchen, or galley, was close by, so the carrying of food to the dining room, still my task, was easy. Finally, I had found a seaman's lap of luxury, but certainly not a life of ease. Work was as hard as ever; watch keeping onerous and unnatural. Sleep scarce and always disturbed by the usual carousing in port.

But my loneliness eased on these ships. On one of them, I became friendly with John, an OS. He was twenty-four, a huge man, enormously strong, a good seaman, but with a violent temper when drunk. And he drank rather heavily at any opportunity. He was known for his skilled fists, and had served time for sending a couple of adversaries to the hospital. The prospects of doing it again frightened him. He wanted me around, hoping I would help him resist temptation or, at least, temper his violence.

John had made one trip to the USA where he had bought a "bomber's" leather jacket and a pair of yellow khaki slacks, army issue. These items were uniquely American and, since he wore them whenever he went ashore, he became, inevitably, known as Yankee John. He was known, feared and, perhaps, respected in the bars of Gdynia. Some of those feelings were transferred to me since I turned out to be his constant companion. I enjoyed that, and his company.

He met a German girl, Gerda, and, through her, I met Kristina from Czechoslovakia. Both were nineteen. They had good friends among the Polish soldiers, and, having seen us with the girls, the soldiers treated us well and in a friendly manner. One day the girls disappeared, and so did the soldiers' friendliness. I don't know what happened, but John's explanation, that he had been preparing to bring the girls to Sweden, seemed a plausible cause. His scheme had been discovered. While no action was taken against John or, by implication, me, the girls were gone. We never saw them again.

As I write this, something curious is happening. Memories of which I have not been aware come surging forward clamoring for recognition. I suddenly remember Kristina's second name, but not Gerda's. I remember the name of the street they lived on (Ulitska Katolska), not the house number. I have some recollections of their apartment, small and over-furnished to the point of being uncomfortable. Big wooden furniture finished in old-fashioned, glossy lacquer, and many religious icons hanging on the walls. But, even more curious, no, painful, is my memory of what finally caused the break between us, that prompted John to try his scheme. These are some of the things that need not be told in detail. Suffice it to say that, to them, as children of the war, coping with life as it unfolded took precedence over principles of living, as we saw them.

A more successful smuggling of people took place on the same ship. On a trip back to Stockholm, one of the engine crew wanted me to vacate my bunk in his favor. It was an absolutely unprecedented request. Who ever heard of an engine crew member bunking in the deck quarters? Was he out of his mind? He was not. It was merely a case of twisted logic. I learned that as he told his story. He had met a family, man, wife and an eight year old daughter. As the father explained to him, they had to get out of Poland. They were Jewish and it was a matter of life and death. Could he, the motorman, help them? They only needed help to get aboard and food and shelter for the few days across the sea. There would be handsome compensation. The motorman agreed, managed to get them aboard and hidden in his cabin. He got the money and spent it that very night. Next day we left port. The family had now taken over the small cabin. The motorman had nowhere to go. In addition, the family needed food which caused another problem. Three extra, unexplained meals were a challenge, indeed. In his hung-over state the motorman was overwhelmed by the responsibility which only added to his very real headache.

Under stress his mind raced and he reached the conclusion that since the family was Jewish, and so was I, common sense dictated that I was responsible for the family's needs, not to mention his own need for a bed. I had little choice. To get food turned out to be no problem. The cook never asked the reason for the upsurge in appetite. Perhaps he was flattered by the sudden appreciation of his cooking. Perhaps he knew the story. For the next three nights I slept poorly, mostly in a chair on deck. The family was very quiet, dared not move about for fear of being detected. The parents were grateful, but distrustful. The girl, though, was only fearful. Fearful, defenseless, trapped with no escape possible, all reflected in her anguished face. The picture of that girl has been with me often, particularly when my three daughters were growing up.

In Stockholm I managed to get the family ashore. The customs agent assumed that the man with his three suitcases had just been paid off from the ship. Having been met by his wife and daughter he was now on his way home. I brought them to my mother's apartment where they stayed a very short time. My mother felt very uneasy around them. On her son-in-law's insistence, they reported to the police and were granted a temporary permit to stay. I never again heard from, or about, them. I often wonder about their story.

One incident that rests strongly in my memory took place on the *s/s Rudolf*. In Gdynia there were always some soldiers guarding access to the ship (or perhaps it was access to the shore). Since we were there for a long time, both the crew and the soldiers did their best to relieve the boredom. One common diversion was a drinking contest. Who could drink the largest amount of pure, 96 percent, alcohol? The trick for success was to take a small drink of the alcohol and chase it with a great amount of water without breathing in between. To breathe would cause a horrible and dangerous cooling effect from the spirit, and the water would dilute it so that there would be no shock to the system. Following these rules it was amazing how much could be ingested at one time.

This time the game had started the previous evening and, for some reason, when cleaning up, I had poured the left over spirit in a large mug which was left on the sink where the drinker would get the water chaser. The drinking started. First a Swede did his part; a Polish soldier followed. He drank the alcohol, drained his water glass, but needed more. Saw the mug on the counter and, believing it to be water, drained it in big mouthfuls. The collapse was inevitable. We thought he had died of shock. So did his friends. But, worse, they thought we had done this on purpose; in their mind, we had committed murder. At gun point they marched the drinkers, I think there were four, onto the pier. I don't know if they, indeed, intended to shoot them. It looked very threatening when suddenly the presumed dead soldier came up on deck trying to get ashore. In his drunken stupor he was at risk to fall between the ship and the pier where he might have been crushed if the ship moved ever so slightly. His friends abandoned their prisoners to help him. Rescue mission accomplished, all were friends again. The game resumed.

Most of the time in port, we had a night watchman posted at the gangway. More often than not I was assigned that job. The duties were to make regular rounds on the deck, check the moorings and wake the people who needed to be up earlier than others, the most important being the cook, and the Chief Mate.

At the proper time I roused the cook, and, shortly thereafter I knocked on the Chief Mate's door. Twenty minutes later, I knocked again. No answer. I looked through the window to see if he was up. He was sitting at his desk with a glass in his hand swaying a bit sideways and forward as if he was trying to put on his shoes. Satisfied I took another round on the deck. Returning to the gangway I was surprised that the mate was nowhere to be seen. He should at least be in the mess room having his first cup of coffee. Another look through the window showed him in the same chair but now slumped over backwards looking straight at me. Something was wrong. I woke the Second Mate; he called for the carpenter and together they broke down the door. The Chief Mate was alive, but not for long. By the time a doctor arrived, he was gone. It was ruled a suicide. He had drunk a large quantity of creosote, the chemical used to preserve railroad ties and telephone poles. That, coupled with his wife having left him the day before, gave both the reason for his death and the method of departure. A new Chief Mate arrived and life went on.

Time is Important

There were two aspects of shipboard life that truly distinguished it from life ashore, and I absorbed them quickly. One was how we perceived the passage of time, the other was the way we addressed each other.

Time, as we perceived it, had more to do with voyaging than with the calendar. In our daily activities we certainly counted by the conventional concepts of seconds, minutes, hours, days, weeks and so on. But it was not so when we talked about shipboard employment. We never said we were signed on for a particular period, say 6 months. Instead, our time aboard a ship was counted by voyages, or trips. For instance, I was on the *Verna* for three trips, but cannot, for the life of me, say how many months that was. Those three trips, although short, became in my mind equivalent to three trips anywhere else, say to the Eastern Mediterranean, or North America or wherever. Our lives progressed, not in discrete time intervals of months or years, but in segments of time measured by number of voyages. Many years later, when I entered academic life, I would take the same approach to time, counting it only in the discrete segments of semesters, quarters and inter-sessions.

However, this approach to time has not worked for my life in retirement. Now I have no guide lines for measuring my time. I have no duties, assignments or activities that, being completed, constitute segments to indicate the progression of my life. Instead, I have settled into a daily routine that, indeed, is measured by the dials on my watch. The only interruptions are the arrivals of birthdays and holidays that mark the passage of the year, too long a period for comfort at my age.

At sea, the number of trips was very important in determining one's status on the ship because it was a proxy for experience. During drinking parties in port, the conversation almost inevitably turned toward our experiences of ships, good and bad.

To get an idea of such a party, picture, if you can, ten to twelve seamen sitting around the dining-room table. Work for the day over, we are well scrubbed and reasonably cleanly dressed. A feeling of well being, general satisfaction with life and good will towards each other is almost palpable, it permeates the air. So much good will that someone breaks out a bottle for all to share. A joke is being told; the kind of joke most people ashore would not understand but, in the dining room, we almost roll off our chairs with laughter. For example (and here I adapt and paraphrase from the Swedish), the carpenter sends the apprentice deck hand all over the ship to find the girl we need to bring up the anchor – it is heavy work and only the wind-LASS can do that. (The windlass is the heavy winch used for hoisting the anchor.) We laugh heartily at the thought of the apprentice's frantic search for the lass.

From jokes, we turn to stories of our experiences on ships with strange captains, mates or fellow crew members. More bottles appear. We drink, we tell, and we laugh. It is, indeed, a happy and jovial exchange of experiences. To back up particular stories, we begin to refer to how many trips we have taken on various ships. Clearly, the more trips there are, the greater is the experience and veracity of the story teller.

To begin with we listen to each other attentively. After all, one of us might be a truly outstanding seaman deserving respect. Soon, however, someone senses that his achievements are not properly appreciated. He can not resist elaborating on his experiences and, particularly, on the number of trips he has taken. The elaboration progresses and becomes boastful embellishment. Well, if he can boast, so can the others, and very soon there is competitive boasting and embellishment. We boast of our heroic endurance on particular ships, usually bad ones, by stating, again and again, how many trips we completed on them.

The more the liquor flows, the more vociferous becomes the boasting, and the more exalted and noble becomes one's heroism, at least in one's own eyes. The experiences of the ship-mates begin to appear trivial, and become more so with every glass emptied to boost self esteem. To verify our claims we bring out our seamen's books and proudly show how many trips we have had on any particular ship.

To begin with, the books are passed around eliciting admiration or deprecation depending on how much courage the liquor has imbued in the reader. Since, as the party progresses, the only worthy claim to heroism is one's own, we sit, towards the end of the session, somewhat apart from each other scrutinizing our documents, counting trips and bemoaning the lack of appreciation from those who ought to know better. The wonderful air of well-being and good will is slowly evaporating. In its place comes disappointment in one's shipmates and elevation of one's own worth. Both conditions benefit much from a still generous supply of bottles.

I remember one occasion when an older shipmate, having spent most of his life at sea, was reduced, first, to tears, and then to anger because his war time voyages were ignored. Never again, said he, would he drink with the likes of us. And so he took his bottles away for his own exclusive use. Others followed suit. With more drinking, renewed self esteem soared, singing ensued and soon it all started over again. An example of scarce skills seemed essential and someone boasts saying that "When I was on the *Karina*, I was the only one who could make a heaving-line end knot, a Turk's Head. Can you do that?" Others try to outdo the one with the knot, and boasting resumes until, again, no one talks to anyone except himself. Liquor begins to ebb and so does the stamina of most of us.

With communication ended and the liquor supply exhausted, we finally part company. Nursing our bruised egos we already plan on how to endure the next time segment, our next trip.

Nightmare at Work

The call comes early in the morning, before day has broken: "Turn to; make ready for sea, we're leaving around noon". I wash sleep off my eyes, dress, have a quick breakfast of coffee and more coffee and hurry out on deck. There is much to do. For me, this is the most dreaded work at sea. To make ready for sea is hard physical work performed under the frenzied urging of the bosun and mates.

First, put the crossbeams on the hatches in the 'tweendeck, then their hatch covers. We have seven cargo holds, each one with a 'tweendeck hatch. There are four crossbeams on each hatch. Each weighs at least half a ton, maybe more. We hoist them into place with the deck winches, and then put on the covers by hand. It is tough work and takes several hours. It's very tiring.

The bosun's nervous energy drives us on to the next task, namely to do the same thing on the weatherdeck. But here the hatches must be covered by water tight tarpaulins put in place and secured with battening irons and wedges, that is, we are "battening down the hatches". Again, it is a couple of hours of arduous labor.

Wiping the sweat from my eyes, perhaps grabbing a cup of coffee, I move, with the others to the next task: lowering the booms to secure them in their brackets; there are eighteen booms. The boom-stays, two to each boom, are tightened and all loose rope ends put in proper place. Everything is checked and, if necessary, lashed or put away. Ventilators are covered. Again, it's a couple of hours of utmost exertion with the third mate adding his energy to that of the bosun's. I am reeling from tiredness. My body aches. Unless we leave on my watch, I can have a long rest as soon as the work is done. The thought of that rest keeps me going.

Finally, most is ready. We hose down the deck and wait for the pilot to come aboard so we can take in the gangway. There is time for more coffee while we wait. Sitting in the mess room I doze off.

I am awakened by a call: "Turn to, make ready for sea, we're leaving around noon".

I raise my tired, aching body from the bed, wash sleep off my eyes, dress, have a quick breakfast and hurry, no, drag myself, out on deck. All the grueling work I have just been through has been for naught. It was a dream! A nightmare of hard work as vividly real to me as the work I have been awakened to do now.

Given that I had this dream quite often and, to me, the work in the dream was real, there were times when I considered putting in for overtime. I never did, but told the mate about the dream, hoping he would, on his own, see the merits of such a claim. He did not.

Name Calling

Already on my very first ship, the brick schooner, I ceased to be Bernhard. I was, simply, Abrahamsson. And so I remained throughout my seafaring career. Everyone was referred to by the family name. This caused some derivative naming because it was very common to have several, unrelated, crew members with the same family name. When that happened, we attached some distinguishing feature to each one. For example, and as unlikely as it may seem, on one ship we were three Abrahamssons. Inevitably, I became "Stockholm" after my home town; another became "Smaland" for his home region, and the third, "Boegen", the Swedish slang word for a gay man.

The habit of only using the family name was common also in a broader context. As a matter of course, wives addressed their husbands by the second name. Less often the men called their wives Mrs. So-and-so.

It was not done in a jocular manner, as I have sometimes heard it used ashore, but as the accepted and proper way of address.

To the credit of my shipmates, I was not often referred to as being Jewish. On the *Verna*, the 2nd mate would, at the beginning, talk about the "Jew Devil", but not viciously so. He did not harass me beyond what was acceptable and considered normal for an apprentice deck-hand. His attitude changed quickly and I became Abrahamsson also for him. Why, I do not know. It may have had something to do with the fact that I did not eat pork. While I had no particularly strong religious feelings, the traditions of home remained with me for a long time. I had never had pork, or pork products, at home, and so could not bring myself to eat them aboard ship where pork chops were served once a week. Instead I traded them to whoever would give me their pancakes, also served once a week. The 2nd, by virtue of his rank, "won" my pork chops most of the time. Perhaps this persuaded him that there were some merits in having me around.

The second incident, though, was enough to poison my memory of the general tolerance and acceptance aboard ship. It was the bosun on the *m/v Virginia,* on the Mediterranean run. He was vicious and ruthless in using his powers to assign difficult and dangerous work to the "Jew Devil". I tried my best to meet his demands no matter how many times I was outright frightened by them. Changing the mast top light in bad weather at sea meant a high climb and the risk of electric shock. Washing the mast with very strong lye solutions, mixed by the bosun, could have the same effects as putting the hands into open fire; it was difficult to prevent burns even when using thick rubber gloves. To paint the flared bow when in port involved swinging rather precariously on a rope, or rope ladder, to reach the scaffolding. I fell into the water several times. The bow flare seemed to need an extraordinary number of paint layers, all to be applied by me. The same with the mast's light and clean appearance. No doubt he meant me harm.

I responded by adhering scrupulously to the union rules. For example, one article said that the "foreman" must give the seamen sufficient time to put away their work tools and equipment before the actual quitting time. Any extension beyond that time resulted in a claim for overtime, much frowned upon by the Chief Mate. In addition, the union contract specified, in essence, that, for any task assigned to him, a seaman must be allowed whatever time was necessary to complete the task to the best of his ability. I combined the two stipulations in such a way that no matter how much time I was given to complete or wind up the work, it was not sufficient for me to do it to the best of my ability. He got very little useful work out of me.

Ultimately he fell into disfavor with the Chief Mate; his dislike for me deepened, and a seething hate took its place. Trying to get to me he promoted his hatred among the others of the crew. But there was no need for me to worry. His spewed venom back fired. He was not a popular man; indeed, no one really liked him. The crew's dislike for him grew as his viciousness toward me became more and more open. Knowing the risks of sudden disappearances at sea, they formed an unspoken alliance to see that I was not alone when venturing up on deck. I left that ship when we returned to the home port; so did he. Our paths did not cross again.

There were a few more, but minor, incidents of anti-Semitism. Some were settled by physical strength, others by studious avoidance of that strength. The older and stronger I got, the less did I encounter overt anti-Semitism. The clinching moment in this respect was prompted by an AB, big, strong and totally unable to control his rage when drunk. In that stage he would often set out to find the "damn Jew" who certainly needed some thrashing. I was very much afraid and stayed clear of him most of the time. But this time he caught me on deck, and I saw no escape. We were just aft of the last cargo hold at an opening called the "tonnage hatch". The hatch was uncovered. Lying on the deck were its small, wooden covers, about 4 feet long, 2 feet wide and 3 inches thick. At each end there was a steel reinforcement with handles for lifting the cover; the weight may have been about 25 pounds. As he came towards me, fear gave me unimaginable strength. My reach was sufficient to lift a cover, and my strength sufficient to swing it back and forth. When I let go, the cover "floated" a couple of inches above the deck and hit his ankle with a satisfying thud. With a broken ankle he was no more a threat to anyone. He did not really hate me; I was merely the most convenient object for his bad temper when he had drunk too much.

My name remained, for the most time, Abrahamsson; occasionally it was Stockholm or Grumpy, and, once, it was even "Beagle Eye", not because of my good eye sight which would have merited the name "Eagle Eye", but, rather, because someone thought my eyes were very sad and reminded him of his childhood dog, a beagle.

Friendship
The Baltic coal trade was a dreary existence. The Polish ports, Gdynia and Gdansk, were devastated, in ruins. Dust and foul smells hung in the air and the expected gay, bright lights of the night spots did not exist. The nights were dark. So was the mood of the people and it all affected the seamen aboard the ships waiting for weeks to get their cargo.

Getting a berth on the Mediterranean run was a welcome change. The ship's name was *Virginia* owned by the Swedish Lloyd, a well regarded company. We expected good food and good living quarters. In neither respect were we disappointed. Work conditions were, generally, good except for me who had to cope with the bosun's hatred of Jews in general, and of me in particular.

Two deck hands, I and Kurt (Kurre), a year older than I, shared a cabin. This was the first time either of us sailed with someone our own age. Both of us knew what it meant to be the youngest aboard ship and how lonely that could be. We were happy to see a possible end to that, and we took an immediate liking to each other. He was also from Stockholm and had gone to sea at roughly the same time as I did. Our sea experiences were similar. We had similar, vaguely expressed, hopes for the future; that is, we wanted advancement at sea and ultimately to go into some shore based employment where a seaman's experience would be useful.

What cemented our friendship, though, was the bosun's ill will toward me. To Kurre it was inconceivable that anyone would expose someone to danger merely to satisfy a personal hatred. To do so in order to save ship, life, and cargo was one thing. Malevolence was an entirely different thing. He took my side without hesitation, and without telling me so in words, only through action. It was he who made sure that all lines were properly secured when, in the beginning, I actually did the assigned work such as painting the flared bow or washing down the masts. When, toward the end of the voyage, I did as little as possible, he was always ready to produce the relevant paragraphs in the union contract. Whenever the bosun turned the conversation in the mess into an anti-Semitic tirade, Kurre would either launch into some other topic, or with terse anger tell the bosun to shove off.

Our backgrounds were, however, as dissimilar as our sea faring was similar. His mother had been widowed when Kurre was about six. He had no recollection of his father, and he was very close to his mother who treated him as an equal and a friend. She treated me the same way, and I felt very much at ease around her. A few times I confided to her problems I felt could not be broached to any of my family. Each time she listened carefully, then told me to take my mother into my confidence; she was sure that there I would get the best advise.

I did so. My love and respect for my mother, her sagacity and wisdom, grew deep and solid. Our relationship moved onto new levels. I told, related, and asked. She listened, advised and encouraged. I have always been grateful to Kurre's mother for steering me in the right direction. The two mothers never met, and I regret that even today.

Kurre's mother was a waitress in one of the better 2nd class restaurants in Stockholm. At this time Sweden had very strict controls on liquor consumption both at home and in restaurants. Outside the home, drinks could only be had in connection with meals. How much liquor one could get, and the cost of the meal, depended on the restaurants. They were classified as 3rd, 2nd and 1st class. Third class had no dress code, no table cloths, the menu was limited as was the quantity of spirits that could be consumed, and prices were manageable. These restaurants were predominant in most cities, and they, generally, catered to the blue collar workers.

Second class was a significant step upwards as they required coat and tie. They had white table cloths and, usually, a flower arrangement, a varied menu and a much larger allowance for drinking. In addition there was, most of the time, live chamber music appropriate as background for refined dining. First class was another, big, step upwards, mainly in price, dress code and the amount of spirits served.

Regardless of its classification, restaurants were hard to get into. There were usually long lines waiting for admittance because this was the only venue for drinking outside the home. Bars, as we know them today, did not exist, although there were beer halls.

A restaurant server was a true professional with many years of apprenticeship training. At work they wore "uniforms". Kurre's mother, working in a 2nd class establishment, earned a good living and had allowed him, from an early age, to visit her at work; he normally had his dinner there. He acquired what we called "restaurant manners", something I certainly did not have. I had never been to a restaurant of that standing, or any standing for that matter. But, with Kurre's help, we set out to remove that deficiency.

I had stayed away from drinking in my earlier ships. What I had seen of shipboard joy and entertainment was more frightening than tempting. Kurre had no such hesitations. He participated, but not in excess. I liked him, admired him and felt good in his company. Slowly I began to participate and, in doing so, found acceptance, camaraderie, a sense of belonging and loyalty that had been absent before. And so began my years of recklessness; a period of melting seamlessly into the seafaring life I had, until then, only seen from the sidelines. I became a full participant. I was seventeen.

For the next few years, Kurre and I were essentially inseparable. Certainly there was drinking and there were women. Kurre was good looking by any criteria. With blond, wavy hair, brown eyes, a slightly upturned nose and an athletic build, he carried any kind of clothing with a flair that can best be described as "eye catching". Many were the times I heard women comment on his good looks, his appearance, and, on getting closer, his beautiful eyes and charm. With such allure, Kurre created his own temptations and readily gave in to them.

Whenever we were in a Swedish port, we did go to 2nd class restaurants. There were some in both Stockholm and Gothenburg where we were so well known that the bouncers, walking down the line to spot unacceptable drunks, would recognize us and, no matter our impaired sobriety, would wave us to the head of the line. These were times to literally spin our heads.

Once we got ahead of the line because of my suit. I never had enough funds for a new suit, nor did I need one until we began going to restaurants with dress code. However, my brother Lennart always dressed nicely. I asked to borrow one of his suits, and he responded generously by gifting me one. It was a beautiful suit, I thought. Only many years later did I realize that my taste was not as impeccable as I imagined. The suit was blue, not navy and not azure, but nicely and clearly blue. It had very thin white vertical stripes about one and a half inches apart, and between these stripes there were bright red stripes about double the width of the white ones. It was a unique suit and, although my other brother, Herman, said that looking at it gave him both nausea and head ache, I thought it nice and becoming.

Lennart's to-be-wife worked at a fine restaurant where Lennart was a steady customer and had stood in line more times than can be counted. Now Kurre and I were going there for the first time. We stood in line quite far towards its end and expected a long wait. But the bouncer, that all powerful arbiter, was checking the line. Without a word he beckoned us to the very front and let us in immediately. We were astounded. Kurre asked why we got this wonderful treatment. The bouncer looked me up and down, "There can't be more than one suit like that and I know the owner. You must be important!" I wore that suit often, not always with the same good result

Just before starting the ships' officers' school I spent a weekend at a resort in the archipelago. I met a girl shortly after arrival and we decided to have the dinner buffet together. To make a good impression, I wore Lennart's suit. It was now a bit old and showed signs of wear. In particular, Lennart had a habit of leaning on his elbows whenever he sat down. As a result the material at the elbows had worn thin. While walking along the buffet table ahead of the girl I was trying to impress by being well dressed and debonair, she moved up to me and said I had gotten some food on the elbow of my jacket. To be helpful she began to brush it off. Much to our surprise, the lining of the sleeve suddenly popped out of the spot she was trying to remove. It was not a food spot but the tell-tale sign of my suit material on its last leg. No more was I well dressed, nor debonair, and certainly not "suited" to contend for that girl's company.

In foreign ports there were bars galore to choose from. I remember one in Genoa where we would have our own private drinking contest. The bottles were displayed on a very long shelf, easily 30-40 bottles in line. We would start with a drink from the bottle to the extreme left, then the bottle to the right of that one, and so on, moving down the line with the goal of reaching the extreme right bottle before the evening was over. Much to our surprise we never got that far. We never reached beyond the mid-point where a bottle marked "VAT 69" was placed. We would take a drink from that bottle and, with heads spinning, or worse, the evening was over for us. We drew the only possible conclusion: "VAT 69" was the most potent drink ever and was an effective barrier to our continuing the contest. It never occurred to us that the real barrier was the drinks we had before reaching the mid-point. Our shipboard friends did not see the fallacy either. They carefully stayed away from "VAT 69", it was too potent a drink.

Everything we earned, we spent. Spending was a great incentive to earn more. Two years after the end of the war, scarcities were huge in the Mediterranean area. Sugar was rare and saccharine was in great demand. In Sweden it was not rationed, fairly inexpensive, and packaged in half kilo paper bags that were easy to carry and did not take much space. Most of us would bring a couple of kilos to sell, or exchange, mainly in Italy. This business was a good supplement to income. On one particular trip, in the northern Italian city of Livorno, we were told of a good market for our saccharine, and we actually identified a buyer. Kurre and I offered to consolidate the ship's supply and bring it ashore.

We dragged a rather substantial, and heavy, load in four suitcases to the place where we had arranged to meet the buyer. He was there, but had no intention of buying. Instead he had brought two armed policemen to "confiscate" the suitcases. It was clear to us that this was simply and plainly robbery. To hang around passively was to invite disaster, so we took off with two of the suitcases, one for each of us. We managed to get away – for awhile. Running for refuge in a culvert under the road looked, first, like a good idea. Once there it looked less so. We felt trapped and so ran out again at the far end. Barely had we cleared the culvert before the policemen began firing through it. That was too scary. We abandoned the two suitcases and took off wherever downhill would take us. There was no pursuit. They had found the remaining suitcases and probably concluded there was no more to be had.

We now had a problem. How to explain the loss of everyone's investment intended for the high life on the water front in Genoa, the next port of call? Talking back and forth, we decided to take the easy way out – run away from the problem. The plan was, in essence, to "jump ship", that is, we would wait till it had departed for Genoa, and then ask the Swedish consul to help us get to Antwerp from where we would get a ship to Sweden or elsewhere.

Decision made it was merely a matter of waiting for the ship to leave. It was truly miserable to wander the streets, occasionally reinforcing our courage in some bar, while waiting for the right time to set the plan in motion.

The longer we waited, the more miserable we felt, and the less appealing and clever did seem the plan. Why not, simply, face our shipmates and, if necessary, repay them for the lost saccharine? That, we resolved, was what we would do. By this time the ship had already left so we took the train to Genoa where we arrived in time to help attach the ship's mooring lines.

It turned out to be a costly adventure. Not only did we have to pay for the saccharine but the Chief Mate docked each of us seven days pay. Our shipmates, however, took it in fairly good humor, merely saying that serious business should not be trusted to children. On the other hand, if we wanted to risk our lives, they said, each one of them was mad enough to give us a good thrashing, we just had to ask for it.

We sailed together on several ships. In between ships we stayed in Stockholm where we independently pursued our search for shore based jobs, and renewed our ties with childhood friends. I don't know the details of Kurre's job search, but, as he had a driver's license, he quickly got a job driving a limousine for an American company. At times he took me with him on errands. That was a treat because I did not know how to drive and, apart from taxis, had not gone anywhere by private car.

The first car I owned was an old, very used German car, a DKW (Deutsche Kraftwagen), that I bought in 1958 just before Varda and I got married. For some odd reason we named it Pflumbaum, and it lived up to its quirky name. It usually started when the engine was cold, but, for some reason refused to do so when it was warm. The trick to keep it going was to never stop the engine en route but do so only at the final destination. Before we caught on to this behavior, the car took us wherever we wanted to go, but it rarely brought us back. As a result we walked a lot at the most inconvenient hours, usually weekends or at night. It was frustrating, but, on the other hand, we saw a great deal of the less well known areas of Stockholm. The color of the car was uncertain. It was originally black, but age and weather had blistered it into a faded navy blue. In sunlight it displayed a shimmering spectrum of blue and red. This wonderful color scheme was interrupted by large rust spots which did not enhance its appearance.

The springs of the car had lost their flexibility. With a load of more than two people (it was a 4-seater), it sagged so much that the under carriage rested partly on the road, giving us a spectacular, fiery transit. The car did not give us joy and freedom of movement; only when I got rid of it did we have that experience.

Both Kurre and I had childhood friends whom we had lost contact with when we went to sea. As we tried to reconnect, the two groups of friends showed signs of drawing together. We had some good times, but ultimately drew apart again. Kurre, however, stayed with me and my friends, or, more specifically, with one of my friends, Mary. She was a beautiful girl, full of life, fiery temper, and a great sense of humor. She also had a friend, B-L, beautiful and fetching. I fell for her, and she fell for me. Our relationship lasted almost two years but ended when she insisted on going to sea as a "mess girl". We parted on good terms.

B-L stayed at sea for a year, became pregnant, married and settled in Stockholm where her daughter was born. I knew her husband as I had sailed with him for a short time. The marriage did not last. She remarried and had a boy.

When I saw her next, in 2002, about fifty-five years later, she was widowed, had four grandchildren and spent most of her time on her son's summer farm. Although age had set its mark, she had retained many traces of past beauty. It was clear that she did not try to hide what time had done to her hair, skin or body. As in her youth, she used no make-up or hair spray. Her lined face was derived from the outdoors. The voice was unchanged, the language simple and subdued. She had been a Jehovah's Witness for a long time, and that informed her life, demeanor and expectations of others. She exuded contentment and happiness.

Life took a different turn for Kurre and Mary. He left the sea, they married, had a daughter, grandchildren and a happy life for many years. It was a joy to visit them and I did so often. Our drinking days were over. He was a changed man who lived only for his family. His doting on them was natural and entirely in character. He was happy.

We lost contact in the 1960's as our lives took different paths. In 2002 I met Mary again in Stockholm. B-L had arranged a "re-union". It was a sad occasion. Mary was in an early, but noticeable, stage of Alzheimer's. She had not aged well. It was difficult for her to move around. She smoked much and nervously, used foul language without inhibitions, and used lewd imagery in abundance.

It was difficult to see her in this condition and envision her future. However, she did remember me and we did reminisce, in a fashion. The story, as best I understood it, was that she had initiated an affair with her landlord at their regular summer retreat some ten years earlier. Kurre had taken it hard and had not been able to cope. He had drowned at that very same retreat; whether accidentally or intentionally was not clear. Mary showed no regrets or feelings of loss. Perhaps, for her, the advancing Alzheimer's was a blessing. I did not see her again. Both she and B-L passed away four years later.

While Kurre drove his limousine, I had two serious opportunities to find a future away from the sea. First, I found a position as an apprentice in a fine pastry bakery. The apprentice time was long, but I would ultimately be a skilled baker. My job was to come in at six a.m. to clean the baking sheets used by the bakers who had started their baking at four a.m. This done, I was to load the freshly baked pastries, Danishes and other sweet rolls, into a small, enclosed, trailer attached to the delivery bike and bring them, in time for the breakfast rush, to the two coffee shops owned by the bakery.

Given my penchant for sweets it was the most wonderful and desirable job I could imagine. On my first day I was informed of the owner's policy to allow the employees to eat, at any time, as much as they could possibly want of any delicacy baked on the premises, provided it was at least a day old. That included sweet rolls, cream puffs, chocolate eclairs, cookies, fillings like marzipan, mousse, jams, fresh fruits, custards, and so on. I liked, in particular, the access to the large bowls of freshly whipped cream which were excluded from the day old rule. The idea was, of course, that any normal person would soon have his fill and would then be able to work without distraction or temptation.

I am sad to say that I was not such a normal person; sad because I truly liked the place and its policy. I did eat, and eat, and eat without end. The others remarked on my surprising capacity for self indulgence, but did not interfere. In due time, they said, I would undoubtedly have enough.

All would have turned out well had I not given in to a more refined taste requiring not day old goods, but fresh, just out of the oven, products. That need was met by an elaborate scheme.

As I delivered the day's baked goodies to the first coffee shop, I picked up the pastries that were left over from the previous day, usually a half sheet. The same procedure was repeated at the second shop. This gave me the opportunity to indulge. When I left the first shop, I would substitute some of the returned pastries for some of the fresh pastries destined for the second shop. The fresh ones would be returned to the bakery as day old and were then available for me, and anyone else, to eat to our heart's delight. That way I would have fresh, warm and exceedingly satisfying food for my sweet tooth. Of course the sham was discovered. While the baker could abide my insatiable appetite, he found my behavior much too flawed for his establishment. I admit he was right. My job ended. Access to the wonderful world of pastries was gone. I still believe I would have made a fine pastry baker!

My second opportunity came at my father's urging. Being a painter, he felt that to become an attendant in a paint and hardware store was a very valuable skill. It would also be interesting, he claimed. After much searching I did land such an apprenticeship. Here my job was to work in the basement at the direction of the inventory clerk. I did learn where various pigments and tools were kept, what they were used for, and retrieved whatever the front desk requested. After the initial flurry of learning, there was little to do but while away time.

Once I was left alone as the inventory clerk had some appointment elsewhere. To pass the time, I practiced some rope work learnt at sea. I tied knots progressing from simple ones to complex, woven knots. One such knot, the Turk's Head, was used aboard ships to make a heaving line. The woven knot, at the end of a rather thin line, was filled with a heavy steel nut to give it weight so it could be thrown from the ship to the pier. A line man would catch it there and, pulling it to him, would also bring the real mooring line ashore as it was attached to the heaving line.

I made such a heaving line and decided to practice throwing it. The basement had several twenty gallon bottles (demijohns) from which we dispensed various liquids in small amounts. They were very heavy but I managed to bring two of them close together so that I would have a defined narrow opening to practice my "marksmanship". Many tries later I had not made much progress. The heavy nut seemed to go everywhere except where I aimed it. But, suddenly, there was success. The nut fell into the narrow gap between the bottles. Perhaps a little bit too much to the right; just enough to break the neck of the demijohn. A heavy odor seeped out. It was ammonia.

Well, it was my lunchtime and it seemed appropriate to take it sooner rather than later; besides, the smell was not conducive to staying any longer. I left.

When I returned from lunch, a rather large crowd was gathered outside the store where the doors were wide open. A fire truck was there and, on the whole, there was an atmosphere of emergency around the scene. I realized what had happened and decided it was the wrong time to return to work. So did my boss. Through a co-worker he sent word that my career had reached its end. He did not wish me good luck for the future, only that I should be gone as far as possible from his store.

Before Kurre settled down, our final ship together was a small one carrying general cargo in the Baltic and North Sea trade. Since we now had girlfriends waiting at home, we did not intend to revert to our previous carousing habits. But revert we did. Slowly at first, but, gathering momentum, we were soon back where we had started. Not without guilt feelings, but still an enjoyable life. The captain was a young man. Having abandoned a wife in northern Sweden, he had a Danish girlfriend aboard the ship at all times. He was a skilled seaman, knew how to treat both the ship and the crew well. We liked him, admired him and would, literally, do anything he asked of us. And ask he did.

The captain was very generous with the liquor and cigarettes he allowed us to buy tax free. We took advantage of it. What we did not use ourselves, we would sell in the small Swedish ports of call. One day, Kurre told me that his watch had helped the captain unload some boxes and cartons into a small boat that had come alongside close to the Swedish coast. I did not pay much attention to it; after all, I had not felt any slowing of the ship's movements or heard anything unusual. But it did not take long for my watch also to become involved. We were, indeed, engaged in big time smuggling of cigarettes and liquor. It only took place between Denmark and Sweden – we could not help but wonder if his girlfriend was the source of the captain's merchandise. Be that as it may. We were well compensated.

Our own attempts to earn money that way ended in failure. We had two cases of aquavit which would yield a handsome price if we could get them ashore. But where could we hide them? Customs officers seemed to know exactly where to look. We decided to hide them in the anchor chain box. As long as we had been on the ship we had never dropped the anchor, so that must be a safe place. The chain was heavy, but still manageable enough for us to move some of it out of the box. Hard work, but finally the box was half empty. We put in the cases and reloaded the chain properly into its place. Perfect! Two days later, in daylight, we entered our port of destination; a tricky approach necessitating the use of the anchor. I had visions of glass, wood splinter and the smell of liquor coming out of the hawse-pipe, but nothing happened. The anchor was left in the water as one of the mooring points and Kurre and I heaved a sigh of relief; after all, the two boxes were still safely hidden.

We went about our usual duties preparing for cargo unloading and, at the break, had our coffee in the mess room. Two custom inspectors joined us, had their coffee and asked one of us to come with them to the fore. We did so, both of us, and there, in the chain box, for anyone to see, sat the two boxes as neatly stacked as if they had just been put there. The captain had stuck out just enough chain to uncover our hiding place. One more fathom and the vision of glass, wood splinters and liquor smell would have been realized. The cases were confiscated, we owned up to ownership, paid a hefty fine, got a mark in our seaman's books and did not try again.

The small Danish ports were heavens as perceived by seamen. There were large shot-glasses and women galore; what more could life hold? Kurre and I lived with abandon. It was as if we knew this kind of life was drawing to a close, that there would be a sharp turn-around.

The agent of change was an old seaman totally destroyed by his war time experiences. Twice his ship had been torpedoed; twice he was narrowly rescued from the waters; and twice he had tried rehabilitation for alcoholism. He was now laying the foundation for a third attempt at such rehabilitation. At this he was very successful: he was drunk whenever not sleeping. I believe he was suffering from *delirium tremens* (DT) because he would wake up at night screaming that the rats were attacking him. To defend himself against these rats, and other vermin, he conjured in his mind a large snake, a boa constrictor. Indeed, as time passed, he, himself, became the snake. He would, in his drunken stupor, assume a sort of twisted gait which he said was that of the snake within him. Peeking around the corners, he would make a hissing sound, use his hands to simulate the snake's tongue, and sometimes grab one of us around the waist as a constrictor might do. He was harmless, except to himself.

However, Kurre and I looked at him with fear. Could our future be hiding our own "Boa" or some other animal? How far were we away from that point when drinking ceased being a pass time and became an unwanted necessity? Would staying at sea, drinking or not, leave us as lonely as was the "Boa"? We had girl friends; we were not alone. Why jeopardize, perhaps uncertain, happiness for certain unhappiness?

We discussed these questions realizing that, unless we changed course, we would certainly end up where we were headed. Almost overnight, our drinking ended and we talked earnestly about what steps to take to change our course. Kurre decided he would marry Mary if she would still have him. I was less resolute. The fabric of my relationship was not only frayed at the edges, but it had worn thin in large patches throughout. Inevitably, it had ended. And the sea still had its allure, just not the way it had been the last few years. Why not have the sea *and* a future tied to it? I decided to enter ships officers' school. It was early 1950.

Laying a New Course

When I made the decision to become a ship's officer, I did not expect much change in my life. I saw it merely as a move to another position aboard ship. Of course, there would be different duties, but I did not believe life would be materially different. How could I foresee that both the path and the content of my life would change? I never reflected on it.

Time for reflection is now as I look at a picture of the 1953 class of Master Mariners. All faces are familiar, but I do have difficulties connecting names to them. Nevertheless, it evokes emotions and memories of a very happy and life transforming time. For me, the picture confirms that my first academic education had concluded. Its broadening experiences would be the impetus for further change, and the shape my life has taken since then. In the picture, I appear at the extreme right end of the first row; to my right and above me, in a stairways fashion, are my fellow graduates. I wonder about them. Has my life been much different from theirs? Where did they go? Did they stay at sea? How did their personal lives progress? Did not the experience at school change them as it did me? For that matter, how did I change?

The only thing I know, as I look at the picture, is that my class mates were a congenial lot. Can't mention even one I did not like. Yet, I did not keep in touch with anyone after graduation. However, in December, 2002, I got a telephone call from one I had been particularly close to during those years. I remembered him, Hasse Norman, instantly and was grateful for his call. Since then, we have been in touch regularly reminding each other of the essentially very happy time spent at school.

The school experience had certainly affected him. While he went back to sea and reached command, his long absences from home and the birth of his first child made seafaring unbearable; it clashed with his perceptions of the worthwhile life. For him, seafaring had become empty, its previous allure was gone and in its stead there was only a longing for the secure warmth of home and family. The sea did not any more affirm life for him; it denied it. He left deep sea sailing to become a ship's pilot on Lake Malaren on which Stockholm is located.

In that capacity he met, and kept in touch with, our class mates. He gave me a broad outline of their lives. Our education had, indeed, affected us all, some for good, some for bad. While there were some outstanding success stories, it was also a dismal recounting of failed marriages, drinking, betrayals, and suicides.

Unlike so many of my class mates, I never felt a need, or desire, for a return to alcohol. It was not an ingredient used in the company I kept and enjoyed. In general, the taste, even of wine, became more and more repulsive as time progressed. I now take a glass once in awhile, but only because it is healthy; and I still don't enjoy it, very much!

Ships Officers' School – I

Shortly after my applying to the Navigation School in Stockholm, my home town, its name was changed to the more respect inspiring, and appropriate, Ships Officers' School. Admission required high-school competence in several subjects. For those who did not have those qualifications, that is, most of the applicants, there was a highly competitive entrance examination. For that purpose, the school offered an intensive three months preparatory course.

Like the others, I had only the mandatory seven years of public school, a shaky base from which to reach high-school competence in English, Swedish, geography, math, physics and chemistry, all in three months. It was a stressful time. A number of students dropped out, but I did persevere and passed the entrance examinations. Studies for the Mate's license started in 1951.

The program was rigorous. Classes were from 8:00 am to 4:00 pm six days a week for, I seem to remember, ten months. Upon passing the final exams in June, 1952, I was eligible to sail on the Mate's License. However, I immediately enrolled for the Master's course and passed those exams in June, 1953. But there was still a long road ahead.

The Master's License would be mine only after meeting further sailing requirements. That is, I had to sail in specified capacities as Mate on ships of specified sizes in specified trades. One requirement was service on a sailing ship. There were few of those and there was a long waiting list for mates who needed the experience to get their Master's License. Luckily for me, the requirement was abolished in 1958. By that time I had met all other conditions and so received the Master's License in April, 1959.

Attending a professional school was a new and enjoyable experience; it changed the premises for my future. I lived in my parents' apartment sharing a room with my brother, Herman. In essence I had returned to my pre-seafaring life. But now I had a goal, a purpose, a daily routine – and my family close-by. My relationship with my mother became more important than ever. Without her encouragement I would probably not have succeeded. She always asked about my studies. How far had I come in any particular subject? She looked at charts unfurled on the table, asked for explanations of navigational problems, nodded sagely and continued asking. I am sure she did not really understand my responses but, by trying to explain to her, I actually explained it to myself and so got a deeper understanding of the nature of my studies. Every evening we had long conversations with my pouring my heart out on every conceivable aspect of my life, studies, school, girls, and future dreams. Her eyesight was weakening so I did, occasionally, read to her. Without our evening conversations, my day was not complete.

My father, on the other hand, neither condoned nor opposed my studies – he may have thought about what an aunt of mine had said: getting the Masters License and, as such, turning fifty, were milestones likely to be feted in the society pages of the major newspapers.

Herman and I were the only siblings living at home. The others, Lennart my oldest brother, and my three sisters, Lilly, Nanny, and Maj, were married and busy with their respective families. As never before, I relished my life, my family and my studies.

A totally unexpected outcome of being at school was a sudden upsurge in my popularity with girls who, in earlier times, would, literally, cross the street to avoid being seen in my proximity. In their eyes I was not anymore a seaman, crude, uncouth, probably drunk, a society's outcast. Equally in their eyes, I was now a serious, goal oriented candidate for success. Acceptance to the Ships Officers' School vouched for that. I had become a potentially "good catch". Relatives and friends of my parents found many reasons to visit them, often with daughters, nieces, or other suitable young females in tow. Imagine, to be surrounded by those "family girls", known ashore as "nice" girls, inhabiting seamen's, not so secret, dreams? What more could a seaman ask for? A seaman could not. But was I still a seaman?

Did I look upon myself through the eyes of erstwhile shipmates or through the eyes of my new social environment? At first imperceptibly, then with increased speed, my concept of myself moved from that of the former to that of the latter. By the end of the first year I was very far, indeed, from my carousing past. The focus for my enjoyment of life had shifted. I very deliberately tried to improve my cultural polish so as to confirm and support my image of being an educated man. I attended museums, a few concerts, some theater and even an opera. Admittedly, there was no depth to my appreciation or understanding of these activities, but I did feel good about such forays into alien territory. With hindsight, they laid a lasting foundation for what is today an integral part of my life.

How much my studies had affected, and changed, me became clear when, during the summer of 1952, between the Mate's and Master's programs, I had my first experience as an officer serving as relieving third mate. The ship was an old ore carrier. I boarded the ship in Lulea, the northern port where once, as a young boy, I had been "kicked off" a small coastal trader. With some funds, summer time, and a good reason to be there, the city was very appealing. But I got only one day to explore it before the ship arrived, loaded and took off. The day was spent, not at a beer-hall, but sightseeing, a totally new concept for me.

The voyage took us to some continental ports and, finally, to the northern Norwegian port of Narvik, at the base of the Lofoten Islands. Life aboard was, as usual, hard work and hard drinking. In port, these aspects were complemented, again as usual, with harsh and hard living female company. I shied away from the "festivities" of my ship mates; I was again becoming a loner.

One afternoon, walking along the street, I heard piano music from an open window at ground level. Someone, it turned out to be a young girl, was playing Mozart's "Turkish March", one of the very few pieces I had heard before. I stopped to listen. An older woman, the player's mother, saw me and, delighted by my obviously discerning good taste and appreciation for music, invited me in to listen in comfort with a cup of coffee. It was a mistake on my part. The mother insisted on my hearing her daughter's whole, limited repertoire. However, when the "concert" was over, she proudly urged a repeat performance. While I enjoyed the initial playing, the first repeat was just bearable, the second less so. The girl played haltingly, and appeared to enjoy herself. But, as her enthusiasm waned, even my untrained ears began to suffer. I finally realized that the mother's delight with my presence was not shared by her daughter. Clearly, her delight would be enhanced by my absence. With many compliments on the music, and the coffee, in a voice I hope was full of admiration, I said good-bye.

Later, I reflected on this, my new, approach to shore leave. It had been a long, essentially uneventful, afternoon. Yet, I felt good. Why? I realized it was the normal, everyday family setting that soothed me, assured me that the waterfront's temptations did not anymore rule my life. I was, indeed, changing.

Two other memories from this trip stay with me, trivial, but strong. The first is of the, nowadays unbelievable, abundance of cod around the ship as we were anchored on the roadstead. We had an easy time catching them with a line from deck. The cook used our catch to prepare an old-fashioned, simply delicious, Scandinavian fish-boil dinner. The taste of it lingers. It would be some forty years before I had such food again, in Bayfield, Wisconsin.

The second memory is of the train ride back to Stockholm. It is less of the scenery, which was magnificent, than of the food I brought with me. It consisted of a whole, small wheel of well aged yellow cheese that I wanted to bring home. But, for whatever reason, the train had no dining car, and I turned to the cheese. The trip lasted somewhat more than 24 hours; the cheese lasted beyond that; but my feeling of well-being did not. To begin with I devoured the cheese in large chunks with great relish. The chunks became smaller as time progressed and my tastebuds rebelled. The relatively small piece of cheese that finally reached my home was well received and appreciated. I, however, did not touch cheese, of any kind, for a long time.

The next summer, 1953, I was, again, sailing as relief mate, this time on a large ship loading at Swedish, Finnish and Danish ports for its outbound voyage to the Far East. From the two summers as relief mate I gleaned one major aspect of my life as a ship's officer. Loneliness!

I realized that my studies, my life ashore, had separated me from my seafaring culture as effectively as if it had never existed. I found myself re-living my early, lonely days as a deck-hand in the Baltic coal trade. No feeling of belonging to the group. My exclusion may have been a natural consequence of my being a relief mate, not part of the permanent team, because I certainly felt differently when I began sailing again after my Navy service. But, in 1953, loneliness was again the key ingredient in my life at sea.

Before I accepted the relief work that summer, 1953, a tragic event occurred. Its effects are still with me.

Lost at sea

The story begins in the early 1940s when I was often invited by a school friend to his grandmother's house on the island of Runmaro in the Stockholm archipelago. There I met Hans, the son of the caretaker, a fisherman.

Hans was short and broad, almost stout, but, nevertheless, lean and strong. He was a silent man not given to small talk, but certainly not unfriendly. The face was round and red, a color given by the network of tiny, surfaced blood vessels on his cheeks. He had a typical weather beaten face, not expected in someone as young as he. He was a heavy smoker, drank moderately and rarely, and had eyes only for his girl friend, the neighbor's daughter. His physical strength and agility were the results of the heavy manual labor entailed in fishing during the war years: rowing long distances to the fishing grounds, hauling the nets and long-lines, and taking care of the landed fish. The hard life of fishing and marginal farming had taught him, from an early age, to rely on his own resources. He responded quickly to emerging situations and acted decisively to resolve problems.

A story told about him related that one winter he had brought his mother, across the frozen waters, to the store on a kick-sled. This was a common means of transport in those days. It was essentially a chair mounted on long steel runners. Standing behind the chair holding on to a handle above and behind the chair's back, the driver kept one leg on a runner and moved the contraption forward by kicking against the snow or ice with the free leg while the passenger sat in the chair.

Returning from the store with a heavy load, the sled broke through the ice. He and his mother were in the freezing water, and so were their provisions. The story tells that he, with enormous strength and cool planning, managed to get his, now almost unconscious, mother onto solid ice, retrieved the sled from under the ice, and brought the mother, by sled, to shelter. The provisions were lost.

He, himself, never mentioned this event, but others did so in admiring tones, pointing out that he did not know how to swim. Deliberately not learning to swim was not uncommon among islanders. It was based on the superstitious belief that the sea is not unfair; it will not take a defenseless fisherman.

Once, or twice, I met his family, but his parents and sister preferred to stay away from "city folks" of any kind.

We did not become friends at this time. There was too large a difference in our ages. I was twelve, he eighteen. We were both at an age where such a difference put us in totally different worlds. Ours was more a case of knowing each other by name and sight. Nevertheless, from our few encounters I learnt much about boat handling and fishing. I had great respect for him.

We did not maintain contact; there was no reason for it. My visits to the island ended, and, except for an occasional greeting passed on by our mutual friend, we were unaware of each other.

Nine years later, in 1951, we met again at the Ships Officers' School. I had just embarked on a two year program leading, first, to the mate's license and then to the master's examination. While the master's license, if and when I got it, would be unlimited, that of the mate's allowed me to command only smaller ships in near trades, coast wise and the Baltic Sea.

Hans did not want advanced certifications. Theoretical studies were not for him. He did not want deep-sea trading. Jokingly, his rationale was that such seafaring was way too dangerous. He wanted to stay safe and close to home and family. And so he attended a shorter program that emphasized skills needed for coast-wise trade. Our age difference did not matter at this time. We had more interests and experiences in common, and the parts of our programs that overlapped, gave us time to develop a real friendship.

He dreamed of his own shipping company. Shortly after receiving his license, he managed, with some partners, to raise funds to purchase a small ship of about 100 tons capacity. With this ship he began cargo operations between Stockholm and the island of Gotland, a one-way trip of about 30 hours. As both owner and commander he worked hard, and the business responded well. The ship carried a crew of six: Hans, the captain; an engineer; a female cook; a mess girl; and two deck hands.

The ship had been purchased with minimal equipment. There was no radar, no radio telephone or other communication equipment. The magnetic compass was unreliable as it had not been compensated for magnetic variations. In addition, the lamp over the chart table on the port side was plugged into an outlet on the starboard side. The excess cord had been wound around the compass stand, making it, in essence, into an electromagnet. Hans considered this unimportant. He did not need the compass because most of the trip was in sight of land, and his familiarity and experience of the many islands extended to the short segment in open waters.

Hans spoke often about his business. He was proud of his early application of a new cargo stowage method. He used pallets on which he consolidated various cargo units. In later years this would be called "unitization"; it would be used extensively and, ultimately, would result in the use of cargo containers and specialty ships for their carriage.

His efficiency was known. He had a good reputation as a reliable and safe carrier of cargo, and the ship's crew admired him greatly. With a booming business he needed time for office work and to stay abreast of his cargo bookings; he needed some relief from the constant back and forth traffic between ports. He asked me if I would occasionally relieve him, perhaps once a month. It would be a cinch, he felt. I had my mate's license so this should not be much of a challenge. I was flattered but pointed out my inexperience with inland waterway navigation, and, importantly, that I would feel uncomfortable with no means of communication. "No problem", he said, "a radio telephone is on order, I need it for the business", and as an afterthought, "the compass will also be taken care of ". It would be some time before the arrival of the telephone, and he did not expect me to take my turns until it was installed. As to the inland waterway navigation, he said, "Why don't you take a few trips with me while we wait for the telephone?" I agreed and did so until I felt comfortable with the inland segment. The next trip would be mine. I looked forward to my very first command.

It was morning, the ship was loaded and I was ready to leave. The cargo was mostly construction material: bagged cement, bricks, lumber, paint and oil barrels, and steel beams; most of it on pallets.

At that point the telephone equipment arrived, but Hans felt there was no hurry to install it. That could be done when I returned. He was eager for the ship to sail while the early spring weather held steady. But I voiced objections. "The equipment is finally here", I said, "so why not put it in?" "Even if it costs some delay", I continued, "I will feel so much more comfortable with it aboard". And, after a pause, "But if you insist, I'll go without it". Indeed, I had prepared and was ready to leave. But he felt my hesitation more strongly than I had intended, and responded, "I'll take her this time. Yours is next".

He asked me to make arrangements for the installation of the radio as soon as he returned. This done, I spent my day in the care-free manner merited by the fine spring weather. The evening brought me home to well deserved sleep.

Next day, Hans was to call from Gotland to his agent; that was standard procedure. It was not easy in those days to contact anyone at will by telephone so it was no surprise that the phone was silent at the expected time. The agent did not worry. I did not worry. Whatever we needed to discuss could wait until the ship returned.

There was no hurry, no worry, but there was also no ship. It did not return at the expected time. Not only did it not return, but it had never arrived. Search was initiated but found nothing. Not a single scrap of wreckage. The ship was gone. No one knew when, where, or how.

I felt the absence of the ship, I did not yet call it lost, as a personal affront. I had been deprived of a command. I actually felt resentment. But soon the ship became, also in my mind, lost. Soon it was not only a loss. It became a catastrophe. I was invaded by an overwhelming feeling of helplessness and loneliness enveloped by a deep sorrow. A crying spell followed and so did sleepless nights and nightmarish images of what the final events might have been.

I saw the crew hanging on to an overturned hull, their hands becoming increasingly numb from the cold water until their hold slipped and they silently, with mouths open wide, sank under the ice flecked water. In another vision they were tossed into the water immediately with no hull to hang onto, but the sinking under the water was as silent and fast as in the first vision. In yet another image, the ship capsized and all aboard were trapped inside as the ship, slowly and silently, without a sign of human beings, sank beneath the surface. While my nightmares were soundless, my waking days filled my mind with the screams of the agony and fear of the drowning people. I heard them. I suffered with them.

What *had* happened? The experts speculated on three possibilities. First, the ship had veered too far north because of the unreliable compass and had met ice drifting down from the north. The ship had run into a piece of solid ice, sprung a leak and sank. Or, the ice had, simply, ground the ship to pieces. I found that implausible. Although the stretch of open water was passed during the night, the weather was fine with calm seas and good visibility. Hans knew the compass deviations well and he, anyway, never relied on it. Also, he was far too experienced to take a chance on drifting ice. He knew well the dangers of being trapped in it, and there was plenty of open water to evade whatever ice he may have spotted. In addition, such an event ought to have left some signs of the wreckage.

The second conjecture was more plausible. The drifting ice may have dislodged and brought a floating mine into the sea-lane. These were not uncommon during the spring break-up of the ice. Avoidance of a mine did not depend on good seamanship. It depended mostly on good luck, although a good look-out with keen eyesight would also help. However, even the best of look-outs would be irrelevant during a night time passage. Given the captain's confidence in his mastery of the ship, and his knowledge of his "home waters", it is likely that he alone stood watch, allowing most of the crew to sleep in anticipation of the hard work expected of them at their destination.

The third possibility was that the cargo had shifted and caused the ship to capsize. This seemed most plausible to me. The cargo had not been tightly stowed or lashed. Using pallets left plenty of empty space for cargo to shift, and we had not made any stability calculations. In general, the heavy cargo should be stowed at the bottom to give a low center of gravity. In this case I recalled the steel beams being fairly high up in the hold. Hans and I had together loaded the ship, but neither of us had prepared a stowage plan. While I always deferred to his decisions, I cannot, today, escape the suspicion that Hans may have relied too much on me and, as he placed cargo in the hold, expected me to catch any unsafe stowage. But I did not interfere. I was inclined to see his knowledge and judgment as superior to my own.

Whichever scenario may be true, access to radio telephone might have made a difference. Unless the ship went down very fast, there may have been time to alert rescuers. The outcome may have been different. If the radio was so important to me, why did I not insist that Hans consider it equally important and spend the time needed for its installation? Even with hindsight, I cannot find an answer.

Much time has passed since this event, well over fifty years, but it is still with me. I have never been able to fully reconcile my gratefulness for having been spared with my guilt feelings for having accepted his taking over the command.

I had a difficult period in the aftermath of the ship's disappearance. The nightmares returned for many years, and are not uncommon even today. The visions transmuted into a lasting, pronounced, and irrational, fear of certain types of ships and spaces. I cannot, with an easy mind, board those enclosed boats used for harbor tours and sightseeing. Images of the boat overturned, passengers trapped inside, overwhelm and frighten me. In the enclosed spaces of theaters, I try not to sit in the middle of a row, and I never mingle with big crowds. There is an underlying feeling of almost panic as I have visions of being trapped in space, or among people, unable to escape.

Six people were lost at sea. I knew them all. No one knows what happened, and few care. There were no burials, eulogies, speeches or memorials; no farewells from the fellowship of seafarers. Only a brief note on the back pages of one, or two, newspapers announced the event that shattered the lives of those left behind to grieve and miss them.

Have those left behind carried the memories and sorrows until today, more than 50 years later? Or, if I am the only one who has done so, then I am glad I have told the story, as I know it, of the captain who took upon himself a duty that should have been mine.

The Lady Wore White

My memories of the Ships Officers' School, *per se*, are sketchy. The building was very old and imposing. While I had never been inside the building, I knew the neighborhood well. It was at the beginning of the southern part of Stockholm, Sodermalm, which rises steeply, and high, from the watery approaches to the city. The main harbor, at that time, was along the waterfront, at the bottom of the rise. The reason I knew the area so well was that the sights and smells of the harbor exerted a powerful pull on me. Again, and again, I would take the long walk from home to watch the ships, imbuing them with life from my imagination and dreams. While the port was the main attraction, I was also drawn to the old, quaint neighborhood located on the top of that, almost perpendicular, rise from the quay. And towering over that neighborhood stood the Ships Officers' School.

I roamed that area as a child, partly because it was on the way to the port, and, partly because there were rumors the neighborhood was haunted. In the distant past, the city's executioner had lived there, close to the hill where once stood the gallows. All that was long gone, but it was a fascinating area for those with vivid imaginations. In particular, there was, at the end of the street, a small, old house we called, without knowing why, "Death's Waiting Room". Certainly, this was a name to stimulate children's imaginings. To us, the whole area reeked of mystery and inexplicable fear.

Some people swore they had seen the restless ghosts of the executioner's long ago victims appearing outside, and around, the "waiting room" area. The Lady in Black had been seen often; the Lady in White less so. Many were the stories of brave confrontations with the Ladies. One man said he had implored one of them to seek peace by accompanying him to the near-by church. He related with amazement that, as he approached the ghost, it had taken on an almost human form before vanishing. So encouraged was he by this, almost successful, salvation that he, thereafter, spent many evenings trying to find that lost soul once again.

My mother said these were just silly "old wives tales", but one evening I did, indeed, see the Lady in White. It was frightening even if she was far away at the end of the street. She seemed to be floating slightly above, and along, the street, her white shroud, like gossamer, swaying loosely back and forth and, where the head should have been, a large mass of ectoplasm as white as could be.

I became somewhat of a celebrity at school because I embroidered the experience with fanciful, scary details. The Lady had beckoned me to come closer. When I did not obey, she came towards me at high speed as she floated through the air with outstretched arms. She came so close, I said, that I could see her featureless face and feel the cold of her ghostly presence. But I managed to escape down the stairs to the port. These untrue details came back to haunt me in nightmares for a long time. Only in those dreams did I visit that haunted street again.

In due time the sightings of the ghosts became scarce and explanations began to surface. The small house at the end of the street was a hospice, a concept we did not understand. The explanations we got seemed to confirm, rather than deny, it as a fitting environment for ghosts. The ghosts may not be seen as often, but, surely, they were there.

The hospice was run by an order of nuns. Since at that time there was much religious prejudice, non-Lutherans kept low profiles and most people had never seen nuns in traditional habits

The sisters running the hospice rarely ventured outside, and did so only mornings and evenings when few people were around. They wore long, flowing white or black habits with white, starched veils, or white-winged head dresses. How could we perceive them as anything but "ghosts"? As a matter of fact, many years later, I still felt uneasy passing the then defunct hospice on my way to the Ships Officers School.

Ships Officers' School – II

The school's rooms, large, high ceilinged, and always cold, brought back memories of my primary school, and like that school, tacitly imposed discipline. That discipline was strict. We were there to learn, and learn we did. Any reverting back to shipboard behavior could have immediate repercussions. Expulsion was a potent threat. It was a privilege to be at the school, and we were not to forget it.

The building included a high, square tower with a mast on which a huge ball could be hoisted up and down. It was the time signal announcing the exact noon time. Every day just before noon, the ball would be brought to the top of the mast; it would then be lowered at a slow pace so that it reached the bottom at precisely noon. Across the waters, at the naval station, the time signal was a cannon shot fired at noon. The signals were widely watched and noted throughout the city. At times we were asked how we knew when the exact noon occurred. We replied that the school's "master of the time" knew it was noon when he heard the cannon shot from the naval station. Well, how did they know the time? Very simply, we explained. The naval station knew it was time to fire the gun when they saw the ball being lowered at the school's tower. In that way, we said, there were two independent sources verifying the correct time. The logic seemed impeccable, but no one believed the story.

The curriculum included navigation, seamanship, instrumentation, and some subjects totally unknown to me. They opened a new world. In particular, I was fascinated by economic geography, meteorology, admiralty law and marine insurance. These topics shed light on many of my seafaring experiences, put them into new contexts and enriched my general education. The teachers at the school had Master's Licenses combined with advanced university studies, something akin to, but a bit beyond, the British Extra Master. To me, their knowledge seemed to encompass everything known to mankind. I marveled at their achievements. After all, they had started as common seamen just as we, the students, had. Although I can't recall their names, I can still see some of them in my mind's eye.

Two math professors, in particular, stand out. One taught the preparatory course. He referred to math as the ultimate revelations of the Supreme Deity in whom he professed his disbelief. He was tall, distinguished looking in an immaculate grey flannel suit matching his thick, grey, and carefully combed hair. Always in white shirt and tastefully colored tie he drew attention to his hair by frequently and tenderly stroking it with well manicured hands. We were fascinated by this display of gentility and taste so beyond anything we had experienced. Whenever he had completed a proof, he would step back, look at the board, then at us, stroke his hair and say, "Is that clear? Or do I have to do it again?" Whereupon he did it again, stroked his hair, and left the room. When the preparatory course was finished, he strode to the back of the room forcing us to turn around to look at him as he, as usual, stroked his hair. He then raised both arms as if blessing us, looked each in the eye and said, "I have done my part. Now it is up to you and God to do yours." Having thus commended us to the Deity in which he did not believe, he turned around and left without another word. I saw him a few times during the school year, but he never showed any sign of recognition.

The other one was our regular math teacher; we saw a lot of him during the year. He was a health fan. Vegetarian and obsessed with physical fitness, he brought a bike with him every day. In good weather he rode it; in bad, he pushed it. His appearance was rather the opposite of immaculate. His scalp was sparsely populated with thin, grey strands of hair resembling sewing thread. A shirt of uncertain color and pattern was the height of his fashion; never a tie or matching jacket. Sweaters and wind breakers sufficed. Usually he wore baggy pants held in place at his ankles with clips enabling him to ride the bike. Hiking boots completed the wardrobe.

The pants did not adhere closely to his waist. They were at least two or three sizes too big in that area because he wanted as much freedom of movement as possible. Needless to say, he would not, and could not, use a belt to hold the pants in place. Instead, he used multicolored, loose hanging suspenders. Seeing him from the back, his usual position as he faced the blackboard most of the time, the pants looked like a barrel with him stuck into it somewhat haphazardly. When finished with the blackboard he would turn around very quickly to face our questioning faces. Because of the loose hanging pants, it seemed as if he turned before the pants did. We found it very amusing. He did not, but said that if his pursuit of a healthy life style gave us joy, then he was all for it. I certainly liked him.

Next to our school was a girls' training center for business secretaries. There was no overt interaction between the student bodies. They despised us, they said. Nevertheless, several from our engineering program dated girls from that school. Most of the dating resulted in weddings, and, toward the end of the Master's program, the girls began to find also the deck officers more appealing.

More promising, in terms of meeting girls, was a school for home economics a few blocks away. There we could have good, large, and inexpensive meals as cooking was an important part of the curriculum. There I met Inga.

We had a long, often stormy, relationship, but remained good friends throughout the years; a friendship holding even today. I still have a woolen, true seaman's, sweater she knitted for me. She also became a devoted Jehovah's Witness.

I showed great aptitude for academic studies. I enjoyed them, and the newfound social status they conferred. I was popular among my peers, be they male or female, as well as among the older generation. I had grown accustomed to living at home, to share my thoughts with my mother every evening. My past seafaring days were just that: past. I did not want to lose the newly found stability, security and warmth of friendships that had developed in my new circumstances. The romance of far away places had been displaced by the comfortable security and, in its own way, romance of the stable existence I had found in the last two years. In fact, I dreaded the end of school and gave much thought to continued studies. However, I was spared from making a decision at that point. The Navy intervened.

For every physically fit male there were twelve months of mandatory military service. My obligation had been deferred while attending school, but that was now at an end. Given my seafaring background I was, of course, according to military logic, assigned to the infantry. I was happy it was not to the cavalry because I did not know how to ride; walking was not a problem.

After some bureaucratic maneuvers, I was finally claimed by the Navy. As a reward for my schooling, the length of service was extended to fifteen months; the extra time allocated for special training. However, there was another path. I could apply for reserve officer's training. If accepted, I would be obligated to serve another twelve months, that is, a total service of twenty-seven months. That option appealed to me. It would allow me to continue studying, to stay close to home and minimally disrupt the kind of life I had come to appreciate. I was accepted to that program and started my service at the Royal Naval War College in the fall of 1953

The Navy

Naval War College

The Royal Naval War College (*Kungliga Sjokrigsskolan*) was located in Nasby Park, a short train ride north of Stockholm. A beautiful campus, the center of which was Nasby Castle, it was sprawling, lush and green exuding an air of peace and tranquility totally at odds with the expressed purpose of the school. We were to spend fifteen months there, the first three in basic training, the remainder to acquire the special skills for a reserve officer's commission. This would be followed by twelve months' active duty.

It was a happy experience. Good accommodations, good food and, most important of all, good camaraderie and a feeling of belonging. The days in basic training were not onerous except for the morning jog. Up at 05:00 to run about two miles before making the bed, shower, shave, and be inspected after which we were ready for breakfast. I grumbled a great deal at this inhumane treatment. Whoever had heard of running an "engine" at full speed without first letting it warm up? Even so, never before, or after, have I been in such excellent physical condition. Once, leaving home to get back to base, I missed the streetcar by a narrow margin. Without hesitation I ran after it hoping to catch up by the next stop. But I missed also that stop, and the next. I was now so close to my destination that I decided to forego the streetcar and jog the remaining distance. My breathing was barely affected by this exertion. The morning jogs had paid off not only in physical stamina, but this time I had also saved the train fare. Mentioning this to my sister, she drily remarked that next time I ought to run after a taxi, the savings would be much greater.

I learnt how to march, stand at attention, and at ease. I was particularly adept at the latter. Squaring the corners of the bed was a major achievement in those first few months. Our commander, Mr. G, was a non-commissioned officer of impeccable integrity, skills and knowledge; a true leader. He was much liked and admired.

Once, not doing very well on the firing range, I complained about the rifle. Obviously there was something wrong with it. How else to explain that I never hit the target? I was not even close. He took the gun, inspected it carefully, and told me, kindly, that he now knew what was wrong. I looked around triumphantly at my fellow shooters, "See, it's not my fault, it's the gun". Mr. G showed me the butt of the gun; that was where the fault lay. I saw nothing and asked what was wrong. Again, very kindly he explained that, when I fired, it was the ass behind the butt that was at fault. My performance did not improve much after that, but I stopped blaming the gun.

The food was generally very good. One day, however, a foul odor hung over the campus. It became stronger, became a stench, the closer one approached the mess hall. We thought something unpleasant would be served. But we were wrong. While the incredible smell suffused the dining room, the food was the usual, tasty fare and we were certainly not going to let our noses spoil the ambiance in the dining room.

It was not until the next day that odor and food came together. A strange looking meat stew, the dark brown color of which seemed to match the still pervasive smell, did not allow us to divorce the food from its odor, no matter what ambiance we tried to evoke. It was, indeed, not a positive experience.

The explanation for this extraordinary feast was whale meat. The odor came from the attempt to boil off as much as possible of the animal's blubber. I have always wondered about the Japanese fondness for this meat. Perhaps they have a special way of making it edible, leave alone palatable. Or, perhaps, their taste-buds respond differently than mine. Given that, for me, sushi and other Japanese fish dishes are to be endured rather than enjoyed, I think both explanations may be true. The odor stayed in the dining room a long time.

The curriculum included artillery, its theory and practice. An intensive period of practice involved a couple of days on an island in the outer archipelago. The island was, of course, uninhabited, except for snakes. We were equipped with walking sticks and cautioned to poke around a bit before entering suspect places, particularly the outhouses. Such caution ensured that these facilities were rarely used, certainly not at night. This set-up was not conducive to regularity and we were a rather disgruntled lot when the stay ended.

To this island we arrived with our trajectory tables, equations, slide rules, class notes and interpretations and calculations of various problems. The target was a silhouette of a small ship towed at a respectable distance from, and behind, a larger ship. Each of us was to take command of the battery and use our own calculations of the coordinates for the gun crew to use. Warned to stay clear of the towing vessel, we had three shots each. No one hit the target; some came close to it, and some came very close to the towing ship. My turn was toward the end of the line and, in the scheme of things, my shots were not bad. We all felt good about our performances, and could not help feeling amused when the next man in line took his place. He was the most unlikely seaman and officer one could imagine. Tall, hunched over shoulders, awkward walk, but even-tempered and kind, he never excelled in any subject. We often joked and poked fun at him, and he took it in good spirits.

He took his place, perused his aids, made a pencil correction here and there in his tables, stroked his chin thoughtfully, and checked the calculations again. Finally he gave out his coordinates. Looked again at his notes and tables, changed the coordinates and paused pondering what he had just calculated. He had already taken more time than allotted to him. The lieutenant became irritated and told him to get on with it. And so he did. In rapid succession he fired his three shots. He could have saved the last two because the first shot obliterated the target completely.

Calmly he collected his equipment and walked over to his awestruck comrades and the speechless lieutenant. Whether luck or skill, he carried it off with dignity and confidence. Never again did we poke fun at him.

The stay at the island ended with severe snake induced constipation.

Ship board life in the navy was vastly different from that in the merchant marine. We were introduced to these differences on the designated school ship, a large mine layer *(Alvsnabben)*. The ship was crowded with the crew being augmented by the officers-in-training. No privacy at all. The sleeping arrangements were long rows of hammocks hung in place in the evening and removed in the morning. It took skill, not only to get into, and out of, the hammock, but also to remain in it. After falling off a few times onto the unforgiving and pain inflicting steel deck, I learned quickly and was soon able to sleep comfortably.

Discipline was tight and individual initiative frowned upon; it was a matter of following orders. Proper forms of address were important. Equally important was the dress code, and the daily routine was rigidly fixed. Within that routine we were relieved of watch standing, as we knew it. Instead, we had to learn the ins and outs of being "the officer of the day".

My first experience in that capacity was harrowing. Requested to wake somebody at a certain time I nodded and committed the task to memory. Another task arose; it was also committed to memory. It never occurred to me to write them down. After all, it was not hard to keep these few items in mind. The officer, under whom I performed my duty, looked at me but said nothing. But soon new tasks appeared at increasing speed: awake this one or that one at a specific time; have a launch ready here or there; prepare for this or that; remind one of this, another of that; report when certain tasks were started or completed, and so on. I was inundated and totally bewildered. I could not remember what to do when. It was bedlam. There was too much to keep in mind, a system was needed. At this point, the real "officer of the day" reminded me of all the things I had forgotten but which had, nevertheless, been accomplished, not by me, but by him. He had kept the log, as mandated, but had allowed me to do everything my own way, thus bound for failure. From then on, the log, that common "to do list", became an important key to success.

Another invaluable experience came also fairly early in the "officer of the day" training. A launch had to be ready, and stand by at seven a.m., to ferry the ship's commanding officer to some on-shore destination. At six o'clock I instructed a sailor to pass the order to the launch operator and turned my attention elsewhere.

Seven o'clock arrived; so did the captain, but not the boat. "Where is it?" he demanded. "I don't know", I answered truthfully. "Well", the lieutenant chimed in, "find out". After much commotion, the launch operator was found, and the captain left, some forty-five minutes late.

The lieutenant took me aside. How could I mess up such a simple task? "I sent a sailor to alert the operator", I defended myself. "That", the lieutenant said, "was not your orders. You were to have the launch in the right place at the right time. That is not the same as telling someone to do it. Your duty is to see the job done! Completed!" That was certainly a good point and a lesson that would soon land me in trouble.

The summer was drawing to an end, so was our ship-board training. For the officers, it was a time of observing end-of-training games, and, when not observing, attending dinners and other parties aboard the many ships at the base. One of the full ranked admirals stayed the nights aboard our ship, in the small guest suit on main deck; our commanding officer's, fairly large quarters, were a deck above, close to the main bridge.

The evening before the games, the captain and the admiral returned to their respective quarters in the early morning hours. An evening of lavish partying had put them in good moods, and the admiral even called me "my good man". The captain asked to be woken up at four am, just two hours away. Duly noted in the log, I waited for the wake-up time to arrive. This was a task I would attend to myself.

At four o'clock I knocked on his door and announced,"Sir, its four o'clock". No answer. I knocked again, this time a bit louder. Still no real answer, only some sleepy murmurs. I was in a quandary. What should I do? The captain seemed to be awake, but was he really up? In a flash I heard the lieutenant's admonishment: "See the job done. Complete it!" That meant: do not only knock on the door; see to it that he is, indeed, awake and up.

I knew what to do. Zealously I attacked the door pounding again and again, determined to have him up, unequivocally awake. Just as I began to achieve results, that is, the captain began to stir, and was actually yelling something indicating he did not appreciate my efforts, just then a familiar voice behind me asked what was going on. I turned around and froze. There was the captain, dressed and ready for action. So, who on earth was the angry man in his quarters? The man who used such intemperate language about me? I suddenly understood. The captain had given up his larger quarters to the admiral. I, a lowly messenger, had not been informed. It was too late to change the progress of events.

The admiral was up, and angry. He continued his ranting. I was amazed. Would not advanced education and high rank vouch for a fine, sensitive personality? And, would such a personality not refrain from using crude language when telling someone, me, where to go? But that was not so. His language was fluent, expressive, and replete with colloquial vulgarisms, all of it directed at me.

The captain took charge. He would hear of no explanations or excuses, and sent me back to my duty station. The lieutenant was not only amused, he actually laughed heartily, and assigned me a place far from the captain's and the admiral's sight lines. The end-of-training games began.

Active Duty

My stay at the Naval War College came to an end in the fall of 1954 when I received my commission as an Ensign in the Naval Reserve. There was a seamless transition into active duty. With special training in torpedo and mine warfare, I was assigned to a destroyer, *Karlskrona*. There were many things I liked about life in the Navy. What lingers in my mind are the many formalities which, without rational explanations, still enhanced life.

There were the dinners in the mess room, sometimes in formal dress uniform, sometimes not. Whatever the case may be, a meal without wine was unthinkable. However, the wine glass could not be touched until the commanding officer, we called him "The Chief", gave permission. This was not given by saying, for example, "Go ahead, gentlemen. Enjoy the wine." No. Instead, at an early stage of the meal, he would, from his sitting position, raise his glass, bow slightly towards one of the assembled officers, usually the most senior one, call his name and look him in the eyes. The toasted officer would act similarly, lock eyes, raise his glass in acknowledgment, and they would both sip the wine. They would again raise their glasses towards each other, make eye contact, nod and put them down. The toast was completed. This procedure would progress down the ranks. The toasted officer was now free to toast the company, but would start with the one who had first toasted him; that is, the one who had so-to-speak released him to enjoy the wine. The glasses could only be raised, the bow slight and the eyes locked intently. To clink the glasses, or avoid eye contact, was crude, vulgar and bad form in the extreme. As the youngest, my wine drinking usually came very late in the meal.

Which piece of silverware, or glass, to use for what, and when, followed its own protocol. In general, I waited to pick my fork, or whatever, until I saw what the others did. Some of them took pleasure in picking the wrong ones merely to watch my embarrassment when I became aware of my mistake.

At that time, Sweden had strict rationing of spirits and wines. The officers pooled their liquor allowances, and some funds, to provide the wherewithal for accustomed dining. As the youngest, I was assigned the management of the "wine cellar", and funds. It was serious business, particularly for me who had very little taste for, or understanding of, the epicurean pleasures of wine. It was a challenge, too, because we usually invited one or more officers from other ships for dinner.

I did very well, though, mainly because of my predecessor's efforts. He had arranged a movable shelf above the steam radiator. On a vertical scale he had indicated the length of time, and distance from the radiator, that various types of wine ought to be set to reach proper serving temperature. I followed it and made a major discovery. The warmer the wine, the better it seemed to taste to my fellow officers. In later years I found this to be true only because the wines I bought were so cheap and inferior that their taste was already at the bottom. Any way of doctoring them could only improve their taste.

And doctor the wine I did. In short order we became recognized for our excellent table, its food and wine. Once I splurged on a really good wine, St. Emilion, and got many compliments for my taste and good management of our resources. What an incentive to continue on my path of excellence. I saved the empty St Emilion bottle. On many occasions I filled it with the usual, inexpensive wine, warmed it way above room temperature and served it as the expensive sort. No one complained. The sudden surge in quality was noted, and, again, I was recognized for my management skills.

One evening The Chief asked me specifically for St Emilion. He had invited another officer and his wife to dinner. The guests arrived. He had the rank of commander. Urbane, witty and exuding authority, he was in formal dress uniform, his wife in evening gown. Hurriedly The Chief ordered us into similar dress.

The dinner progressed in the most formal of manners. When the steward served my version of "St Emilion", the guest exclaimed, "St Emilion, my old friend and favorite". I was gratified by his obvious appreciation of the wine we served. Toasts were exchanged in the usual manner, conversation flowed easily; the evening was a success. After the dessert, formality dictated that the guest should give a "thank you" speech.

He tapped the glass with a spoon for attention, stood up, and from that position, extended a toast, first to The Chief, then to his wife and then to the whole company. The speech was gracious and witty. He commented, in turn, on our hospitality, the excellent food, and the skills of our cook. Notably absent in that first round of praise was the wine, his favorite, St Emilion. It began to occur to me that I might have reasons to feel uneasy. True enough. He now turned to "praise" the wine. He was very diplomatic. In essence, he had enjoyed the excellent food which certainly had enhanced the wine, an important aspect as wine is not always of uniformly good quality, no matter the name. Therefore, he cautioned the officer in charge of the wine to question his supplier so as not to be charged for what "he might not receive". A few more comments and he ended with the same toast as he began with. It was hard to believe what I had heard: 'The food had enhanced the wine'. Should it not be the other way around?

As the guests were ready to depart, he took me aside. "Thank you", he said, "for giving us a memorable wedding anniversary. I will never forget your wine. But, don't do it again, there are too many who know the difference between warm wine and good wine".

Later on, The Chief related that his guest was a well known wine specialist. Not only had he studied wine making in France and elsewhere, but he was a senior wine trader for the State Monopoly of Wines and Spirits.

Amazingly, none of my fellow officers caught on to the guest's references to the wine, but, nevertheless, that was the end of my serving my version of St. Emilion.

More Naval Life

Life in the Navy agreed with me. Whether I was agreeable to the Navy, is another question. These were happy days. I liked everything about being on active duty. Certainly, life was structured within a strict set of routines, but, even so, it was not a routine life. The length of the work day was indeterminate, sometimes very short, at other, more frequent times, very long. No nine to five days, no rigidly prescribed daily tasks and, for me, very few administrative duties. Each day brought new activities and experiences. I learned, grew and enjoyed.

The year was essentially a period of training and study. I had to serve in many capacities for short periods of time in order to get a firm grasp on the many aspects of a functioning war ship. To be in charge of damage control was a most useful training. It focused on the unexpected, on emergencies, and honed my abilities to deal with such problems. Among other things, it included evacuation of injured people, fire fighting, ship repair, and the improvisation of steering mechanisms, all of which could be useful also in the merchant marine.

The same held for the intense exercises in archipelago navigation and small boat handling. To learn, not to mention to use, the navigational aids and landmarks specially constructed for the navy took time, skill, and cool nerves. The aim of the training was to transit at the highest possible speed among hundreds of small islands and shoals. The sense of achievement after successfully completing this course dwarfed any other success I can recall.

Advanced training in torpedoes and mines, at the time called "robotics", gave me a good grounding in electronics, radar guidance, and automation. So did my continued training in artillery and communications. Indeed, I was so intrigued by "robotics" that I considered, for awhile, to become a radar engineer.

One incident left a lasting impact. I was in charge of communications and had been issued, and signed for, the master code book, a secret, color coded, document to be handled according to very specific rules. At the end of my assignment, the book was nowhere to be found. I was grilled extensively as to how I had handled the return of it to the higher officer in charge of the code inventory. I described in minute details how I had complied with the rules recounting both place and time for each step: I had brought the book to the designated collection point; it had been inspected for completeness, that is, no pages missing; I had then sealed it in the collection box where it would be in safe keeping until we returned to base.

In my mind I remembered everything: the people in the radio room, where each one stood, the movement of the ship, lighting conditions, the lightly folded page corner to ear-mark the day's code, the bright red color of the book, and so on. My certainty was unshakable. My memory was perfect; I could, at any time, recollect what had happened. The book's missing was inexplicable. For whatever reason, I faced no consequences beyond the humiliating questioning and low marks for performance.

Some time passed and we went to the shipyard to install, among other things, new communications equipment. The Chief called me to his quarters and asked if I still remembered the details of the code book's return. I did, indeed, and described, once again, what had been done. He listened carefully, then asked for the color of my book. "Bright red", I answered without hesitation, and added, "There was a slight watermark on the back". "So, it can't be this one?" he asked and pulled out a pale orange book. "No", I answered, "it does not look like it." "Check it out, anyway", he said, handing me the book.

Embarrassment of embarrassments! It was my code book. My signature acknowledging its receipt was there for anyone to see. No bright red color, no water mark, no ear-mark; just a plain, well cared for, orange code book. It had been found behind the collection box when the old equipment had been removed. Again, much to my surprise, there were no consequences apart from humiliation.

There were many other aspects of naval life that appealed to me, particularly our social life with formal balls and dinners. To invite a girl to such an affair was not only a pleasure, it changed my standing with her. It advanced my cause even with girls I would scarcely dare to approach for a date. The formal invitation, arriving by mail, in a beautiful envelope with an impressive sender's address, contained plenty of stilted language and gold script that could not fail to make a good impression on both the girl and her parents. I was popular beyond anything I could have imagined.

The reactions of the girls puzzled me, though. Some were obviously drawn to the uniform, others were not. In one instance, I asked the invited girl for more dates. She agreed. We met a few times and all seemed to go well. One evening I was delayed and had no time to change into civilian clothes. Choosing to be on time, I arrived in uniform. Somehow I broke an unspoken demand of hers: never to be in uniform when seeing her. She suddenly claimed headache, went home, and disappeared from my life.

Another girl, much more important to me, took the opposite stand. She liked me in uniform, and I obliged. I liked her; I loved her and she reciprocated. We were inseparable and became engaged to be married. For reasons that are not important any more, we broke up after two years. I have fond memories of Marta, as I know she has of me.

There were twelve, sometimes fifteen, officers on the ship. The Chief had commander's rank. I idolized him. He came from the merchant marine, had his master's license and had been accepted into the regular navy after illustrious service in the reserve. He often delegated responsibility to me way beyond my abilities to perform, but was always there to bail me out.

One early morning the ship was to move from its anchorage to the dock. I had the watch and arrived on the bridge expecting to assist The Chief with the maneuver. He was not there. After waiting many long minutes, I realized he wanted me to do it by myself. Supremely confident I weighed anchor and began approaching the dock. Yes, approaching, but not reaching it. I miscalculated the distance, stopped engines too late and drifted beyond the pier. Trying to return to the original point to repeat the action, I ended up behind a not so welcoming island. Full astern avoided closer contact with it. The vibrations of the ship as the engines worked hard brought almost all officers to the deck. At this point The Chief emerged from some hiding place where he had observed my skillful handling of the ship. Calmly he took over and we docked soon thereafter. I got many, undoubtedly insincere, compliments from both fellow officers and crew for my having saved the ship from the hostile island.

The medical officer also had commander's rank, but all the others were lieutenants. Only The Chief and I came from simple social backgrounds; the others carried prominent family names connoting both wealth and social status. While I was treated well aboard the ship, as an equal member of the team, off ship there was no contact whatsoever. Once out of the navy, I never saw, or heard from, any of them although I did make some attempts to stay in touch.

Many years later a most unbelievable event took place. Today, with hindsight, it seems even stranger than it did then. It happened at an academic meeting in San Francisco. One evening a group of us went for dinner to a nice, upscale, restaurant. Leaving the table for the room of necessity, I ran into the sommelier who, as it turned out, was actually waiting for me to leave the table. He was Swedish and said he recognized me from the navy. How was that possible? Had I not changed during the last dozen years? I did not believe him, and certainly did not recall his face or name. But he insisted, and I could not doubt his veracity when he continued.

He had been the chief steward in the officers' mess on the *Alvsnabben*, the mine layer on which I had my naval shipboard training. Serving the officers he became privy to their dinner conversations which, much of the time, centered on the cadets' doings, particularly their mishaps. He remembered me very well, he said, because of two incidents.

The first was my awakening the admiral instead of the ship's commanding officer. That story was told often, and seemed funnier the more it was repeated. So funny that he decided to find out who was this cadet. He got to know me by sight while remaining anonymous to me.

The other story was about my serving pretend "St. Emilion". He had heard about it a few years later when he served on a larger ship, a cruiser. Both events had been topics for dinner conversations for some time and had circulated, to great amusement, through the fleet. He, himself, liked, particularly, the wine story. I had no idea that anyone but myself would remember these incidents so long after, and in a place so far from, their origin. I don't remember the sommelier's name, but still marvel at the meeting.

Active service ended in the fall of 1955 and I returned to the merchant marine. On October 1, 1957, I received my lieutenant's commission, to be followed by that of commander on November 1, 1966. My status as reserve officer in the Swedish Navy ended when I became a US citizen in 1974.

Return to the Sea

With my formal maritime education and training finished, my career as a merchant ship's officer began. It was not an easy decision to return to sea. The Navy had, essentially, given me a life style where I could be both at sea and at home. I liked that; the satisfactions of a rich social life and, at the same time, earning my living from sea-faring, albeit the military kind.

And, of course, there was Marta. We were to marry, but she had no desire to have her prospective husband away for months. If the Navy was not an alternative, she thought I should pursue other, shore based, options. I, however, did not want to abandon the career I had not yet begun, and for which I had prepared so long. As an old saying went, I wanted "to dip my mate's ticket in salt water". We let the issue rest, but parted soon thereafter. I was, again, bound for the sea.

The next two years were rewarding times. I advanced from 3rd to 2nd mate and the future looked good. My first ship, the *Seattle*, traded from the north European range to the US west coast.

The *Seattle*

It was an eventful trip for me and the captain. Less so for the others. We left Sweden in mid-June for a four month round-trip to the US. After calls at several ports on the way to transiting the Panama Canal, we arrived at the turning point in Seattle, the city for which the ship was named. So far all had been routine. Fine weather and predictable arrivals and departures. Almost peaceful days as we crossed the Atlantic. "Almost", because, for me, the third mate, it was not entirely so.

The Captain had decided to be my mentor, and thus my life took a turn for the worse. It was my first ship after being discharged from the Navy with a commission as ensign in the Naval Reserve. My new employer, the Johnson Line, preferred officers with naval experience. It, presumably, lent to the ship a refined atmosphere of class and spic-and-span efficiency. The Chief Mate, the Second Junior and I had that background. The Captain and the Second Senior did not. The latter could not care less, but the Captain saw it as his duty to remove from young officers the harmful effects of naval service. He approached his task with enthusiasm and no planning. The main objective seemed to be to harass me as much as possible.

I had few navigational duties when on watch and, therefore, focused more on manual work to keep the bridge well maintained and clean. About one hour into the watch the Captain arrived to inspect the general going-ons on the bridge, and, particularly, what I was doing. Invariably, no matter what I was doing, he ordered me to do something entirely different, usually meaningless busy-work.

The Captain's behavior became routine and predictable, and I became increasingly irritated and morose around him. One morning I reacted. Not in anger or out of peevishness. I simply thought a response was needed. So, when he arrived on the bridge, I said matter-of-factly, "Good morning, Captain. I am working on the signal flags, airing and putting them in order. What should we change it to today?" I believed my voice was cheery and without sarcasm. He did not think so. Muttering something about insolent naval attitudes, he left the bridge.

Next morning I greeted him, again without thoughts of malice, "Good morning Captain. A fine day we have. Don't we?" He looked me straight in the eyes and answered, "*We*? *We* have a fine day? *I* have a fine day!" This exchange set the tone of our conversations for the rest of the journey and started speculations among the crew that I would ultimately break and try to get back at the Captain. They were wrong.

Captain Hogberg was old and was expected to retire at the completion of this trip. He was fairly short, had a full shock of grey hair and the bushiest eyebrows I have ever seen. He was truly a seaman and commander. While each deck officers had his assigned duties, there was never a question of who was on top. His was a pervasive presence; he was in essence the ship. Except when passengers were around, he never wore his uniform; that was too much naval style. Instead he dressed in baggy slacks, a nondescript sweater, rubber boots or slippers, sometimes a shirt, and a tweed jacket, all of which had seen too much bad weather and contact with greasy equipment he used in his hobby work, carpentry. Also, he did not drink. He was straight forward, honest, and harbored no long term grudges. Although he attributed several later incidents to my actions, he told me he was certain I had not caused them deliberately. And, of course, he was right. My inexperience, undented by his continuing mentoring, was at fault.

Our encounters on the bridge – I rarely saw him in other contexts – continued as they had started, his changing my work, I obeying with some "smart Alec" remark. His insisting on his, in singular, enjoyment of beautiful, good days; I insisting on plural enjoyment. Although he never smiled or laughed, I believe he actually enjoyed our exchanges. I certainly did. I began to like him.

Many stories were told of his odd, but endearing behavior. One was particularly poignant. At an afternoon coffee in his salon while at sea, and with a number of passengers in attendance, the steward who was new in his position, poured the coffee and, as he perceived courtesy, served the ladies first. The Captain stared in disbelief, then, in a stentorian voice, declared, "I am the Captain, I am served first". The steward obeyed. But the cups were only half filled because of the movements of the ship. Again the Captain made himself heard, "What's this? Don't you see the cups have rims? Fill'em up". As this was done, the inevitable happened. The coffee spilled over onto the tablecloth. After his previous outbursts, the air in the salon was somewhat confused and uneasy. Certainly, the jovial mood had to be restored. The attempt was made by one of the women who coyly and jokingly said, "Oh, Captain, the tablecloth is stained. What a pity. What would your wife say? What shall we do?" No answer. Hogberg beckoned to the steward to bring him the coffeepot. Without a look at the company he poured the whole content of the pot all over the tablecloth. Then, looking around him, with a smile he stated what was obvious, "I am the Captain". No one ever doubted that.

His disheveled, but grand-fatherly appearance prompted some to refer to him as a "kindly old man". That infuriated him. "Call me anything," he said, "call me old, but never say I am kind". He did his best to prove the point, but did not succeed well.

On our return trip we called at San Francisco. Late one evening the night watchman called me for advice. The guard on the pier had found an elderly, drunk man outside the gate. He insisted he belonged to the ship. Was this true? Should he be let in? I thought quickly. We had no drinking elderly crew member on this ship. This man, whoever he was, did not belong. He could only mean trouble. Without hesitation I told the watchman, who in turn told the guard, to take him somewhere to sober up. With no more disturbances, I slept well that night.

Shortly before lunch next day the Captain, accompanied by the agent, came aboard. I thought nothing of it until I was called before the agent. He told me the Captain had spent the night in a police station because I had refused to let him aboard the ship. Why? My explanations that we had no old crew member and the Captain did not drink sounded hollow to both him and the Captain. Did I not know that yesterday had been the Captain's birthday, the only time of the year when he, indeed, drank, and heavily at that? I did not.

The Captain was not particularly upset by it. Perhaps it had happened before.

The Captain had a hobby. He spent much time carving decorations on a little dinghy kept on the boatdeck. From time to time, in port, he would launch it into the water to keep the wood moist and tight. He took care of it all by himself, sometimes helped by one of the crew, but the officers were never privy to anything related to the dinghy.

Some time after the San Francisco birthday bash, we were in Long Beach. Shortly before departure I was on the bridge when the engineer on duty requested permission to turn the screw in preparation for departure. This was standard procedure and the request was merely to make sure that no one was working close to the propeller as it was turned at slow speed. I sent a seaman to check that all was clear and with the binoculars checked that no ropes were attached to the railing. Ropes so attached would indicate something going on over the side. All was clear from my vantage point and the seaman's return confirmed it. I so informed the engineer and the propeller was turned.

Departure was imminent. All was ready for sea and the pilot aboard. At the last moment the Captain remembered something. His dinghy was in the water astern and had to be retrieved. A couple of seamen were sent to do so. They returned saying there was no dinghy to be found, but they had gathered some wooden debris in case the Captain wanted it for a memento.

I, as did most of the others, and certainly the Captain, realized quickly what had happened. The dinghy had been tied up astern with the rope attached to a bollard on the pier. Hence my scan with the binoculars showed no sign of it, and the seaman sent to check had not seen it as it was hidden between the hull of the ship and the pier. I was genuinely sorry for this mishap, apologized profusely and tried to show my empathy. The Captain looked at me with sadness and, being in his mentoring mood, stressed the need to check, and check again, until absolutely sure of the answers. He never touched on the topic again, but did resume his hobby.

To a seaman a ship is feminine, a "she". It is, therefore, perhaps natural that many parts of the ship and its equipment are named, in seamen's vernacular, after various anatomical features of the female body. On this ship the crude slang word for a woman's most intimate part was attached to a small workboat. It was used for tasks requiring nimble maneuvering along side when in port. It was propelled by sculling with one oar in the aft. Logically, the oar became known by the similarly crude slang word for a man's most intimate part, and sculling became, of course, the joining of these parts.

These slang words came so naturally, and were used so often, that the proper, common words for the boat, the oar, and sculling sank into the subconscious and were hard to retrieve if needed. And should the proper words be used, one can question if the seamen would understand their meaning.

We had several Swedish passengers, male and female, on the return voyage. One lady was a well known sociologist, particularly interested in "the sociology of the ship". She often spoke to, or formally interviewed, officers and crew. She wanted to get the real feel for, and understanding of, our sub-culture, she said.

Before entering the Panama Canal, the agent requested that we verify the draft of the ship. To do that, we had to launch the workboat. The Captain was on the bridge, as was I. He told me to use the public address system to give the order to launch; he even gave me the mike. It was ostensibly a simple order: launch the workboat with the oar and scull around the ship to read the draft at each side. I called out, "Attention on deck. Get the ..." Here I stopped. A group of the passengers, the sociologist among them, were on the foredeck eagerly waiting for the entry into the canal. The words froze in my mouth. If I gave the instructions in the language of the seamen, everything would be routinely and properly done. But the same language, over the PA system to boot, would mean something entirely different to the Swedish passengers. I felt embarrassment reflected in my face.

I fumbled searching for proper words. They did not emerge. I tried again, "Attention on deck. Get the, the, the..." I could not find the words. My face got redder and redder. The Captain seemed amused. The passengers looked intently up towards the bridge probably wondering who was to get what. The Captain said, "Get it done. What are you waiting for?" I thought I saw a faint smile as he looked me in the eyes and gave the words –– in seamen's language. I complied, it had to be done. "Attention on deck! Get the c--t wet, f--k around and let me know how deep she is." Later I was told that the message, as heard, was imbued with much feeling.

I tried to avoid the passengers when I left the bridge, but ran into the sociologist who clearly had been waiting for me. She was pleased, she said with a wide smile, that I had not given in to modesty but stayed true to my culture. Her understanding of the sea had deepened. What did she mean "staying true to my culture"? Was it a compliment? However it was meant, she had, unwittingly, confirmed the success of the Captain's battle against naval polish. A huge chunk of that had been removed from me.

Towards the end of the journey we left London for Antwerp. The sea was totally calm, no wind at all, but a thick fog covered the whole stretch across the English Channel.

Fog is a terrifying encounter at sea, particularly in heavily trafficked waters like the Channel. It renders you essentially blind. There are no landmarks indicating movement or direction. Sounds are muffled and the moist air penetrates everything. Everyone feels uneasy, alone in the world. Tension rises as the sound of the fog horn reminds us we cannot see. There are other ships around. Will we encounter them? Will we be able to avoid them? We don't know.

These were the conditions we entered into.

It was tricky navigation and the pilot remained aboard for the whole trip. A sharp look-out must be kept according to the Rules of the Road. The Captain, the pilot and I were on the bridge, one seaman on each bridge wing and one in the bow.

Somewhere along the way, not sure of our position but closing in on the shore, the Captain and the pilot decided to anchor and wait for the weather to improve. The depth soundings indicated a suitable spot and we slowed down to drop the anchor. It is usually the Chief Mate's duty, together with the ship's carpenter, to accomplish this maneuver. It was almost time to change the watch at which time the Chief Mate would be on duty. To avoid calling the mate too early, and perhaps to save on overtime, the Captain asked me, "Have you ever dropped anchor?" I certainly had in the Navy. Not only that, but I had earned high marks in seamanship at the Ships Officers' School.

My solid book-learning and limited practical experience combined to give me a totally unwarranted confidence in my abilities. So I responded affirmatively and, together with the carpenter, went forward to prepare the anchors. The order came, "Drop starboard". The chain rattled out and the next order came, "Stick two shackles". The anchor chain consists of segments, each 15 fathoms, or 90 feet, in length. The segments are clamped together with shackles which are U-shaped with a bolt at the upper end of the U. When anchoring, one must know how much chain is in the water. The trick is to keep track of the shackles as they run out of the chain box and over the windlass' gear. As they are usually painted white, it is a simple matter to identify and count them. Or, it should be.

I looked for the shackles, but saw none; and so I continued to let out the chain. From the bridge, "How much is out?" From me, "No shackles seen". From bridge, "Stick out a bit more". This conversation was repeated a few times and, although the carpenter voiced concerns about the length of chain already in the water, I waited until the bridge ordered us to "Hold as is". This was not so easily done. It was difficult to stop the chain's outpouring. The chain already in the water was very heavy and put much strain on the windlass. Nevertheless, we managed to set the brakes.

The watches changed and the Chief Mate came forward. I was sent to check how much chain remained in the storage box. Horror and shame gripped me

Horror, because there was very little chain left. We would have lost the anchor and the chain had we stuck out more. The end of the chain, as it came out of its box with great force, would undoubtedly have whiplashed the whole area around the windlass gruesomely making memories of me and the carpenter. Shame because there was action I could have taken but did not. I was aware of the stress on the windlass and the carpenter was visibly worried. That should have told me that the weight of the chain in the water was excessive whether or not I saw the shackles, and of this I should have informed the bridge.

Meanwhile the Chief Mate had assessed the situation correctly and began to retrieve the chain; hard and dangerous work. What if the chain, under immense stress, slipped out of the hoisting cogs? But, raw non-human power conquered the raw non-human opposition. The windlass creaked and groaned like a seaman called to hard labor without overtime pay. With a good amount of chain back in its box, the Chief Mate explained the mystery of the missing shackles. Ours was a new ship equipped with a "patent chain". There were no shackles. They had been replaced with oversized, but regularly shaped, links. One could not possibly see them when the chain ran out at high speed. The Chief Mate timed the run of the chain with a stop watch. Not even the Captain seemed aware of this method.

The Captain was not in a forgiving mood. But, even so, he could not abandon his mentoring role, and take a shot at naval training. The situation had been precarious. It had been resolved by his decisions made with no input from me. Why could I not think and act for myself rather than having others, that is, the Captain, do it for me? I must, he said, remember more of my "real" seafaring. I had to learn to rely on my own judgments. Only then would I leave my non-thinking, rule-obeying, conformist naval conditioning behind and become a real ship's officer. In essence I would become more like him. These were sobering thoughts. I did like him and there were many aspects to be admired: his seamanship, straight forward manners, honesty, quirkiness, and most of all, his generous letting "by-gones be by-gones". I took his comments to heart and he, true to form, never again mentioned the anchoring incident. In the years to come, I would strive for a more realistic view of my abilities.

There is an air of festive excitement when the ship arrives in the home port after a long voyage. This is the final destination. Another segment of time, as we count it, is completed. Even without family in this port, I have come home. The language, the food in the restaurants, the streets and neighborhoods are familiar. There is relief, albeit temporary, from the vagaries of the sea, its wind, rain, cold, or heat. A wonderful feeling of safety and security mingles with curiosity and anticipation of what may come next.

Soon customs formalities are done with, and it is time for home, family and friends. The usual port entourage will appear a day or two later to entice those of us with roots elsewhere. The pastor from the Seamen's Mission and a group of decent, well meaning women will compete vigorously with the less decent, less well meaning women we seem to prefer. It is truly a home-coming with serious partying to make up for lost time. But this is a special home-coming. The Captain is retiring and there will be promotions, not certain, but very likely. Much, not to say all, depends on the marine superintendents.

The superintendents are older, experienced captains or engineers who have excelled in their careers and, as a reward, have been given high positions at the head office. They are powerful, not to be crossed in any way. They will be the first to come aboard.

One is concerned with the deck department, the other with that of the engine. Their function is to assess the condition of the ship, its maintenance, and the officers' overall behavior and management skills. Each officer's performance is evaluated and reported to the head office. The evaluations are absolutely crucial for our future careers with the company. They determine promotions and assignments to desirable ships and trades. Everything we have done, good or bad, is documented in the ship's log and in written performance reports kept by the Chief Mate and the Captain. The superintendent's own observations and impressions, gained over time or on the spur of the moment, supplement the reports and are, in reality, what makes or breaks a career.

The Captain has left. The Chief Mate, who is in line for promotion, is having a lavish reception for the superintendents, their ladies, and a large number of influential executives from the company and the port authority. His day-room is crowded and the guests spill over into the outside passageway. The conversation is getting louder and louder in response to the generous supply of high quality liquor and delectable food.

No doubt, the Chief Mate is making a favorable impression on the superintendent and others of importance. As the Chief Mate's promotion becomes more likely, so do the prospects for the Second Senior's elevation to Chief Mate. But, unlike the Chief Mate, the Second has no part in the reception. He and his wife, named Brynhilda, are in his cabin below the Chief's quarters. I am with the Second Junior in my cabin at the end of our passageway. All doors are open as we listen to the party noise and try to deduce what is going on. There is much to learn about how to behave when, in the future, we may be in the Chief Mate's situation close to promotion to the highest position on the ship.

Our quarters are connected to those of the Chief Mate's by a wide, open staircase, rising from an open space resembling an atrium enclosed by smooth, sound reflecting walls. It is a good acoustical box. Sound carries far, clear, and loud.

The party is very noisy. Much talk in loud voices, laughter, singing, clinking of glasses (this is not the Navy), and the occasional attempt at a witty toast. But, as often happens at large parties, there is a sudden silence. All sounds cease. All seem to catch their breath at the same time. The silence is pronounced and palpable. But it is broken by an unexpected, strange, moaning sound that starts fairly weakly but increases in strength and, amplified by the good acoustics, thunderously fills the whole silent space. There is no doubt. This is the result of flatulence, perhaps long repressed, given its force. The silence deepens, but soon the din resumes, hesitantly at first, then with renewed vigor as if to catch up on lost time and drown the memory of the strange sound.

Suddenly the revelry is interrupted by a loud knock on the Chief Mate's door. Again, total silence descends to be broken by the Second Mate Senior, whose voice, used to overpowering howling winds and waves, is loud and penetrating as he says, "Chief Mate, I want you to know it was not I who farted. It was Brynhilda". He stays silently in the door waiting for assurance that his prospects for promotion have not been impaired. That they have not gone with the wind.

When there is no reaction to his honesty, he returns downstairs. The party resumes, this time with great hilarity.

The Second Senior stops at my cabin and explains, as if we had not heard, "It was not I. It was Brynhilda. She is not used to shipboard food".

The voyage is over.

The House with the Veranda

The house with the veranda facing the sea was of ill repute. One of several in the city, but the only one in this upscale neighborhood. For the uninitiated there was nothing obvious or distinguishing about the house. For others it was the veranda. It was larger than those of surrounding houses. Top and side coverage gave shade and prevented insight while the view to the sea was open and gave an impression of exclusivity to those using the veranda. Furnishings were ample, elegant and luxurious. Strategic arrangements of flowers and potted small trees provided for numerous small private areas around a larger open space.

The veranda was rarely empty. Few people were there during the early part of the day, but it filled up as the day progressed and by evening there was a full house. The women were youngish and well dressed in a leisurely elegant fashion; sometimes scantily so, and suggestive, but there were no vulgar, or explicit, displays. Any of them could, without embarrassment, easily fit in at any casual beach party.

This mid-morning a man of indeterminate age sat in a chair on the side of the open area. He wore black pants and a tidy white shirt. His appearance could have been improved by a haircut, but the bushy mop did go well with the large beard that covered much of his face disguising any recognizable feature. Even the closest of family would hardly know him. He sat still, occasionally closing his eyes as if he was trying to sharpen his thoughts by retreating from the surroundings. He did not seem to notice the women who tried to catch his attention. Carnal desire was not on his mind. Why, then, was he there?

He had, simply, come in to get out of the sun after a very long walk that had taken him only half-way to his destination. He needed rest, shade, and a drink. How he had gotten there is a longer story.

Three months earlier his ship had left port for a five-month round trip. As was his custom, he had then begun to grow a beard which would be shaven off five months later, when the trip was completed. But plans changed, and yesterday he had arrived in the port on a ship different from the one on which he had left three months earlier. For whatever reasons the company had ordered him back, and so he returned two months earlier than expected.

He was eager to get home, rushed ashore and made his way to his house on one of the hills above the port. His wife was not home, but he was not perturbed by that. He knew that, when he was away, she often visited her sister some distance away but still in the same city. She would undoubtedly return sometime during the day. Meanwhile, he took out the many presents he had bought for her and put them in various places around the house; places where he was sure she would notice them. On the table in the living room he placed, prominently, the largest item, an ivory jewelry box with a string of pearls inside. Surely she would appreciate that expression of his love.

Most of that day he spent waiting. Apprehensions grew so that most of the night he spent sleepless and waiting. By morning he had persuaded himself that she was staying at her sisters' for more than a day, perhaps for a few days. He had no telephone to confirm her whereabouts; few homes in the city did, but so convinced was he that he had found the answer, that his earlier apprehensions were replaced by a keen feeling of anticipation. In a calm and happy mood, he set out for his sister-in-law's. Walking would take him there a bit before lunch and would give the women plenty of time to be up and dressed.

Just before mid-morning he was in the vicinity of the house with the veranda. Hot, tired, thirsty, and ahead of his planned lunch arrival, he stepped in to rest. As he rested, he thought how sweetly surprised his wife would be when he showed up, not only at her sister's home, but two whole months before he was expected. He thought of the presents left at home that she would discover. How she would marvel at his thoughtfulness and his love for her. He thought of her tenderly, her warm, welcoming smile, and her excited exclamations of pleasure at his early return. These were the reasons his eyes were closed; lost in reverie he did not notice the women around him. He was in his own world.

He must have dozed off with his pleasant thoughts, but awoke with a jolt. He felt a soft hand stroking his hair and neck, and heard a seductive voice whispering indecent suggestions in his ear. For a brief moment it seemed that what he felt, and what he heard, was part of his dreams, but then he was fully awake again. He stood up, turned and saw the young, quite beautiful, woman who had already turned towards one of the little alcoves expecting him to follow her. He sighed heavily, as if regretting a lost opportunity, and started towards the door. After a few steps he turned to cast a last look at temptation. He gasped loudly as she turned around to face him again. His beard did disguise his face and her dress, scanty as it was, drew attention away from her face. Yet recognition was quick and almost simultaneous. He had found his wife!!

* * * * *

All this he told me years later when I sailed with him. He also told me he spent a rather long time in a place he called an "attitude adjustment institution". After seeing a number of "adjusters", he went back to work at sea. He proudly displayed on his cabin wall a document certifying that he was sane; he knew of no one else who had such a document. Hence its prominent place on the wall.

There were rumors that he had reconciled with the wife, and I asked him about it. What he told me did not stretch credibility as seafarers perceive it. The wife, he said, had opened her own establishment outside the city. While her employees served customers rather indiscriminately, she, herself, catered only to a select clientele. He went to see her, and was rewarded by being admitted to that select group.

He was not embittered by the experience and pursued our female passengers with greater vigor and purpose than ever before. His pursuits were such that I could not resist asking him if he would consider marrying again. He paused pondering his response. Then, looking far away, with a wry smile and a wistful sigh, his answer was a question, "Why subscribe when you can buy single issues?"

The *Bali*

Measure for Measure

In the early 50's Hong Kong was a very desirable port of call. Not only could one buy many things not available elsewhere, but anything could be replicated, or made to order very quickly. It was common for ships' crews to order clothing, usually shirts, suits and shoes immediately upon arrival in Hong Kong. Instead of bothering with measurements they often left an old, worn out piece of clothing with instructions to copy it. So faithfully were the orders filled that if a defective item had been left, a defective copy was delivered. A story circulated about a shirt on which a cigarette had burnt a hole. The owner wanted it replaced and so gave it to be copied. Much to his surprise the new shirt had also a cigarette burn, just as did the old one.

The clothing orders were usually ready in a day or two which was about the time the ship stayed in port. But Hong Kong was rarely the final destination. Normally, the Swedish ships would continue north to Shanghai which was the end point for the outward journey. Returning home, the ship would call at some ports in the Philippines and Indonesia before coming back to Hong Kong. This schedule allowed the tradesmen fairly long time to make larger and more complicated items than clothing.

On one particular voyage I was third mate on a large liner of the Swedish East Asiatic Company; a wonderful berth. The *Bali* was well maintained, had comfortable quarters, good food and a friendly and competent crew.

Captain H., in his mid-60s, was an odd choice to command such a large ship, or any ship. He was short and stout, always immaculately dressed in white suitable for the tropics. Physically he did not make any impression, be it strong or weak. A most notable feature was his glasses; lenses as thick as the bottom of a heavy soda bottle. Even with those glasses he needed high resolution binoculars to inspect his surroundings on the bridge. How he had been allowed to ship out was a mystery to me. He was the most indecisive man I had ever met. Although he was known as a good seaman, he hesitated to take over when on the bridge, hesitated to give a firm order, hesitated to give even an opinion and preferred to stay out of sight in his quarters as much as possible.

Thus, rarely seen and, knowing his own, age-set limitations, he happily relegated the running of the ship to the Chief Mate. He, in turn, relied heavily on the 2nd Mate who, being a fisherman's son, was born to seafaring. In my view, he was the soul and matter of the ship. I was essentially a flunky to the 2nd and learned a great deal from the fact that he seldom made mistakes.

The Chief Mate, on the other hand, made many mistakes and, often, bad decisions. He compensated for these shortcomings by never admitting to them. Instead, he persisted and compounded his mistakes until the 2nd quietly resolved them. Equally quietly he let the Chief Mate take the credit.

The Chief Mate was, however, a kind man. His name was Karl, nick-named Kalle. He walked with a slight, yet noticeable, limp. Years ago, the story told, he was walking along a country road when, in the middle of the road, he came across a small wooden cube, about 2 inches in each dimension. He was in a relaxed and playful mood, took a running start and kicked it as hard as he could merely to see how far it would fly. It didn't. The little cube was what had been left above ground of a large stake driven several feet into the ground. It did not give way; his toe did. He broke it. He did not like to tell that story, but felt that his limping required some kind of explanation. The one he gave was that someone had maliciously dropped a heavy weight on his foot. Sometimes the weight was a box; at other times a hatch cover, or a mast block falling from above. These explanations elicited sympathy and compassion, something the true event would not. He told that story often enough to earn the name "Kalle the Toe". By that name he was mostly known in the company and on some of the Swedish waterfronts.

Shortly before the ship left Sweden, Kalle had married. His wife was a cute girl with a bubbling personality. She adored Kalle. In her eyes he could do no wrong. They had a new apartment, sparsely furnished. This set Kalle to thinking in big terms. No plain pine or beech furniture for his bride. Solid, well cured, first quality, mahogany was the only fitting tribute to her who was the essence of his happiness. The first purchase would be a dining room set made to order in Hong Kong. He thought about it, calculated, measured and planned. He had all the measurements done, checked them a second time, drew some elementary sketches and noted everything down in his "to do" file. There was to be a table, eight chairs, a sideboard and a tea cart.

We arrived in Hong Kong and Kalle asked the agent to find him a good carpenter. To be on the safe side, in case the carpenter could not be found before our departure, Kalle gave his list of items, their measurement, and the sketches to the agent to forward to the carpenter.

Departure time was coming close and no carpenter had shown up. But just before slipping the moorings, he did appear. From a distance, he on the pier, Kalle on the ship, they engaged in a shouted conversation. The carpenter in good English, Kalle in Swedish with some key words in English. Communication was difficult. The essence of the exchange was that the carpenter said the measurements were all wrong. Kalle told him to follow instructions. He bristled at someone's questioning his ability to measure and, by implication, his decision to have a dining room set unequaled in the whole of Gothenburg. To emphasize his authority, he pointed to his three gold stripes, straightened his cap, put his arms akimbo and fell silent. After a few minutes we slipped the lines and departed. The carpenter shrugged his shoulders and slowly got along on his way as we did on ours. Kalle was very proud of having asserted himself and did not tire of telling the story to anyone patient enough to listen.

We continued our journey and, several weeks later, returned to Hong Kong where we anchored on the roadstead. Not long thereafter, merchants arrived by boat to deliver whatever had been ordered. Only Kalle's order was missing, no boat carried his furniture. He was upset, but could do nothing, only wait and see.

Cargo began arriving by barges when somebody pointed out to the 2nd that a barge had been lying alongside for some time with a tarpaulin covering a large shipment of some kind. Examining the barge, the 2nd found Kalle's furniture; but a strange lot it was. There were, indeed, a dining room table, eight chairs, a sideboard and a tea cart. But they were monstrously large! To give just one example, the chairs' legs were 45 inches high, and those of the table and cart were 75 inches. Horizontal surfaces were proportional to the heights. Were they intended for an amusement park? Was it a joke? What had happened?

It turned out that Kalle's measurements were in centimeters while the carpenter had assumed they were in inches. He had tried to come to an understanding with Kalle. But the language barrier and the Chief Mate's inability to concede the possibility that he could make a mistake had resulted in the order being filled as filed.

The furniture was brought aboard and stored on deck. Kalle paid as agreed, and insisted that he had gotten exactly what he wanted; it was merely a matter of adjusting the dimensions to fit his plans for his apartment.

Kalle spent most of his free time trying that adjustment. Not an easy task as anyone knows who has tried to fix uneven legs of a chair or a table. In addition, there were no power tools, and no work bench, or vise, that could hold steady such heavy and awkwardly large pieces. No wonder that Kalle's furniture became progressively shorter and shorter as well as more and more uneven. The horizontal surfaces, table tops and chair seats, became increasingly disproportionate to height. What plans he had for adjusting these surfaces was not clear. Kalle worked hard; well cured mahogany is not a forgiving medium for handicrafts.

His efforts had great entertainment value for the crew. We would gather around to give advice and moral support. We would watch him work, take meticulous measurements, work up a sweat with the handsaw that became duller and duller until the ship's carpenter took pity on the chipped and splintered wood and sharpened it. Kalle finally conceded defeat and one night, as we approached our home port, he dumped the remains into the North Sea.

His wife was disappointed when he told her how the stupid carpenter had been unable to follow simple instructions. But she was comforted by the thought that there would be other trips to Hong Kong, and she would confidently wait until he found an intelligent carpenter, his equal, who could follow instructions.

The Madman

On the return trip from Shanghai to Hong Kong we called at Manila where a male American professor, and four younger girls, graduate students, boarded. They were bound to a European port from where they would continue to the US.

Next stop was Balikpapan, a port in East Borneo, to take on bunkers, that is, fuel oil. Normally we would bunker in Hong Kong, but there was another reason for our stopping in Borneo. We were to take on a new crew member. His name was Gunther, a German who had been third mate on a sister ship still on its outbound voyage. For reasons soon to become apparent, he needed to get home and, as was customary, would work for his passage. His Swedish was poor; my German good. Accordingly, the Chief Mate ordered that he would share watches with me and, in general, make himself useful under my supervision. His bunk was in the cabin that served as our sick bay and which was next to mine; we shared a wall. The arrangements sounded reasonable.

Gunther was quite ordinary looking. In his late thirties, he was slightly balding, tall, muscular and strong. He had a round face and wore glasses. Rimless, round lenses gave easy, visual access to his eyes which were grey and brown and exuded warmth and friendliness as did his whole demeanor. With such a likeable addition to the crew, shipboard life could only improve.

But even before leaving Borneo, Gunther started to behave strangely. While in port we had a lifeboat drill, mainly for the benefit of the passengers. The boat had been lowered into the water, and I was in it unlocking the falls, i.e., the blocks and tackles used to hoist and lower the boat. The aft falls had already been hauled up on deck to be out of the way, and I was tending to those in the bow. For whatever reason, perhaps premonition, I looked up and saw a grinning Gunther about to drop the falls back into the boat. I was just underneath and, on instinct, jumped overboard. The falls, weighing some 20-25 lbs and dropped from a height of about 30 feet, crushed the rowing bench where I had been a few moments ago; a narrow escape, indeed. My lasting memory of the incident is his grinning face, so at odds with our first impression of his friendliness. No one believed it had been done it on purpose, but we, nevertheless, became leery of him and began to observe him more closely.

We did not have to wait long. He started to talk to himself, avoided personal contacts but inspected each one of us closely as if he was looking for someone lost, checked every door he saw, opening and closing, opening and closing, opening and closing.... He seemed particularly fascinated by the fire stations. These were glass enclosed cabinets with a ready-to-use hose and two fire axes. He inspected them carefully and, as they were not locked, spent much time with his favorite activity, opening and closing, opening and closing....

Whenever in his cabin, he banged fiercely on our common wall. I checked it out, and found that he was trying to carve an opening in the wall with a bread knife taken from the dining room. Why he tried this was beyond anyone's understanding; the wall was, after all, made of steel. I removed the knife as soon as I could, and he did not seem to miss it.

Gunther spent much of his time declaiming German poems or texts that I did not fully understand because of the highbrow language. He must have had a good education. Often he would sing sentimental seamen's songs, waltzes. These were familiar to me, but I have forgotten most of them. Relating the story now I am struck by the juxtaposition of his highbrow spoken language and the simple sentimentality of his songs. His favorite song, repeated again and again, expressed a longing for a seaside home filled with the sounds of rushing waves and shrieking seagulls. It ended with "...da ist meine Heimat, da bin ich zu Haus" ("...there is my home ground, there I am at home"). He had a pleasant voice, and sang with much feeling. Under other circumstances he would have been a popular and welcome guest at any party.

He became more and more irrational and violent. His mood shifts were announced by his eyes. They told us what to expect. Their light color would quickly change to black as the pupils expanded as if hit by total darkness, no matter how much light there was around him. With the normal color gone, all warmth and friendliness were gone as well. Only rage and violence came forth. I began to lock my door as did the others.

With all his strange behavior, one thing surprised us. Except for his times of violence, Gunther did obey orders; he did as he was told. The 2nd told me to keep Gunther occupied as much as possible with manual work; that might forestall problems. I did my best. Since Gunther shared my watch, I assigned him the work to scrape, sand, and varnish the teak railings on the bridge wings. He did so willingly and worked hard. The scraper was a triangular piece of steel attached horizontally at the top of a wooden handle about 12 inches long. The steel was sharpened along the edges so the points of the triangle resembled a bow huntsman's arrowheads.

At first, both of us worked on the same bridge wing. But soon his eyes began to blacken and, muttering something, he would whack the scraper into the railing where it would stick. It was done with ferocious strength, teak is a hard wood, and I worried that I had given him such a potent, potential weapon. I was afraid to be close to him, or even to be in the same area. So he was left alone on one wing while I stayed on the other. It was a workable arrangement except that the frightened helmsman did not want to be in between us. It became necessary to lock the door to the wing where Gunther worked. He did not like it and responded with many attacks on the railing.

The closed door meant also that Gunther was beyond my immediate supervision and that he had a certain freedom of movement. At times he disappeared and I would be quite concerned, but he would return without causing troubles. I worried about the scraper, though. It had to be removed and that was done although he resisted for a while. By the time I did this, he had whacked away at the railing so much that it was destroyed in parts. I gave him a new "weapon", a wad of sand-paper. He sanded with patience and without anger; the monotonous work seemed to soothe his mind.

At night, with no work to be done, I asked Gunther to stand lookout on one wing. With the door locked, I stayed on the other wing or indoors with the helmsman and watched Gunther's every move. But he never did anything alarming, only checked the door once in awhile. He talked, sang and gesticulated but showed no violence. Nevertheless, the helmsman insisted on having a heavy wooden bat at his side. No one of the crew moved around, or went to bed, without having such a bat provided by the ship's carpenter. Fear began to grip the ship. No one wanted to be alone; at least two were now required for any task or purpose. Showers were taken "under guard", and so with everything else. The first question asked before going on watch was, "Where is Gunther?"

The cook and the two stewards were petrified and armed themselves with meat cleavers. One steward stood watch while the cook went about his duties. Only a fool would approach the galley without giving some form of advance notice. Taken by surprise the cook would undoubtedly protect himself with deadly force. No more visits for us to the galley in the early morning hours for a cup of coffee with freshly baked buns. That the cook managed to maintain his good and plentiful menus was remarkable and appreciated by all.

The radio officer's station and quarters were just under the bridge. He had to maintain radio contacts at certain periods each day. He usually made his way alone from his cabin to the radio room. There he locked himself in but would call for someone to check the outside before exiting his post. No more chats for him on the bridge with the mate on duty. The social fabric of the ship was disintegrating; we spent much of our time off in locked, very hot, cabins.

The passengers, though, were unaware of the situation. As was customary, the areas of the ship set aside for them were out of bounds for the crew. Even Gunther had adhered to that custom and we did not worry that he would break it. But change was coming.

One evening, on the 2nd's watch, Gunther came up on the bridge carrying a fire axe. The mate quickly closed and locked the doors to the bridge wings and called a warning to the captain whose quarters were just below the bridge. Gunther, meanwhile, tried to pry the door open with the axe. Could not do it and, in anger, attacked the railing chipping away big chunks. Somewhat mollified, he threw the axe overboard. He seemed perfectly normal again. But we were not to take any chances. The captain was as usual indecisive, feigned sickness and would not come out of his cabin. He called on the Chief Mate to do whatever he thought necessary.

The Chief Mate acted. All axes were removed from the fire stations. Two were missing. One had been thrown overboard by Gunther, but where was the other? It was not found, and the thought that Gunther might have hidden it somewhere, prompted Kalle to have Gunther followed by one of the heftier seamen equipped with an especially heavy wooden club. At any sign of dangerous behavior, he was to knock Gunther down. But nothing extraordinary happened, and the vigil relaxed. Then, suddenly, after a visit to the bathroom, Gunther came out stark naked, threw his clothes overboard, and took off for the passengers' quarters. Before the guard managed to subdue him, one of the girls was attacked. She was frightened but not harmed. Suddenly Gunther's rage was spent, and he was, again, his docile self. Although the guard's club drew blood, no one dared to get close enough to examine him. Since he looked as he usually did after a rampage, we assumed he was physically OK. We managed to persuade him to put on clothes again. But what to do now?

The passengers were worried. Before the attack they enjoyed the trip; eating well, sunbathing, and resting. That the captain was rarely seen did not bother them; his English was, anyway, not good enough for interesting conversation. Whatever else they may have seen, or surmised, was put down as the natural outcome of the unnatural life and environment of seafarers. Now, however, they perceived this event as the basis for the captain's seclusion in his cabin, and they began to do likewise. Fear had taken over the ship.

We had to do something. Why should we, the many, be locked into our cabins, when Gunther, the threat, was not, and he was only one? He should be locked up. And so he was. He literally did not take that lying down. He did not object to enter the cabin, he felt at home there. But the locked door enraged him. He ranted, raved, and destroyed whatever he could get his hands on, his bed, the bedding, curtains and the washbasin; most other items had been removed. The concomitant noise, violence, and threats, and my being afraid of him, made it impossible for me to stay in my cabin. I spent much time in the dining room and on deck. The others, however, finally returned to a semblance of normal life.

Trying to serve him food, and to let him use the bathroom, forced us to have a guard of three or four men, and they had their hands full. How to calm him down? Could we sedate him? We had morphine, but were not allowed to use it without company and medical approval. A new idea came up. We were, after all, in the tropics and the heat had made us all a bit lethargic. Why not increase the heat, at least for Gunther, so that he would be too exhausted to fight? Perhaps he would calm down, perhaps sleep. So the heating system was turned on and set on high. The problem was, of course, that there was only one heating zone – the ship. We did close all vents leaving open only the one in Gunther's cabin. But even so, the pipes gave enough heat to complete our version of a living hell.

The tactic worked, somewhat. Gunther did, indeed, become exhausted and tired, but not calm. Within a very short time he was naked again, urinated, defecated and smeared the waste all over himself and the cabin. We did not know how to clean up the mess; no one was willing to enter that cabin. The stench was abominable, and the heat did not help. I had long since moved out and slept on deck; I was even frightened to go into my cabin to get clothes and other necessities. Everyone avoided the passageway outside Gunther's cabin.

The passengers told the captain they would leave the ship in Singapore and he so informed the head office. The company still wanted us to bring Gunther home. The management did not seem to understand the situation. Perhaps the captain, close to retirement, minimized both Gunther's and our tribulations to curry favors with the management.

In Singapore the passengers left; we took on cargo and proceeded through the Malacca Straits. Gunther seemed to have adjusted to the heat treatment and, during a quiet spell, we had been able to give him and the cabin a rudimentary cleaning. But as soon as we had him back in the cabin, and the door locked, he became even more violent and threatening than before.

The captain finally took the initiative. The responsibility was too great, and we had a long trip ahead of us. The prospects of spending another three weeks, or more, at sea with this madman were too much. The passage would take us around Africa, and that was a new route. On our way out, we had been the last ship to pass the Suez Canal; it closed shortly thereafter because of the 1956 Middle East War. The captain accepted that it was his duty, and responsibility, to protect and keep safe the crew, ship, and cargo.

In the final analysis he and he alone, could, and should, decide if Gunther remained aboard. He ruled against it. The company was informed, and in Penang, north of Singapore, Gunther was taken ashore by a medical team to be returned to his home for treatment.

The routine of shipboard life returned. Fear disappeared and I, like most of the others, actually looked forward to a long, tranquil sojourn at sea. But it was not entirely to be so for me.

Shortly after leaving Penang, I came down with a strange illness; fever, headache, chills alternating with profuse sweating, and general aches. A couple of days in bed did not improve conditions. Kalle, the Chief Mate, thought I ought to get medical care in Colombo, the main port of Ceylon, today's Sri Lanka, but I resisted that idea. I simply did not trust the doctors outside of Sweden, and there were stories, probably untrue, about sailors being kept in hospitals merely for the income their stay generated.

My symptoms did not subside. Kalle earned my gratitude for the attention he gave me. He took over my watch duty for awhile, and, on off-time would relieve my fever with cold water compresses. This he did on top of adjusting his furniture. While not well, I still managed to return to watch keeping after a few days. As we proceeded northward, I sensed improvement and, suddenly, I was myself again.

I described the symptoms to the port doctor in Gothenburg, but he was at a loss to explain what had hit me. The answer, malaria, would be revealed much later.

The rest of the journey was uneventful. The weather stayed fine until the North Sea where high winds and rough seas gave relief from the monotony of the long trip. After thirty-two days at sea, we finally arrived in Gothenburg, our home port. The terror of the madman at sea began to fade, and was soon forgotten as we prepared for a new voyage.

Foul Weather Friend

I am no fair weather sailor. I actually like bad weather. Some sunshine cheers me up. Heavy doses make me gloomy, and incessant sunshine depresses me. The heavy air and dark skies of a low pressure have the opposite effects. Rain, thunder, and lightening are bonuses to boost my well-being.

A sun-lit, calm sea is indescribable because there is nothing to describe. What can be said about light on a reflective water surface? A moon-lit sea is somewhat more impressive, but I still don't know what that impression is.

Foul weather is entirely different. To experience it at sea is to experience spirituality. There is the color phenomenon. The sea is not blue or green, no matter what poets say. It is grey bordering on black. It is a fearful color that changes from lighter to darker hues in response to the winds' bearing down on it. The watery surface is like a black satin sheet which is being moved up and down so that undulating waves move across it. That sea, that black water, is moved and ripped apart by the high winds; the waves become ridges and, as they fold into themselves, white foam outlines the crests of the waves as they chase each other toward their ultimate destruction and transformation into the spray lashing my face. These are sights to see, and they cheer me.

Not so cheerful are the movements of the ship. The winds and waves push against it, and it begins to roll, pitch and yaw, all at the same time. This is the realm of seasickness. The ship rises and falls, rolls and swings rhythmically and mercilessly. Sometimes the rhythm is interrupted when the ship suddenly stops with a bang and a shudder as if it has run into a wall. But it has merely slammed into a rouge wave. The pitiless movement is not interrupted, though. One moment the tilting sea raises the bow toward the sky. The next it is pointed downward and buried in an oncoming wave while the stern is flung into the air and the propeller spins wildly out of the water. The noise and vibrations of the propeller's churning air instead of water add to the wild movements of the ship. The feeling of mayhem and bewilderment becomes tangible and frightening, but it is soon replaced by the confidence we have in the ship and our own strength to overcome whatever the sea throws at us.

To me it was, indeed, man against the sea. What could the sea do to us? Good seamanship meant to know just that, and to know how to meet the challenges; how to ride out a storm, how to position the ship against the raging sea. Should the ship take the waves head on, the safest defensive maneuver? Or side ways, the most dangerous choice? Or, perhaps, go with the waves? Or somewhere in-between? It all depends on the strength of the wind, the height of the waves, knowledge of the ship, its stability and handling characteristics. Seamanship also meant to know how to navigate and determine position in conditions of poor visibility and physical stress. And, very important, how to read the weather signs. Will the storm abate or become worse?

The dangers are real and tangible. As the ship moves over the waves, it is for very brief moments still when it becomes suspended on two crests, one under the bow, the other under the stern, with the midships unsupported by the water. Those moments end violently when the ship becomes draped over one crest amidship with the bow and stern hanging free. The ship is bent, repeatedly, up and down, and can snap apart, much like a paper clip that is bent back and forth.

I was unaware of these dangers. It was still me against the sea. It was a beautiful struggle. The black sheet of water, rippled by waves is transformed into a landscape of moving mountains. The ship plows into the mountainous water giving the impression of smoothing the way, very much like an iron smoothing out a wrinkled cloth. Driving rain and windswept spray slap our faces trying to tell us to give up. But we carry on. We will reach our destination.

Searching for a fixed point to counter the violent movements, the horizon disappoints; it is also in motion. So eyes turn skyward where the wind drives the clouds in constantly changing, rolling patterns. It is like looking through a kaleidoscope, the view of the heaven is one of turmoil. At night, the ship's swaying masts draw circles among the clouds and stars tracing out a new, imaginary zodiac. The old zodiac looks brilliantly lit because the darkness, the kind of darkness seen only at sea, brings the sky closer, brings the stars closer so one absorbs the mystery of the sky without explanations or prompts. The Milky Way and major stars hang in the air, occasionally touched by the wandering masts. These are the fixed points in our stormy existence.

This, then, is foul weather. Its forces have entered my innermost being. I feel renewed, rejuvenated, at peace, and elevated from my ordinary existence. Can it be an aberration to feel this way? That it is a driving life force? Many of my friends certainly think so. But I cannot accept that. I cannot deny the spiritual experience of it. I have glimpsed Divine power, and have been allowed to live and see it again, and again. And so have my seafaring colleagues; and they seem to have similar feelings. Bad weather confirmed our worth as seamen. We were, justifiably, proud of arriving in port after encountering severe weather. That we celebrated in our usual fashion, with wine and women, was, in our eyes, merely a complement to, and acceptance of, the other forces of life that drove us.

Nor is the fascination with nature's forces exclusive to seafarers. One November day in Duluth, Minnesota, strong easterly winds hit the harbor with monstrous waves. My daughter Nili and I decided to watch the fury from the water front. We expected to be alone. Why would anyone, except a forlorn seaman and his indulging daughter, want to see water being swished around? Much to our surprise there was barely standing room along the more exposed watching spots. But we found a good one. The waves came crashing in, broke over the pier, washed over the draw bridge, and the wind-carried spray lashed everything far, far inland. The spectators were soaking wet, but loud cries of delight went up when especially large waves approached. Around dinner time the lines of watchers began to thin. They left slowly and reluctantly, but in exuberant moods. We did and felt the same.

I then understood that we, who appreciate bad, really foul, weather, may be a minority, but a large one. It is good to know that I am not alone; I am among foul weather friends.

Fog

To me, fog at sea is a terror only surpassed by shipboard fire. In both cases, it is the helplessness, the utter irrelevance of my actions to master the events that creates the fear. Fire is uncommon, and I have not experienced it. Fog, on the other hand, is common, and the fear it instills is strong, chilling and unsettling depending on its nature.

In a light, or patchy, fog I can see the surrounding waters from time to time. The air is usually still and slightly damp. Without radar, visibility is limited as there is no horizon. But, because there are still some focal points, I do have a feeling of being in control of movement and action. From the wake of the propeller I can see, and from the bow swell I can hear, the ship's motion. It is not pleasant, but this fog does not induce fear or feelings of helplessness. Even the foghorn's bleating is without edge and significance. I operate it manually and infrequently, not so much to warn other ships, but to break the watch keeping routine. I imagine the ship as a knife cutting through a cream cake where the sea, with its dark color, is the cake bottom and the clumps of drifting, whitish fog are decorations of whipped cream. The image, while not truly cheerful, does take the edge off the uneasiness the fog evokes.

This image does not hold when the fog is uniformly very dense and unyielding, hiding even the fore of the ship. Again, there is no horizon to be seen, but now the wake and the bow swell are gone as well, one being hidden by the fog, the other's sound absorbed by it. The surrounding waters have disappeared, and an eerie silence has descended. Where am I? Where are we going? Indeed, are we on the go? Looking out, the only sight is an unchanging, grey, featureless monotony of what could be a concrete wall. As we close in on this wall, it yields and enfolds us. We are in it, embraced by it, and see nothing; in essence, we are blind. The moisture is heavy, so is the air; it muffles all sounds as if a huge, soft, wet, blanket has been wrapped around me. It is almost hard to breathe, the absence of sound spreads across the ship affecting even its engines. They sound different, soft and apologetic as our forward movement brings us further into the yielding wall. I alternately squint and open my eyes wide hoping to enhance vision. It does not help. I rub my eyes and use my fingers to open them wider. Nothing helps. My eyes begin to hurt, so does my head. Now the foghorn is not merely a routine breaker. It is set to warn of the ship's presence every third minute for thirty seconds. It is, to me, an ominous sound. It is loud, gaining strength towards the end of the blast; it is deep, somewhat blurred, and comes often enough to appear as a monotone staccato. My mind hears echoes of Verdi's "Requiem", the doomsday trumpets in "Dies Irae" proclaiming the Day of Judgment, and I feel accordingly. Although most of the ghoulish, braying sound is swallowed by the fog, enough of it bounces back to reinforce my head ache, deepen the ensuing silence and my bleak mood.

The tension becomes palpable. Nerves are frayed. The unease begins its transformation into fearfulness. Although there is nothing to see in any direction, I peer intently at that nothing. The uniform color seems to become more nuanced with patches of lighter and darker grey. Soon I begin to see and hear what is not there. Was that the shadow of a ship? If so, why did it not sound its horn? Was that a foghorn answering ours? From where did it come? Did you, too, hear the bell of a ship at anchor? And where did that come from? Tension on the bridge is almost unbearable. The captain has been there since the fog joined us. The mate on duty is standing by, ready to order the engine to slow down, stop, or reverse. The captain chooses to stop the engine, hoping that the stillness of the ship will help reveal answering horns or bells. The silence is deep, the captain decides, and we proceed again slowly forward. We are silent, nervous, and in "the dark", hoping for wind to disperse the fog, or sunlight to burn it off.

It is miserable to be outside. Even rain gear cannot prevent the raw dampness from penetrating the clothing that becomes heavier and more uncomfortable the longer I stay on deck. When relieved, I hesitate to go below. I am too tense, or, to be honest, frightened by the fog. If I do go below, should I go to bed? Or should I remain dressed for an emergency? In any case, I have to relieve my aching eyes, and so I go below. My sight now returns; there is comfort in that, but both comfort and eye sight vanish when I again venture outside.

I feel none of the exhilaration of foul weather. This is not man against the sea. There is no sense of achievement, conquest and victory. There are no encouraging visual effects. There are no howling winds and rushing seas to rejuvenate me, to remind me I am young and alive. Instead, the fog has aged me. In the mirror I see an old man's tired, bloodshot, rheumy eyes. But it will not last; it can not last.

The wind picks up, the fog eases, leaving floating patches to be burnt off by the rising sun.

Normalcy reigns again. My eyes regain their youthfulness. How wonderful to see with clear eyes, to take in the surroundings with a single glance; to sense movements and sounds as they are. To breathe moist, not wet, air; to again be part of the world.

Under Israeli flag

The *Zion*

While still on the *Bali*, I initiated a new job search. From Manila I applied for a position with the major shipping company in Israel, the ZIM Lines. The country's Consul General was very helpful, and we remained friends for many years to come. Every year, until his death in the early '70s, he sent me a case of special San Miguel Christmas beer, no matter where I was. Sharing it made me popular in many quarters.

ZIM Lines' response, a position as second mate, reached me after arrival in Gothenburg. A few weeks at home in Stockholm and I left for Marseilles to join the *m/v Zion*. On Israel's Independence Day, 1957, we arrived in Haifa where I formally signed on the ship. It immediately set out on its scheduled run to the US East Coast. The ship's capacity was some 250 passengers and 6,000 tons of cargo. It was new, traded from Haifa to New York and called at several ports in between.

This was a new challenge. I did not speak Hebrew and my English was poor, at best. Over time, I learned some basic Hebrew and my English improved to become mostly understandable. The beginning of the voyage, from Marseilles to Haifa and then on to New York, was not auspicious.

The officers and crew were mostly Israelis. But there were also Italians and Norwegians in the engine room and the catering department. The first engineer would, years later, become a professor at MIT and a world leading authority in nuclear propulsion. He was also a much sought after expert in port and shipyard designs, ship operations, management and technological progress. Our academic interests would overlap and, in later years, we worked briefly together. It was a group of good, competent people and the ship's success and well-being depended more on them than on the captain.

The captain was in his forties; slightly built with a full head of grey hair. Not a remarkable face in either features or expressions, although, at times, he would look at people under half closed eyes as if he tried to hide his observing them. My response to that look was to tap him gently on his arm to make sure he was awake. He did not take to that approach, and usually said something, probably deprecatory, in Hebrew or English.

I understood neither. His most prominent, physical feature was the right arm. It was frozen at the elbow forming a ninety degree angle, the result of a WWII injury. It provided him with a formidable weapon. He would jab me with it when he wanted my attention. It could be painful, and I developed a habit of staying to his left. That did not help much as he was very adept at turning around to his right so the elbow would hit me in the back; very painful, indeed.

The captain was a hero and a legend in Israeli maritime circles. Not only had he served with the British Navy during the war, but had later brought Jewish refugees from Europe to what was to become Israel. Running the British blockade had required skill, daring, and a degree of ruthlessness, all honed to perfection by heavy and persistent drinking. These characteristics stayed with him when, in more stable times, he was the captain of the *Zion.*

His drinking was not obvious to the casual observer. He carried himself with dignity. Well dressed in immaculate uniform, no staggering walk or slurred speech. But many of his decisions had the hallmarks of impaired thinking. That became evident on my first trip from Marseilles to Haifa.

Just before dawn, we were closing in on the port of Haifa. The weak, emerging day-light from the east outlined the port's mountainous background, and the flashes from the lighthouse at the entrance began to be discernible. This sight, the first view of the Holy Land for most of the relatively few passengers we had, was announced on the public address system. Notwithstanding the early hour, people streamed to the decks. Excited comments, much pointing, some hand-clapping and even attempts at singing, when, suddenly, the ship veered sharply to starboard and, at high speed, left Haifa behind. I, also seeing Israel for the first time, began to suspect the improbable, which turned out to be the truth. It was not Haifa we had approached. It was Beirut. Shortly thereafter we reached our destination. The captain had a good laugh at his mistake and did not mention it any further. However, thinking about it in the light of later happenings, I could not free myself from the suspicion that it was not a mistake, that he could not resist getting an adrenalin rush by, in this fashion, re-living his past blockade running.

Bound for New York the cargo was, mostly, Russian military equipment captured during the 1956 war with Egypt. I believe it was intended for US military research. The importance of the cargo may explain the captain's strangely arrogant behavior when we arrived at the New York pilot station.

It was customary for the US Coast Guard to approach incoming ships with a question, signaled by Aldis lamp, in Morse code: "What ship? Where bound?" to which, also customarily, we should respond: "Zion. Bound New York". For this procedure I did not need to know English. Without even trying to read the signal, I would respond appropriately. But not so this time. The captain told me to signal, "None of your business." I could not spell that, so he took care of it himself. The response from the Coast Guard was immediate. We had to anchor in a designated area until further notice.

A day later we were let into the port. The damage was substantial: delayed disembarking of the passengers; delayed unloading; and delays in the whole turn-around itinerary. The captain, though, felt good, as he always did when drunk and the unexpected happened. He had asserted his rights of command. What business was it of the Coast Guard's where he was going? He had informed the port authority and that's what counted. How all this was perceived by the company's management, I do not know.

After loading in Philadelphia and Baltimore, we returned to New York for more cargo and passengers, various supplies, bunkers, and large volumes of fresh water required on passenger vessels.

The last day in port, I was on loading duty. The captain was aboard, but all other deck officers were attending to personal business ashore. Everything was done, only a hundred tons, or so, of cargo remained to be stowed. It was fragile and sensitive material urgently needed in Israel.

I was happily taking a break when the stevedore foreman broached a problem: the ship was down to the fully loaded marks. Should he stop the operations, or did I have something else to suggest? This was a serious problem. A decision had to be made, but not by me. Get the captain.

He was in his quarters, but would not answer his phone or knocks on the door. Time passed, cargo operations continued, the loading marks were under water. I had to act, stopped the loading, and was discussing with the foreman what items to unload when, suddenly, the captain appeared, clearly under the influence. I explained the situation to him; the foreman did so, too. The captain seemed to enjoy the dilemma, it appealed to the dare-devil in him. Again, he was re-living the past. Without hesitation he ordered the fresh water tanks emptied to make room for the cargo. I protested. A passenger ship could not depart without sufficient water. He insisted we could manage using the ship-board desalination equipment. The cargo was essential for the country; surely the passengers could bear some sacrifice for a higher cause.

I was now concerned that my license might be compromised and marked carefully in the log book the captain's taking over and his decision. The water was discharged, the cargo loaded, but the marks were still under water. The passengers began embarking. Coast Guard inspection before departure brought to light the lack of water and the over loading. Enough cargo had to be removed to allow full water supplies. Again, there were costly delays. At this point I decided to request a transfer when we returned to Haifa; this captain could be dangerous for my license.

But I did not dislike the captain; on the contrary, I liked him and, in some respects, even admired him. In a truly dire emergency, I would follow him without questions. For such situations, he was a true leader. On this trip, though, there had been no real emergencies. In their absence, I believe he reacted to imaginary circumstances, and so created the problems we had. His misfortune was that he could not let go of the risk-taking behavior that, in war times, had brought him fame and reward. Such behavior in peace time, on a commercial passenger liner, was to court disaster.

The return sea passage was uneventful with respect to the captain's actions. He was a perfect gentleman among peers and passengers. So were the other officers and crew. A few days after arrival in Haifa, I had another attack of malaria, missed the ship and was assigned to another vessel.

I don't know what happened to the captain. Unconfirmed gossip related many mishaps before he put the ship on the rocks outside Yafo, incurring millions of dollars in repair; was transferred to a cargo ship which he ran aground in the Mississippi delta; and, ultimately, enhanced the safety of the sea by retiring.

The Love Bug

The return trip to Haifa was momentous. I met Varda. She was returning to Israel after a convoluted departure from the country a few months earlier. She had arrived in the spring of 1956 to visit family and friends and to find work. When the Suez war broke out, she was evacuated in the middle of the night. She and a handful of Texas oilmen were flown, by an army helicopter, to Rome from where she made her own way back to New York.

On this, her return trip, I spotted her carrying a book, Goethe's *Faust*, and, having the uneducated man's respect and admiration for the educated woman, I was immediately impressed by her intellectual taste, not to mention her good looks. I did my best to put myself in her path as much as possible. The strategy worked. We went from nodding acquaintance to spending a great deal of time together, talking and listening to classical music in the well equipped music room on main deck. As she was born and raised in Jerusalem, it seemed natural that I would ask her to show me that city when the opportunity arose.

That opportunity came the second day after arrival in Haifa. I had deck and cargo duty that night, and we decided to go to Jerusalem as soon as I was relieved early in the morning. I was tired after the long night shift and, with a slight headache, fell asleep in the car. It was difficult to wake me when we arrived in Jerusalem. The headache was roaring, relentlessly piercing my brain and eyes. I was sick! Really sick; delirious; drifting in and out of consciousness. High fever, severe, but intermittent, chills and muscle aches. While not in good shape, I was still able to resist any attempt to take me to a hospital. Instead, Varda managed to get me to a hotel where I passed out.

Varda had attended kindergarten with a boy whose father was a well known doctor in Jerusalem. He remembered her and agreed to make a house call. Next day I knew what was wrong. Malaria! That was also what I had experienced on the *Bali*. A couple of injections and a longer cure of taking pills, and the doctor assured me that this type of the sickness would not return. I have never had a relapse.

Varda sent a cable to the head office explaining the situation. She stayed with me for two weeks as she nursed me back to health, and, before my returning to Haifa, showed me the city sights. We returned to Haifa two weeks later where I found an upset supervisor. Where had I been? I had missed my ship and had to be reassigned. Did I think I was on holiday? Did seeing the sights take precedence over shipboard duties? As I sat there being harangued and speechless, a telegram arrived to the supervisor. It was the cable Varda had sent 14 days earlier. Luckily it was dated and he knew the shortcomings of the postal service. He actually laughed, sent me to a doctor for a check-up, and cleaned up my file to reflect the facts.

That was the beginning of my courtship of Varda. We married in Sweden a year later in October 1958.

We had a lot of fun together. Varda was always keen on exploring new sights and places. She laughed easily, particularly at my jokes. I drew the only possible conclusion: she had, and still has, a marvelous sense of humor. After all, laughing at our jokes, is that not how we define someone's sense of humor? In Varda it manifested itself all the time; sometimes self deprecating, sometimes earthy, sometimes sharply to the point, but always it gave us fun and laughter.

Later on, when people asked how we met, I would say, jokingly, that the ship was just too small for me to escape Varda's determined pursuit. She would say, more truthfully, that the meeting was inevitable because wherever she went, there was I, clearly not on behalf of my duties; she actually began to believe that the second mate's duty station was somewhere close to her cabin door.

In the period leading up to our marriage we, lightheartedly, even jokingly, talked a great deal about the pros and cons of the step we were about to take. I told Varda that I, at the tender age of almost 29, was too young for marriage. Did she not see that I was like a flower being plucked too early, in mid-bloom, losing the prospect of reaching full flowering? She retorted that, to her, I was less a flower in mid-bloom than a wilted plant, not a flower, mind you, in serious need of the watering and care she would give. Whether flowers or wilted plants, we were in love and needed no discussions to convince us to marry.

The time for the wedding ceremony grew closer, and, in my nervousness, I could not refrain from taking a jocular stance. Before the ceremony at the Stockholm City Hall where the mayor would marry us, I told Varda that the Swedish language has some peculiarities. "When the mayor turns to you", I explained, "and says something unintelligible in Swedish, you may think the answer should be 'Yes'. Don't be fooled", I said, "in the Swedish ceremony the right answer is 'No'". She nodded, she understood. The moment arrived and, much to my feigned consternation, Varda answered "Yes". Before she could rectify her mistake, if, indeed, she had any intention to do so, we were pronounced husband and wife.

I questioned her afterwards how she could foul up the simple advice I had given. "I must have misunderstood" she said. A misunderstanding so early in our life together? We both realized it was a case of failed communication. The implications for our future were grave. How long could our marriage last when it had started in such a manner, with a lack of communication? We have pondered that question for the last 50 years.

Farewell to the Sea

Other Israeli ships

After the *Zion*, I served on several other ships under Israeli flag. The *Artza* and *Jerusalem* were passenger ships, in Mediterranean and Atlantic trades respectively. The *Tappuz* and *Tamar* carried cargo wherever the charters took them. All were good experiences.

One trip on the *Tappuz* took us to Prince Edward's Island in Canada.. We were to load potatoes in the holds, and breeding stock cattle on deck.

It was late fall with winter not far off. Very cold, wet, and miserable, more so for the cattle than for us. A specially trained man joined the crew to care for this valuable, live, cargo.

The bad weather followed us across most of the Atlantic with relief coming only near Gibraltar. The animals, however, were sick even when the seas subsided. The caretaker was also sick and, while he fed the animals, he was unable to clean the stalls. The stench was not too bad as long as the winds carried most of it away. It was pathetic to see the sea-sick caretaker, but, to see the animals in that state, was outright heartbreaking. I never thought I could feel such empathy for non-human suffering. They bleated incessantly, were thrown about in their small stalls in sync with the ship's erratic movements, and, as would humans, undoubtedly wished for an early demise.

The winds blew to and fro but did not fully dissipate the stench. In self defense, the crew cleared out the mess. It took a couple of days, but it gave only temporary relief and the work had to be repeated many times before the voyage ended. For months my cabin and my clothes reeked of the smell. No amount of cleaning and airing seemed to work. In due time, the horrible odor gave way to a more mellow smell, that of pure manure. Today a whiff of that fertilizer reminds me of the voyage, but strangely enough it does not repel me in the least.

In 1958 I had to do naval reserve duty in Sweden. This is when Varda and I were married. Our paths parted immediately after the ceremony; she took off to New York and I to Marseilles where I was to join a new passenger ship, the *Jerusalem*. We knew we would soon be united as the ship was to be employed, first, in the Haifa to New York run and, later, in the West Indies cruise trade.

The *Jerusalem* was large, some five hundred passengers, if I recall correctly. Nothing of interest transpired on the Atlantic crossings. They were all routin. The cruise trade, however, was different. The first cruises were great. Very good food, served amply and often. The entertainment in the night-club was fun, and the comedian, was hilarious. The island ports were idyllic, way different than any other ports I had seen, and mingling with the passengers was interesting and fun.

Slowly, my perceptions began to change. First, my girth increased noticeably. I had to hold back on the food. After valiant attempts, I gave in; it was easier to let out the uniform than to exercise willpower. The comedian, who so taxed my laughing muscles the first time I heard him, and with whom I had an occasional drink, began to get on my nerves.

Were there really no other jokes, gestures, and innuendos? At times I felt like planting my fist in his mouth to see if that would effect some change. By the fourth trip, those feelings had become so strong that, for his safety, I stayed out of his way.

The ports, so wonderful at first sight, became totally uninteresting. Little to see or do except shopping, and that was done for its own sake. The food in the restaurants was much inferior to that on the ship. Everything ashore catered to the casual, but eager, one-time visitor. For us, who manned the ship, the ports became only interludes, pauses in the circular voyage. Soon I did not bother to go ashore.

We were allowed to mingle with the passengers, particularly at the organized "fun" activities. Indeed, on some occasions, such as the dancing sessions arranged for solo-traveling ladies, mostly elderly, we were ordered to attend, to augment the supply of male partners. It was not fun. It was not a venue for meeting interesting people. In my status as newly married, I was taken aback. The frivolous, morally loose, behavior of the passengers, be they male or female, seemed boundless when we were at sea. There were instances when my memories of the Baltic coal trade paled by comparison. And those memories were of life in port, not at sea.

This was unexpected, and I did not want to be part of it. It was not my kind of seafaring. My field, and dreamed of career, was in cargo transport, not the "hospitality-turned-everything- goes" business. I was tired of it. I wanted to move on. I wanted a cargo ship; and I wanted my own home with Varda.

Relief came in the summer of 1959. I had applied for permanent US resident status based on being married to a citizen. The papers were being processed in Curacao, but it seemed logical to me that I should be able to wait for the documents in New York just as well as in Curacao. Varda checked at the information desk of the INS, and was told it was perfectly alright for me to leave the ship and process my status from New York.

On that basis, I informed the captain of my decision to leave. He refused to sign me off the ship's roll. I left anyway. He then turned my seaman's book over to the Coast Guard which classified me as "having jumped ship", that is, I was in the country illegally. At the same time, the INS informed me that also in their eyes I was illegal. They were not responsible for erroneous oral information, no matter where obtained. Did I have anything in writing? No! Hence I was, incontrovertibly, an "illegal alien resident."

Some legal wrangling followed, resulting in my getting a student's visa, but no work permit. While waiting for the resident papers, I took advantage of the study permit and took courses at New York University (NYU). A short while later, I had an offer to sail on a small ship carrying bananas between Costa Rica and Miami, but declined so as not to jeopardize my permanent residency. It arrived a couple of months later, in early 1960. By that time I was committed to further study. Again, a new course had been laid. Life at sea was behind me; a new, uncharted world lay ahead.

Beyond the sea

New York

meant coming home for Varda. For me it meant a new, unexpected turn in my life. While as a child I often had romantically colored thoughts of living in Canada's Northwest Territories and Alaska, the continental USA and, particularly, New York City held no allure. Yet, there was excitement and anticipation as we settled into a small, third-floor apartment on upper Riverside Drive.

The apartment house exuded dilapidated grandeur. The original huge flats had been subdivided into smaller units. The former dining room and pantry were now our living room, bedroom and kitchen, respectively. In the back of the kitchen was a tiny bathroom adjoining what was once the maid's room, now a small essentially unusable space. Our two windows, one each in the kitchen and the living room, faced the back wall of the Museum of American Indians about twenty feet away. That wall stretched upwards so far that we had no view of the sky unless we leaned far out of the window, a hazardous feat we did not attempt.

Varda's parents lived in a larger unit on the fifth floor with a great view of the Hudson. It was natural to visit them often, to have dinner and together watch their television, a fascinating gadget for me. Over time this became an expected routine, then a habit. These arrangements were not good for a newly married couple, but at the time they did not bother me very much. There were too many exciting things to see, explore and experience.

I had been to New York many times, but had never lived there, never been part of its life, its rhythms ranging from the hectic to the frenzied – and therein lay a difference. There was the city, said to be the biggest in the world. Varda knew it well and together we set out to expose me to all its beauty, charm, and flaws. The excitement of seeing the huge hordes of people soon turned into unease, then into a pervasive feeling of threat as I had earlier developed a wariness, not to say fear, of crowds and closed spaces.

At first I managed to subdue this fear and actually enjoyed riding the subway. I would look around, laughing, boisterously joking and talking with Varda. Neither of us had that typical New York "subway voice" pitched sufficiently above the noise of the train to penetrate all open spaces, so we enjoyed a conversational niche of our own. It surprised me that fellow passengers seemed totally unaware of the marvel of traveling at high speed under ground. Why did they not show their excitement as did we? Why did they not enjoy the ride? They seemed to be in their own worlds staring ahead with a stoic expression so blank it reminded me of pools of stagnant water left in the hollows of rocks after a storm. Were their minds breeding ugly thoughts as does stagnant water breed ugly insects? It was strange, indeed.

The subway gave me a sense of adventure, more so than did the buses. In time this would be reversed as I tried to escape the heat, the crowds, the smells of sweating bodies in polyester clothing, all enhanced by the closed-in spaces of the train.

The physical aspect of the city enthralled me. Not the streets or stores, but the houses; and not the houses as a whole, but their cornices. I discovered them by sheer happenstance. We could not see the sky from our apartment. Except for heavy rain, we had no idea what the weather might be. So coming out of the building I automatically looked upwards to get a bearing on the weather. Once, for no particular reason, I scanned also the top of our house and saw a most beautiful series of decorations circling the roof. From then on, that is what I saw on our walks – cornices, one more elaborate than the other, and rarely duplicated. There were gargoyles, snakes, lions and other animals, statuary, flowers, vines and writings mostly impossible to read. I marveled at the builders' decorative skills and imaginations, but wondered why they were displayed where they were least likely to be noticed.

There were, of course, the more well-known features and landmarks of the city that I had not seen on earlier visits by ship. Empire State Building and Rockefeller Center were awe inspiring. The city seen from the top of the Empire State stirred my imagination; it made me wonder what giant had thrown together all those large rocks that, on closer inspection, turned out to be massive buildings.

The large department stores, notably Macy's, Gimbel's, and Klein's on the Square shocked my system. They were too large for comfort. Too many people trying to get "a good deal" regardless of need. It brought out, to me, the difference between shopping and buying; the former being a pass-time, the latter the satisfaction of a need.

We walked, walked, and walked; truly explored Manhattan, its ethnic neighborhoods and restaurants. From the sights of the river, full with ships of all kinds, I could feel the life of the big port that was New York. But that life was not apparent; it seemed invisible. The finger piers jutting out into the river could be seen only from above, from a high vantage point like the Empire State Building. The ships tied up along them, and the cargo moved into the piers' enclosed warehouses were not part of the city's life and scenery. An exception may have been the large passenger liners, but they would soon disappear as jet airplanes became common.

Most New Yorkers seemed unaware of their city's being also the world's largest port. I did not want to lose that awareness, but had no choice. While the river and the ships hinted at ties to the sea, they were just that: hints. Because they were not part of my every-day life, these ties became weaker and weaker until my removal from the sea was almost complete. But, what was left of my awareness gnawed at my inside leaving a hollow in my breast, a longing for a change back to what had been my life. It lent an undertone of sadness to my existence in the city.

Like Stockholm, New York was held together by many bridges. It was popular to weave in and out of Manhattan to the boroughs by walking the bridges. We often walked to, but never crossed them and so did not become familiar with these boroughs.

But reality soon impinged on our life. Varda's work limited our excursions to week-ends, and I explored the only avenue open to me, the university. That was the beginning of my sadness turning to disenchantment with the world's largest city. It ended with my certainty that New York was neither nice to visit nor to live in.

Logic defied

Registration at New York University was a time consuming, frustrating, and disappointing experience leaving a lasting memory. We arrived at a late stage in the registration period and, as we had no class catalog, had to rely on material available at the Registrar's Office.

The process was straight forward, just awkwardly implemented. First, Varda would explain to me what courses were available. It took much effort on her part as I had no idea what many words meant. This took place outside the Registrar's Office. With our list ready, we went into the office to complete the registration. But, lo and behold, this, the most logical place to register, was not it.

The staff could merely tell us where the point of registration was for each of the four courses I had selected. They were all in different buildings. The first one was on the other side of the square, far away. There we got into a long line snaking slowly to a table where the actual registration took place. Once there we were told the class had been filled two hours ago. It was hard to understand why we had to stand in line for that information. What logical construct prevented them from informing the students before they reached the end point?

We had to pick another course. So back to the Registrar's Office to repeat the process for the new class and, of course, for the others we had chosen. Much running from building to building, standing in line, and finding the classes closed. At the end I was registered for a set of courses that had little bearing on the original choice. And so started my academic career.

Disappointment

Even the instruction was not what I had expected. It was not the "reading" system I believed Swedish universities used. That is, a certain level of achievement required knowledge of certain specified materials presented in a reading list. A higher grade required a longer reading list. Mastery was demonstrated by lengthy discussions and elaborations with the professor on the material in the reading lists. Also, I believed students attended lectures at their own discretion. I probably had the wrong perception of the Swedish system, but that is what I expected at NYU. I was disappointed.

We used one text book and some supplementary readings on which the instructor elaborated and explained. Attendance was mandatory and achievement measured by "true/false" and "multiple choice" questions. Given my language skills – acceptable reading, poor writing and speaking – that was a good system and I did well. My English improved rapidly. I did enjoy the courses, but not the old, disorderly and dirty appearing rooms and buildings. That physical setting seemed merely an extension of the misery of the subway ride necessary to arrive there. Some professors impressed me; many appeared indifferent and, at times, arrogant. Most disturbing, though, was the cost. One year and our funds were exhausted. Was it worthwhile to borrow to complete the studies?

In truth, I had enough of both the city and the studies. The traffic, noise, crowds, dirt and ugliness of daily life had begun to affect me. Yes, the early excitement was gone. The subway was now a necessity, not an adventure, although the daily conquest of my fear of closed-in spaces was an achievement. I now had joined my fellow passengers. Like them, my face carried a blank look. Like them I ruthlessly pushed myself into the train at rush hour; no hesitation in shoving the weaker aside. I did not see my surroundings anymore; I had withdrawn into my inner world where the sea still loomed large. Most things in the city bothered me. No exhilaration when looking upwards, in taking long walks or exploring new neighborhoods. The summer with its heat and humidity was an ordeal. The air was as dirty as the rest of the environment. Rain cleansed it somewhat, but the drops left sooty spots wherever they fell, on buildings, streets, skin, hair and clothes. With a strong wind chill factor from the river, the winter was equally miserable. The spring and fall were too short to make up for the other seasons.

Added to it all was our being too close to Varda's parents. I became increasingly unhappy with their attitudes and perceptions so at odds with those of my own. The old canard that "...we have not lost a daughter but gained a son", did not sit well with me. To me it implied giving up independence and submitting to a new parental authority, an authority I had left behind a long time ago. I felt strongly that they wished for a greater, even dominant, role in our life. I saw it in their strange expectations for my behavior. For example, Varda's mother would say, "I'm freezing, you better put on a warm jacket today." Or, if I decided to go to a movie, she would say, "Not tonight! I wouldn't". In either case I had to assert my independence, my free will, and so dressed lightly, and went to the latest possible show no matter how cold or tired I was.

Varda's father was orthodoxly observant attending services every Saturday morning, occasionally also at other times of the day. He expected the same from me, but I was not inclined to do so. I know he was disappointed, perhaps even hurt, and that I regret, but I had to affirm my own life style.

Their meddling became increasingly burdensome. They simply did not understand my world. I was miserable, but not beyond endurance because I had Varda's firm support and understanding

I missed the sea. I missed its wide expanse, the clear air, the essential silence aboard ship, the spiritual charge of a storm, the soothing solitude of standing watch, of being in charge of something I knew and understood, of being independent. I was ready to leave the world's largest city to be its dismal self, to take Varda and myself in a new direction, perhaps to Stockholm. I was tired of being in a place where my only dream was to be somewhere else.

Decision
The arguments for leaving were weighty but, after much searching and discussion, our decision was based on one consideration only: seafaring was not compatible with our marriage. A shore based position would be

my goal. A new apartment in one of the boroughs might restore the magic to our life and the city, we thought.

But the only thing I had to offer a prospective employer was my experience at sea and that, I was told, was not enough. Most US ships' officers, certainly those graduating from a maritime academy, also had a college degree. I needed the same.

NYU was out of reach. A great opportunity and alternative was offered by the City College of New York (CCNY). It was well reputed, was competitive with high admissions standards. There were doubts that I could meet those standards. But, if I did, there would be no tuition, and the final degree carried weight.

On the basis of good grades from NYU, a high score on my High-school Equivalency Diploma and, I assume, a good interview, I was accepted for the 1960 Spring Semester to the Bernard Baruch School of Business and Public Administration.

I now had a definitive goal: to graduate as soon as possible. New York was the right place for success. The city held no diversions for me, no temptations. Therefore, it was a good place for single-minded, hard studying laying the foundation for the change we so desperately needed. The next two and a half years would be difficult. I developed an even deeper dislike of the city and everything in it. It sucked the life out of my existence, and gave little in return. Indeed, I would refer to this as the black period of my life; a black hole into which my joys disappeared not to escape again to illuminate future memories.

In my later professional career I avoided the city, did not attend meetings or conferences there, and declined out of hand two academic offers. The third, many years later, at the United States Merchant Marine Academy (USMMA), I did accept, albeit with some misgivings.

Nevertheless, there were many events which, when I search my memory, seem worth mentioning.

What about music?
There was, of course, entertainment. Once we happened upon a theater on Second Avenue giving *HMS Pinafore*. It was my first experience with Gilbert and Sullivan. It opened a new world of pleasure and delight. Since then we have seen most of their plays many times, but nothing can replicate what I felt discovering "musicals" for the first time. We saw other Broadway productions, but, except for *My Fair Lady*, none was memorable.

Classical music had always been part of Varda's life; it was now entering mine, but not entirely without setbacks. We were friendly with a high-school teacher who lived in the penthouse of our building. He, in turn, had a friend with access to free opera tickets; to the old Met before it moved to Lincoln Center. Once he passed some tickets to us; to *The Meistersingers*. We were ecstatic, there can be no other word to describe our delight. Varda liked opera but was not familiar with Wagner's works; hence she looked forward to a sophisticated, satisfying musical event. I looked forward too, but had no idea to what. Wagner was known to me only by hearsay. While I had seen some operas in Stockholm, they were forgotten. Now the opera reference point in my mind was the recent excitement with Gilbert and Sullivan, no matter that sophisticates did not consider it real opera.

With much anticipation we counted the days to the performance. The day finally arrived. Ensconced in very good seats, we could barely contain our excitement.

The performance started. It went on; and it went on; and on, and on... Not even Varda was prepared for such a long performance. On my part, I wondered why it was so different from *HMS Pinafore*. Where were all the rousing melodies? The funny people? Would not a Meistersinger excel in presenting something like *I'm a Modern Major General*? Perhaps it would come towards the end? It did not. Would it ever end? It did. For me it was not an experience to be soon repeated. My appreciation of opera was set back many years.

One winter evening we entered a subway station in Times Square. Close to the entrance was a store with a juke box featuring classical records. Two men, best described by their appearance as derelicts, or vagrants, were huddled in front of the box raptly listening to the music they had chosen. It was an opera selection by a popular tenor. The listeners were totally absorbed in the music. They nodded to the tune, tried to hum, or even sing, in accompaniment; they were clearly transported to another world, warmer, more friendly and beautiful than the one to which they returned when the recording ended.

We had stopped as well to hear the tenor. At the end we lingered as the two men began to comment on what they had heard. One said "You should hear that sung by Caruso. No one can match him." "Not so", said the other. "Have you heard Bjoerling, the Swedish tenor?" The lines were drawn. A spirited discussion followed as to the relative merits of Caruso and Bjoerling. They knew whereof they spoke. Language was florid, musical terms abounded and they included snippets of singing to make their points. Since they apparently had nothing else to attend to, it was clear the discussion would last a long time. We left.

I could not help but reflect on this event as quintessentially New York. With their unshaven faces, dirty looking clothes and general skid-row demeanor, their roles as classical music lovers and critics seemed preposterous. Yet, they had spent money they could ill afford to hear the music they loved and that brought them escape The garish, noisy surroundings did not bother them. It was only after returning to the dreary present that they began to reminisce about other, even more sublime singers, and the pleasures they had given them. Where can such a juxtaposition of material poverty and intellectual riches be seen? Only in New York, I believe.

Of language and social life

Our penthouse neighbor and friend, the teacher, played a great role in my learning English. By now I spoke fluently and without hesitation, but not necessarily all in English. Whenever I lacked a word or concept, I simply substituted the applicable Swedish expressions. I spoke, what I was told many years later in Wisconsin, Swenglish. For example, discussing my English teacher's comments on my essay, I wanted to say: "He ought to read my paper again because I know what I am talking about". What I might actually say was: "He ought to read min uppsats igen because I know what jag talar om." Or, "...underordnade klausuler are not that hard to forsta" for "...subordinate clauses are not that hard to understand." No one ever questioned me on these curious sentences. Perhaps they thought mine was a higher form of English, and they did not want to appear ignorant. Perhaps they thought it too low-brow to merit comment. Perhaps (most likely) they were simply polite.

The only exception was our neighbor. He immediately asked for the meaning of the many strange words I used. He insisted that I explain them in English. Doing so gave me much practice and my vocabulary improved by leaps and bounds.

I have few recollections of our social life. Many of our friends were going to college. We proudly put our newly found knowledge to immediate use. Our conversations inevitably descended, or became elevated, depending on one's perspective, to analyses of whomever in our group was absent at any particular time. Psychology 101, inadequately understood, provided all the input we needed.

The terms we used, the depths of our believed psychological insights, all lent strength and a scientific veneer to what was, in essence, gossip. We were very pleased by our scientific approach. One day, who knows, we would even understand what we were saying.

Hazardous occupation

One of the requirements for matriculation at the Baruch School was my attending an evening, non-credit course in American history. It was a large class, all foreign born and with a poor command of English. The content was good, the teacher even better. It was a wonderful course.

We, the students, gathered in the intermissions to discuss and clarify the material in our accented, at times grammatically broken, speech. Misunderstandings abounded and, at times, frustrations spilled over into shouting and peevish sulking. But we got along well and some of us became lasting friends. There was a young man from Columbia, about my age. He had studied for awhile at a seminary in his native country. Now he was enrolled to study philosophy at the CCNY Uptown Campus. We talked often. He was very likeable. We were friends.

The day of finals arrived. We were seated in a large room, row upon row, trying to answer essay questions. It was difficult for most of us to convince the teacher, in writing, that his efforts had borne fruit.

Toward the end of the allotted time, students began to hand in their papers which the teacher started to read immediately. He was hunched over reading intently when my Columbian friend approached, laid his paper on the desk and walked to the door in the back of the teacher. At the door he hesitated for a few moments, then turned around and walked up to the teacher whose back was turned toward him. Without agitation or hurry he put his hands on the instructor's shoulders, bent down and quickly bit him on the neck drawing blood. Screams, turmoil, and confusion ensued while the student simply stood by as if this was no concern of his. His sedately folded hands on his stomach evoked an odd sense of piety and tranquility.

The teacher got medical attention; the student police attention; and I made a mental note not to become a teacher. I lost contact with my Colombian friend as he ended up in a psychiatric hospital.

Hoyt Street

Other requirements for admission to CCNY entailed various tests of the students' command of spoken English, pronunciation, vocabulary, and grammar. Everyone took a turn to read a passage before the testing panel. A number of freshmen from Brooklyn and the Bronx passed without difficulty although I thought they spoke rather strangely. I was confident that I, too, would pass easily. Although I had an accent, I did not think I spoke as funnily as did those from Brooklyn and the Bronx. No such luck. Three words and I was immediately put into remedial speech class.

There I learnt not to say "noyvus" for "nervous", "woik" for "work", or "hoyt" for "hurt", and so on. I became much aware of these kinds of words and took pains to pronounce them correctly.

One day on the subway I overheard two women talking in Danish. Feeling that we, as new immigrants, must have a certain bond, I initiated a conversation. But the only common, understandable language we had was English. After a brief, uninteresting exchange of words one of them said they were getting off at the next station, at Hoyt Street. I immediately picked up on that name and with, what I thought was a winning smile, said, "Since you are new to this country, you might as well learn the proper pronunciation of the street where you live. It's not Hoyt Street. It's Hurt Street".

Suddenly the vocabulary of the ladies changed. Using words, both Danish and English that I had not heard before, they made clear to me that they had lived on Hoyt Street for some 30 years. I, they said, using a Swedish expletive, was an arrogant SOB. They left no doubts as to where they thought I ought to go. Since then I have never tried to tell anyone how to pronounce anything English; I have my own problems in that area.

Getting out

Graduation came in June 1962. In the absence of real news, *The New York Times* thought it fit to print a "human interest story" about me. Titled "Swede's Ambition Turns From Sea" (June 3, 1962), a synopsis of which was printed in the Stockholm paper *Dagens Nyheter*, it mentioned my plans to obtain a doctorate in economics three years hence. Behind that ambitious plan is a story of rational decision making.

About a year before graduation I began looking for a position, preferably in the management of shipping. My major professor, Harold Keller, whom I liked and respected very much, arranged for me to meet with a well known Danish ship owner, Jacob Isbrandtsen. He received me early in the morning in his large office the trimmings of which were almost intimidating in their display of tokens of successful shipping ventures: hand carved furniture of exotic woods, highly polished ships' lanterns, walls covered with models and paintings of, mostly, his own ships through time. It was stunning and I worried about my mundane errand in such a setting. But, as the elderly gentleman he was, he set me at ease and we had a pleasant, not too short a meeting. He arranged for me to see his personnel manager for lunch that very day.

The manager was exceptionally frank. A first university degree did not make me competitive with other graduates who were some 10 years younger. The heart of my experiences was still the sea. If I wanted a job on a ship, he might, and he stressed the word might, be of help, but, because of my age, he would not consider me for a job in the office. However, a graduate degree would go a long way to close the age gap. For example, he said, the average age for a Ph.D. was 35. If I had that degree at that age, or a bit beyond, I would, indeed, be a desirable candidate, particularly if I included a heavy dose of international relations and politics in my program. The closing of the Suez Canal in 1956, he continued, and other political developments had prompted forward looking shipping companies to assess the positioning of their ships so that they would not all, at the same time, be closed off from trading by being in the wrong places. This kind of planning put a premium on those able to do "political risk assessments."

He made a strong impression on me. I decided to have the doctorate by 1965, if at all possible.

Making a Living

We lived less than adequately on Varda's salary of $48 a week. I needed a job. Taking the clue from my summers in Sweden, a relief mate's position would fit the bill. It seemed an easy solution.

But the Coast Guard did not recognize my Swedish documents and so I could not be hired by an American ship. I tried several other flags, including those of Scandinavia, but their needs were, of course, for relief duty in their home ports, not in the US.

That avenue closed, I tried to be certified as a regular seaman, an AB. This time the Coast Guard would be happy to issue the relevant papers; I only had to produce proof of being a union member. Off to the union I went. Certainly, they would gladly accept my membership but I had to produce proof of, or promise of, employment by a shipping company. The companies I talked to would be delighted to have me, they said, but I had to be a union member which required seaman's papers. The circle was closed. To be hired, I needed seaman's papers which required union membership, and for that I needed a job offer which I could not get without the union card. What now?

There were plenty of ads for house painters. I applied, but was turned down for being over qualified. Also, I spoke funnily; too many strange and long words; I clearly did not belong. But one of the painters thought I might have a chance to become a member of, as I recall it, the Tug and Bargemen's Union. After so many set-backs, calling them was a huge boost to my self-esteem. "Great! Welcome! Be here at seven tomorrow morning for a briefing." Joy of joys. I had prospects of a sea related job. Life was truly taking a turn for the good.

At six thirty I was on the spot eagerly waiting to begin the process to become a union member. A small crowd had assembled by seven.

There was much talk; I understood little. That phase over, we were given placards attached to sturdy wooden sticks. The placards had inscriptions such as "Moran is Unfair", and "Support your Union". I was all in favor of supporting the union, but wondered what Moran's unfairness had to do with my membership and possibility of a job. I simply did not get it. It took a few hours of walking up and down the pier with the signs held high before it became abundantly clear what I was doing. This was not paying work, nor was it likely to lead to it. My attempts to further social justice for the union and to improve the ethics of Moran ended by lunch-time. My job search took a different turn.

The only noteworthy event in picketing Moran was a very brief encounter with a Frank Brainard who was at the time writing a history of the Moran company. Many years later I would again meet him at the US Merchant Marine Academy where he was the director of the Merchant Marine Museum and a big name in maritime history. There was no reason for him to remember me, and he did not.

A job was needed during the academic year as well as the summers, so I welcomed working in the mail room of a small company publishing medical texts. It was owned by a husband and wife team the latter of which was a niece of Varda's mother. The company was successful but the owners were an odd couple. He was originally from Germany and she from a small town in Wisconsin. Each had a strong will and an ego impervious to any influence by the spouse, or anyone else. The resulting clashes were ferocious; their appeals to the employees to take sides made it a sorrowful place to work. Many of the personnel spent much of the working day looking for other positions.

I assumed that their home life was peaceful, perhaps even harmonious, because the behavior in the office could not possibly leave much energy for continued confrontations at home. However, visiting them, as we did from time to time, showed that there was no peace to be found in either place. The mail room was quiet, though, and I learnt a great deal about office intrigues, and earned a whole dollar per hour.

Another close friend of Varda's family thought my technical abilities were neglected in the mail room and offered a position as a draftsman of electrical circuits. He was ill informed about my skills, but with a pay of two and a half dollars an hour, I did not feel it necessary to set him right.

I had some familiarity with the reading of electrical diagrams and did not think it would be hard to draw them. After all, they were mainly straight lines interrupted by various squiggles and boxes. An instruction book from the public library was immensely helpful; so was the foreman who allowed me to come in two hours early to practice my skills. The shift was from four p.m. to midnight, so in the beginning I started at two p.m.

The greatest benefit of the work was the dinner break. I discovered *Tad's Steakhouse* on 42nd Street. One and a quarter dollars bought a T-bone steak, baked potato, Texas toast and a bowl of salad. I had never had anything so tasty. Especially the salad. It was served with blue cheese dressing something I had neither heard of nor tasted before. Equally tasty was the rind of fat adorning the steak. I always asked for the fattest one available.

A couple of months of that daily fare increased my waist quite noticeably and I adopted the old attitude that a fat person is a happy person. I did nothing about my girth as I did not want to be unhappy. Only by quitting the job did I break the habit of eating myself to happiness. Henceforth, my weight and happiness stayed essentially unchanged: the former high, the latter low.

Not fitting in

My studies were enjoyable; they were my escape from the present and our hope for the future. The professors at CCNY were engaged, knowledgeable, accessible and helpful. Through my major professor I had several opportunities at internships in international trade companies.

One, International Selling, Inc., was a subsidiary of a French company, had many employees and was very noisy. The air was filled with well accented voices yelling orders, questions or answers over the low walls separating the desks. I had the elevated title of Rate Clerk. My task was to find freight rates for various commodities and relay them to the salesmen who worked by phone. Speed was of the essence. I had just a few minutes to find what was needed.

I did not last long. I was fired for two reasons. First I was too slow. Accurate but slow. Too late did I realize that speed took precedence over accuracy; it was always possible to adjust the rate quotation once the deal was closed. And adjusted they were. The rates I found were never the final ones, no matter how accurate I tried to be.

The second reason was more circumspect and was revealed to me much later by one of the executives. It had to do with not fitting into the unspoken hierarchical social system. Simply put, I dressed inappropriately.

I had a nice, high quality custom tailored suit from Sweden where I had absorbed the attitude that a suit ought to be kept for as long as possible, perhaps twenty years, or more, if let in and out as needed. Naturally, I wore it to work with a nice shirt and tie. This outfit was complemented with my very fine black woolen overcoat and Italian Borsalino felt hat. That nice, perhaps elegant, appearance earned me deferential treatment from the building's service people. In their eyes I was clearly an executive of the company. At least I dressed like one. This irked my office mates and, particularly, superiors.

Why, they asked, did I not dress as behooved my station? Lower echelon employees wore visibly cheap suits, shirts and ties; same with overcoats. These should be raincoats of cheap quality, easily wrinkled and rumpled. I, the very lowest of employees, was totally out of place. Such pretensions and arrogance deserved only one response: dismissal. I put my finery away to be used only on holidays and other major occasions. While such major occasions never occurred, I was nevertheless prepared for them and felt good about it.

My next job was located in the Empire State Building. There I tried to verify this "sociology of dress" by observing the men in the lobby and elevators. The truth was depressingly clear. Appearances ranged from the cast offs from Klein's basement, a large group, to a small number of picture perfects from *Gentleman's Quarterly*. A clear case of "the clothes make the man."

I encountered this kind of unspoken social ranking in other contexts as well. Somewhere along Broadway was a car dealership displaying the latest model of the Ford Thunderbird. I had never seen such a beautiful car and wanted badly to see it up close. One day I entered the store wearing a rather shabby jacket well suited for the weather. I walked around the car relishing what would certainly be out of my financial reach for a very long time.

A salesman approached and without preamble or courtesy told me that what I was looking for was next door, just a few yards down the street. I assumed that the car I was looking at was for display only, not to be touched or inspected in any way; that should be done next door. There I went; it was a store selling Vespa scooters!

Fitting in

Hunter Trading was a small import firm occupying three rooms in the Empire State Building. Each of the two partners had his own office. The secretary, Rose, and I shared the third room which was also the reception area. One partner was from Holland eking out his American dream, while the other already had reached it as he carried a well-known New York family name. They were good friends and great people to work for. The company imported wood products, plywood from Taiwan and Italy and knocked down furniture from Yugoslavia and Poland.

I had learnt my lesson in my earlier job. Now I tried to dress and appear appropriately. Cheap shirts and slacks from Kleins, unpolished shoes, a nondescript weather jacket when needed and, once in a while, a scarf and an unshaven face. I fit in.

My position entailed many and varied functions. Like any respectable large company, which we were not, we had several departments. There was one for finance, another for letters-of-credit; others for customs clearance, customer relations, marine insurance, claims, and shipping and freight forwarding. With the partners engaged in buying and selling, it fell to Rose and me to handle the affairs of these departments. We took turns to assume the role of being the head of whatever department was relevant for a specific issue. It was mostly routine. In cases where correspondence was needed, the partners chipped in doing the writing. Since I read the letters carefully before signing, I gained valuable insights into persuasive writing.

The work schedule allowed for much leeway. That is, I could come and go as I pleased, as long as I arrived before 1 pm, left after 6 pm and stayed in the office in between. How much freer could one be? I liked my bosses and the work.

The partners decided to seek new business in Scandinavia and naturally turned to me for information on local customs and, particularly, when to go. I suggested mid-June till end of July that being the height of the Swedish summer. In my mind I saw the Swedish mid-summer celebrations, long days, sun drenched bays, sailing boats, and great outdoor cafes, all so unlike the unpleasant heat and humidity of New York. My descriptions waxed lyrical. Their faces reflected my enthusiasm. They took my advice, left the office in care of Rose and, hesitatingly, me and went overseas.

They did not know, nor did I, that Swedish businesses go on reduced hours in the summer and, during the time I suggested, closed down entirely to give workers vacation during the best part of the summer. The result was no business contacts whatsoever. But they were not angry with me. Indeed, they brought gifts. A gold-wire money clip (nothing clipped to it) for me; and some jewelry for Rose. They joked about the good times in Stockholm and in Holland where they stayed on the way back

I was embarrassed and braced myself for being fired. It did not happen. If anything, the partners seemed to appreciate me more than ever giving me more responsibilities such as relieving Rose from her coffee making duties.

The firm expanded. An office manager was needed and, if I wanted it, they would hold it open until my graduation. The salary would be huge, just under six thousand a year. It was tempting but I had my plans and was determined to get out of the city and to go to graduate school. The new office manager arrived and I left the firm shortly before graduation.

The Pier Superintendent

One of the partners recommended me for a summer job with the Hudson River Day Line. I had no expectations of success as I went to the pier for an interview, but the elderly gentleman who met me proceeded as if I was already employed. There was no ship in sight so he gave me an uninteresting tour of the pier which looked like any other of its kind. A huge cargo shed with a clean area for passengers to gather, wait, embark and disembark. Beyond this area was a much larger one with a jumble of stored items and materials providing numerous out of sight nooks and crannies. My job, he said, was to inspect these areas and ensure that the clean one stayed clean, and that the storage area would not become a destination for the love-sick, nor a home for derelicts. To give me authority, he gave me the title Pier Superintendent.

This elevated title also entailed some duties relating to the ship. I was responsible for all the complexities involved in tying up the ship, having the gangway in place and secured, and seeing to it that the passengers stayed properly in line as they flowed into and out of the ship. It sounded trivial. It was.

While I was given my instructions, the ship had arrived and he gave me a fascinating tour of it. I had never seen anything like it, nor had I any idea that such ships still existed. *Alexander Hamilton* was a paddle-wheeler, one wheel on each side amidships. It carried tourists on the scenic route along the river from Manhattan to Bear Mountain State Park and West Point, a trip of about two hours each way. With a capacity of, I believe, some 400 passengers, it was a comfortable ship with numerous decks and cabins. I had many conversations with the captain. He talked much about his impending retirement. Naturally, dreams of succeeding him began to form in my mind, but they were brutally destroyed by still vivid memories of my trying to get Coast Guard documents. Nevertheless, I knew this would be an enjoyable summer, a fitting, finally positive, experience in the city I so disliked.

The ship spent most of the days on the river, so I focused on the pier itself. There were instances where couples bought tickets for the ship but, once inside the gate, abandoned all thoughts of river travel. Instead, they took off for the far recesses of the pier. Again and again I was in the difficult position of telling them to leave because they were out of bounds not only in terms of space but, perhaps more importantly, because they had shed too many confining garments. Depending on the stage to which the romance had progressed, they would obey me quickly or less so. It really did not matter. I had made my point, although I was as embarrassed as were they. I must admit, though, that my embarrassment was tempered by a sense of power and authority as I imagined my having dictated the conditions for their meeting deep seated natural urges. This perceived power gave me confidence in my ability to handle delicate situations.

Once I came across a professional and her customer. They were not embarrassed. They were unpleasant, rude, vulgar and threatening, and I tried to respond in kind. After all, the power was mine. "What do you want?," the man asked. "Yeah, what is it?" chimed in the woman, and continued, "If you wanna watch, you gotta pay." "Never mind," said the man, "you damned Peeping Tom, get lost, fast, or ...." Clearly they did not know who I was. An introduction seemed appropriate. "I'm the Pier Superintendent. I'm in charge here; not you. By the time I return," I said, cautiously increasing my physical distance from them, "you better be gone. I just have to dock the boat; it's coming in now." Whereupon I hurried to the berth where the ship was not due for another few hours. I simply did not have time to check that they had followed my stern advice.

As to more permanent residents, the derelicts, I never saw any.

One day the ship was chartered for a large party. It would depart early evening and return at a non-specified, but late, time. As usual I was to oversee the embarking and disembarking. This was normal, except for the expected late return. What was not normal was the list of telephone numbers I was to rely on in case the need arose. The numbers were to various police stations and hospitals. This was strange, not to say ominous, but it did not fully register with me.

Around six o'clock the passengers began to arrive. Men and women, young and younger, racially mixed and all well dressed. Nothing unusual to my eyes which were drawn to two particularly cute girls with boyishly cut hairs, in shorts, high heels, and carrying large, stylish handbags, holding hands as they boarded. How adorable. I remember them because next time I saw them, on the ship's return, they were not cute, not holding hands and, who knows why, they were shoeless. They were drunk, using their handbags as weapons and the hands to tear at each others hair and clothes. What a sad end to friendship.

I also remember a tall, slim, handsome black man with a mid-size valise giving the impression he was going to stay somewhere over night. He was striking. The reason I remember him is that he embarked a man, but disembarked a beautiful woman. However, he was not alone carrying a valise. Many did so, and I assume they carried clothes in them to facilitate the gender transformation that clearly took place aboard the ship.

The embarkation was smooth and event free. Mostly they entered in pairs, much like in Noah's Ark, just not one of each gender. The return in the early morning hours was different. I never had reason to use my telephone list. An hour, or so, before the ship returned a number of police officers materialized taking up positions around the passenger area, some also deployed in the back of the pier. A number of police cars, vans and ambulances were there as were one or two fire engines. And so was the manager of the company, the man who had hired me. We stood there watching the unfolding spectacle, his knowing what it was about, I surmising it.

My boss filled me in. The charter was a "meet your soul-mate" gay-lesbian affair. With so many passengers aboard, opportunities abounded for finding new partners and romance. Drinking started soon after leaving the dock and quickly escalated to being too much. Facilitated by the drinking, dancing and courtship had given way to unruly free-for-all groping and manhandling. Couples that had come aboard as partners had begun to split as the sexual tensions and opportunities mounted. Soon fights erupted, blood was drawn and the captain cut the trip short. He alerted the manager who, in turn, called in the police. I called Varda to come and see this extraordinary happening, but she was not ready to enter the subway at that time of night.

The passengers came down the gangway often reeling, singing, cursing, some bloodied, many with clothing missing or in disarray. Much fighting continued on the dock with both knives and knuckle-irons in use. Many were arrested, many sent to hospitals, and it was a long time before some semblance of peace reigned on the pier.

At that time, we followed some police officers who boarded the ship to clear it of remaining passengers. There were many of those in cabins and secluded deck areas flagrantly displaying nudity and sex. While they were disgruntled at being told to leave, they were not belligerent or aggressive. Their disembarkation was almost as decorous and orderly as had been the earlier embarkation. As they came down the gangway affectionately holding hands, or with arms around each other, they seemed to have found what the arrangers had promised and hoped for.

Nothing noteworthy happened during the few more weeks I stayed in this job before departing for Madison, Wisconsin, at the end of August, 1962. Again, I was on a new course leaving the sea behind.

Unbound by the Sea

My life has always been bound up with the sea. Even now, in my old age, I remember my seafaring years with fondness and nostalgia. But I know those times are irrevocably gone. My experiences can not be replicated because the seafaring world has changed.

The very ships are different. The beautiful flowing lines of the ships that were part of my world have given way to the boxy, clumsy outlines of today's fast, high capacity technological wonders.

The crews are smaller. Shipboard operations have been automated. The sharp distinctions between deck, engine and catering departments have become blurred. The social relationships on board have changed. And the large ships and the huge volumes they carry have altered the ports, their natures, their sizes, and their locations. The ports of my youth with their waterfront bars and unusual life style are hard to find. But it is no wonder that the waterfront bars are getting scarce. I remember a visit to a ship on which I knew the radio operator. I caught him just as he was shouldering his golf clubs to spend the afternoon on a game together with several of his shipmates. Golf? What seaman had even heard of the game in my times? Just a few more years and the very position of radio officer would become obsolete and disappear.

The high speed of the ships and the efficient ports mean that very little time is available for the enjoyment of either shore leave or the vast open seas. The smaller, exotic ports I experienced are inaccessible for large, modern ships. Today's seafarer can not see the world as I did.

The physical challenges posed by the sea in my time have also changed. The allure and romance of seafaring lay to a large extent in man's struggle against the sea. Survival required skilled seamanship. The overriding concern was: What could, and would, the sea and weather do to the seaman and his ship? It was in overcoming these natural forces that the seaman excelled; in overcoming his fear of the raging waters and winds. The sea was invulnerable. The ships and their crews were not, but they fought to overcome whatever the sea could throw their way.

Today it is different. Technological change has weakened the powers of the sea to do us harm. And so our perspective has changed. We do not ask anymore, as a matter of course: What can the sea do to us and how can we fight it? The odds of our surviving the wrath of nature have improved so much that we now ask: What are we doing to the sea, and how can we control what we do? Concerns for the environment--for the sea--have taken over and have brought with them voluminous regulatory paperwork and legal liabilities to plague the officers and crew. Good seamanship to save the crew, ship and cargo may founder on perceived violations of such rules. There have been many instances of imprisonment for the captains involved in such issues.

Another new aspect is modern piracy, which has become a problem on many trade routes. Of course, I many times experienced thievery and illicit boardings, but they were non-violent and occurred only in ports or when transiting narrow waters at slow speed. It was vastly different from today's heavily armed pirates who use speed boats to attack ships at full throttle on the open sea. Piracy has no bearing on seamanship, but its life threatening presence must be added to the many new challenges and hardships at sea.

Even the majestic beauty of the forces of sea and wind are now tied too often to the devastation and suffering from tsunamis and hurricanes. In the face of such forces it is difficult to extol the beauty of being a foul weather friend. The romance and rewards of seafaring are the casualties of all these changes.

It is a truism to say that the present molds the future. That is the course of life, and so it has been for me. Now I am old; the future of my youth is behind me. But as I write my memoir, my past has been brought forward and has become my present. I think often of the essential fullness of life at sea: the dark nights of standing watch, the crisp close-by stars, the fog, the storms, the hard work, and the camaraderie. It was a time when the ship was my world, my secure point in life, when the heaving surface around it and the firm sky above were the foundations and spiritual sources of my life.

I treasure my memories of the sea. Although they are of a time long gone, they enrich my life even today. But no matter how vividly I have been brought back to the sea, it is the past; I cannot dwell there. I will not allow my past to become my present when the implied future is simply not there. A different future is now mine and, as I face it, I will not be bound by the sea as I was in my youth. My memoir is finished. What was must now rest; what is must be free to shape what will be.

The changes wrought by time have finally unbound me. The sea beckons me no more.

BOOK TWO
"DOUBLE OCCUPANCY" AND OTHER STORIES

Linguistics

My accent, pronunciations, and cultural background have, at times, led to unexpected outcomes and funny situations. Here are some that stand out in my memory.

Not far from the apartment building where I grew up, in Stockholm, there was a lighthouse on a small island in the waterway. I went to the same school as did the two children of the lighthouse keeper. Every school day, one of the parents would row the children to the mainland. In my youthfully romantic mind that family lived the most desirable life. Could anything be better than to live on an island and have a boat of your own? I felt resentment toward my father. Why could he not be a lighthouse keeper? I developed a strong yearning for the life in a lighthouse. That dream has stayed with me throughout my life, although today, of course, lighthouses are automated and unmanned.

As Varda's and my relationship developed, we reached the point where we did confide to each other our most cherished dreams and hopes. Somewhat hesitantly, I told her about my romantic view of lighthouse keeping. Imagine my surprise and happiness when Varda's eyes lit up, widened to resemble those of an owl's and, with barely constrained emotions, said that she fully shared my dream. Imagine our feelings, we were truly soul mates. Our relationship was cemented as never before; we were heading toward a future of shared dreams.

Many years later it became clear that our different backgrounds had filtered our words. While I had talked about lighthouse keeping, she had heard that my dream was to become a light house-keeper and that was, indeed, a man to dream of.

My first visit to the US was in 1947 aboard a ship of the Swedish-American Line. We docked at Greenpoint in Brooklyn. It was a wonderful experience. I tasted real coffee for the first time in my life; it was awful. My very first hamburger was different. That was worth writing home about; that, and the strange thing called ketchup. And, not to be forgotten, that wonderful, fluffy, crustless, "never-touched-by-a-human-hand" white bread.

But other things were even more exciting. One was the Radio City Music Hall which we had heard of, but never really expected to see. However, the ship's electrician spoke English and was willing to take the younger crew members, as a group, to see Manhattan and, of course, the Radio City Music Hall. We were eight seamen who set out to find the subway to take us to the city. A couple of blocks from the dock we were lost and the electrician looked for someone to show us the way.

He spotted a small bearded man wearing a fedora and asked him in his very best Swedish public school English: "I beg your pardon, sir. Can you tell me the underground way to Radio City Music Hall?" The man looked at him, and us, with an expression that combined both fear and astonishment, thought for a long while, and then decided he understood the question. He stroked his beard and said, in Yiddish: "Muss men geyen zwey block do ariber un folgen di zeygen"; that is, "Go two blocks that way and follow the signs". More questions and answers followed. All unintelligible to the electrician. He was dumbfounded and began to look desperate. I, however, understood most of the instructions since my parents had spoken Yiddish at home. I translated and even tried to get some further clarification, in my rudimentary Yiddish. The impact on the group was enormous. They were impressed; my prestige was at an all time high. Aboard the ship word spread that I was fluent in English.

Many years later my ship, now an Israeli vessel, was, again, docked at Greenpoint. Varda came to get me at the end of my shift. Up the street was a little luncheonette where I usually indulged my taste for hamburgers. The owner was a pleasant man who spoke with a rather strong German accent. He and I got along well, but he had never seen Varda. Now was the time to introduce her to him.

He looked at her and said, "Sharmin." Varda said, "Thank you." A moment later he said again, "Sharmin", nodded his head and looked kindly at Varda. And again she said, "Thank you." Now he looked very intently at her and, once again, said "Sharmin." Varda responded as before, "Thank You." I wondered how many more times he would tell her she was charming. He repeated it once more and got the same response from Varda. Then, almost in desperation, he blurted out, "You're Sharmin. Are you not from Sharminy?" We finally understood. He thought Varda was from Germany.

When first I arrived in Israel I would be asked about my country of origin because, it was clear, they had difficulty understanding me. That did not bother me much because I knew my English was shaky. However, they asked, if I was from Sweden, why did I speak like a Welshman? That question surprised me. I took it as a great compliment. Wales is, after all, part of England. Imagine how flattered I was that people thought I spoke like an Englishman from Wales. Perhaps I had underestimated my knowledge of the language. Perhaps I did, indeed, know it as well as my

Swedish shipmates once thought. I basked in my new status as an almost native speaker of the English language.

Sometime later, at a lunch at the Maritime Club in Haifa, I was seated next to a man who had a prominent position with a ship broker in town. We engaged in conversation about maritime matters. He would say something to which I would respond, "Can you, please, repeat that?" He would look at me and say, "What?" I would say something and he would respond, "Again, please?" and so on.

Our conversation consisted of mutual incomprehension, misunderstandings and frustrations and a total lack of communication. It lasted a long time, though. I finally admitted to him that I did not understand what he was saying. Although I knew he spoke English, I could not understand his accent, or inflection. Where was he from? He told me he was a Welshman!!!

After my bout with malaria, which stranded me in Jerusalem, I was assigned to an old passenger liner, the *Artza*. She was in trade from Haifa to Limasol in Cyprus, then to Genoa and Marseilles after which we returned to Haifa. The main purpose of the trade was to bring immigrants to Israel from, mainly, Hungary, Rumania and Poland. The ship was essentially empty on the outward trip. The few passengers we did have, and they were few, indeed, were either tourists or businessmen from Haifa and Cyprus.

The captain was an elderly Hungarian. He spoke several languages fluently, English not among them. That is, he spoke it but had no feeling for the nuances of the language. A true gentleman of the old hand-kissing-school, immaculately groomed and always in white dress uniform, he kept his distance from both officers and sailors. But he took his duties as captain seriously with regard to the entertainment of the passengers, particularly the women. There was the Captain's Dinner, his cocktail parties, dances and whatever else he could think of to please his guests. The officers were included in these activities, but only as he directed them; heaven help anyone who might upstage him.

On one trip a very important lady boarded in Limasol for England via Marseilles. Rumors had it that she was the wife of the British Governor of the island, but I doubt that. However, that she was important was borne out by the manner in which she arrived. She was escorted by a number of men and women who looked very "upper crust" and included several high officers. A mountain of luggage followed.

The captain issued orders for our behavior. At all times we were to be in white dress uniform; we were to keep a low profile and should minimize our presence in areas used by the passengers. These orders did not prevent me from witnessing the next event.

Shortly after departure the lady was sitting at a table in the salon. The captain approached her, performed his version of heel-clicking, bowed and kissed her hand, then sat down at the table. No small talk followed. The silence began to be embarrassing. Finally the captain had decided how to proceed. With a well practiced flair he retrieved his gold cigarette case, and, with a gold lighter at the ready, he offered her the contents. Courteously, she declined, "Thank you. I don't smoke." Somewhat put off balance, the captain recovered and asked, "May I offer you a drink?" To that she replied, "I don't drink!"

This was as far as the captain had planned his approach. But, again, he recovered and paid her what he thought of as the ultimate compliment: "My, are you a cheap lady!"

Name Dropping

After graduate school I worked at the International Monetary Fund in Washington, D.C. as a "desk economist" covering Sweden. Part of the work entailed travel, with high level IMF officials, to that country for meetings with economic policy makers.

Befitting our important missions, and elevated status as international bankers, the Fund was very generous with travel. First class was a requirement easy to comply with. I had not experienced that luxury before, and was excited to make my first trip. As the departure date came closer, my excitement was complemented by feelings of importance and growing self worth. It was a totally new me that boarded the SAS plane for Stockholm. A new suit, white shirt and blue tie added to my well-being as I took my aisle seat of ample size, took out my science fiction pocketbook, and surveyed my surroundings.

To my right, in the window seat, sat a woman. Quite beautiful, older than I, handsomely dressed, she gave me a brief, indifferent glance and returned to her book. With each of us engrossed in books, there was plenty of comfortable space between and around us. Snacks and drinks were served with real china and silverware, and a great deal of attention. It was, indeed, going to be an enjoyable trip. Only much later did I realize that the attention was prompted by the lady next to me, the lady to whom I paid no attention, and who did similarly to me.

Well into the flight an attendant brought her a copy of the *New York Times* which she eagerly began to read. She read fast, but in a curious way I had not seen before. First, she read pages one and two, then turned to the last page of the section and, finally to the penultimate page. Having read these four pages, she had no use for that large, loose sheet of the paper, and so dropped the sheet to the floor in the space between us. The rest of the paper was read, and disposed of, in the same fashion. The space between us was fairly filled with paper.

The rustling of the paper in her hand and on the floor began to irritate me; it detracted from my escape into science fiction. Finally, I remembered whom I worked for, resuscitated my feelings of self worth and importance, and turned to her, asking, "Why do you put the paper on my side? Why not fold it the way it was so others can read it, too?" She recognized immediately my accent, smiled and explained, in Swedish, that she was used to read quickly and, somehow, to put the paper together again did not fit into that scheme. Besides, there were plenty of copies aboard. The paper on the floor is no problem, she said, and raised her hand to call for the flight attendant. Before she reached the button, the attendant was there and picked up the papers. That was truly first class SAS service. "With the papers gone", she inquired, "is all OK?" It was a kind and sincere concern of hers, but I felt I had been rude and, therefore, apologized. The silence between us broken, we had a good time talking about nothing in Swedish.

She was charming and gracious. Soon she asked me what I was doing, and the purpose of my traveling to Stockholm. I responded, probably not with modesty, then asked her the same questions. She said she sang professionally and traveled often all over the world. Perhaps I had heard of her? My brain raced trying to identify some singer known world wide, but found no answer. Seeing my puzzled look she asked if I know anything about opera. I did, I said, but not much. The places where I had lived lately had no opera houses. "Well," she said, "then you probably have not heard of me, Birgit Nilsson." I certainly had heard that name, but wished she had not told me, because knowing who she was tied my tongue. We continued to have a pleasant conversation although, now, she carried most of it until it ended naturally and easily, and we fell into comfortable silence and, in my case, sleep. Before landing, she bid me farewell and good luck; I wished her likewise.

Arriving in Stockholm, she was the first to leave the plane, other passengers were held back until she had reached the tarmac where she was received with flowers and a limousine. As I began my descent on the ramp, she waved me good-bye.

In the fields of maritime law, environment, economics, and policy, Elisabeth Mann-Borgese was a giant. The daughter of Thomas Mann, she had established her fame independent of that of her father's. A forceful speaker and writer, her concerns were with the oceans as "the common heritage of mankind". She was a passionate proponent for the preservation of the marine environment and its usage for the benefit of all. This must be achieved, she believed, through law and without confrontation among nations. To that end she created several institutions throughout the world.

She was a professor at Dalhousie University in Halifax, Nova Scotia, where I met her in 1978. She was small, grey haired, with keen, twinkling eyes and a wrinkled face, all exuding grand-motherly charm. Her life style was modest. Dinner at her house meant very simple, but tasty, fare enhanced by an abundance of excellent wines. I was invited several times to her home overlooking the sea. Before my eyes reached the view of the sea, they passed over the far part of her backyard garden where, taking the pride of place, was a cemetery for her much loved, departed dogs. She talked about them quite often, but never of her children..

Each year she convened a conference named "Pacem in Maribus" (Peace in the Oceans). In 1990, Varda and I were invited to the eighteenth conference held in Rotterdam. It was a major affair lasting the whole last week of August. There was a huge maritime trade fair; there were papers, symposia, speeches and, at regular intervals, overflowing social grace. Elisabeth, through her International Ocean Institute, had commissioned a symphony from Franco Mannino. At the end of the conference he conducted the Prague Symphony Orchestra as his "Sinfonia n. 8 'degli Oceani' " had its world premier in Rotterdam's De Doelen Hall. It was an exciting event with many well known, perhaps even important, people from Holland and the international community. We enjoyed the feeling of being part of something not given to everyone. But, more important to me was to be part of the circle of friends surrounding this, most remarkable, personality in my field.

For me, the true high point of the "Pacem in Maribus" conference came when the writers of the major papers were invited to be presented to Queen Beatrix. I received my invitation with amazement, joy, and disbelief; no one had ever told me that any of my papers were good, leave alone of major importance. But, of course, I accepted the accolade. At the appointed time Varda and I arrived to see a dense crowd around the Queen. But, I must have been better known than I expected. Someone from her entourage recognized me, and escorted me to her. Varda intended to take pictures of the event, but was not able to get through.

The Queen wore the kind of hat one expects of royalty, wide-brimmed and uncommon. She received me with a gloved outstretched hand. From my demeanor she clearly understood I was in a quandary: what does one do with a Queen's outstretched hand? Kiss it? Shake it? My confusion was not eased by another lady in her company, who, with an equally magnificent hat, smiled and, believe it or not, winked at me. Was she trying to give me courage? Or did she mischievously enjoy my predicament? I have no real recollection of how the situation was resolved, but remember having decided to take her hand, bow deeply and see what happened. The Queen, however, put me at ease before I could implement that strategy. I believe she briefly and lightly touched my shoulder, unstretched her hand and engaged me in conversation.

She knew a great deal about shipping and asked me about my conference paper, my seafaring days and about Wisconsin. Amazing how much she knew, and how easily the conversation flowed, at least on her part. It went on somewhat beyond the allocated time. She said she had enjoyed my visit with her and hoped I would leave Holland determined to come back. On my way out of her presence, the other lady again smiled and winked. Both of them made my day.

In 1954 I was a cadet at the Royal Naval War College, the Swedish counterpart to the US Naval Academy. Each year there was an elaborate formal ball to which the cadets could invite their girl friends. In this particular instance, one, or two, of the princesses of the crown would be there as well. Many senior officers from the various branches of the military would also attend. All in all, a very illustrious affair demanding immaculate social behavior from everyone, particularly the cadets.

Royal ladies do not dance indiscriminately. They use dance cards prepared in advance, in this case by the commandant's office which identified each cadet's place on the card. This posed an implicit problem. Social graces were not taught at the college. Soon-to-be naval officers were assumed to come from "good" families where social grace was as natural as breathing. But what about those of us who came from the merchant marine, the common seafarers? We did not get this kind of manners from our homes, nor did we study it. Instead, we absorbed formality through knowledge of, and familiarity with, naval traditions and customs. We learnt when and how to wear formal dress uniform; how to behave at a formal dinner; what silverware and glasses to use, how to toast properly, and how to introduce yourself and your escort at formal events. I had no difficulty with these aspects of naval life.

As to ballroom dancing, the powers-that-be simply assumed it to be a universal skill. And therein lay my problem. I had some rudimentary notions about waltzing as my sister had told me that the movements were the same as those of ice skating. However, I was far from confident of the accuracy of that description. Yet, I was assigned a place on the dance card of, I believe, Princess Desiree, and was absolutely petrified by the honor.

White gloves on, unusually hot and nervous, I waited for my turn. The girl I had invited for the evening waited impatiently for it to be over so she could also have some fun. Soon I was perspiring; the jacket felt very tight and the gloves were already moist. All went well, however. There were so many cadets to be honored that only a few minutes were allotted to each one of us.

That I managed to get through a few steps without stepping on her toes was due less to my dancing skills than to her "avoidance skills"; she must have had a lot of training. Conversation was minimal, but fluent on her part; I limited myself to some mumbled compliment on her dress. I doubt she heard what I said, but she looked interested and engaged for the few, but very long, minutes I was honored.

On Saturdays, Ships Officers' School ended in the early afternoon. On these days, I usually went to the nearby communal bath house which had both a swimming pool and a sauna. It was a new facility located in the Citizen's House (Medborgarhuset). The House had many other amenities such as a coffee shop, library, lecture halls and a theater. Because it was new, large, and impressive, it was also popular, and a "must" for out-of-town visitors. On Saturdays, one could usually count on a fair number of people in the bath house.

One such afternoon, in 1952, I sat, uncharacteristically, alone in the sauna, contemplating my bad luck because there was no one to rub my back, the customary favor sauna bathers do for each other. But my bad luck did not last. As I was ready to give up, a couple of men, speaking Danish, entered the sauna. One in particular caught my attention because he was intricately tattooed over large parts of his body – obviously a fellow seaman. Here, clearly, was a suitable person to ask for a back-rub. I did; he complied, and I returned the favor.

A shower, a dip in the pool, another shower and it was time for my usual coffee and pastry break. That ritual over, I left the building. Coming out of the front door I saw a crowd watching a black limousine with a low registration number indicating a royal car. This was not an ordinary event, so I joined the expectant crowd. We speculated aloud on who it could be, but no guess seemed credible. We had to wait and see. A few minutes later a couple of men came out of the building and entered the car. No one knew who they were. It seemed disappointment was the reward for our waiting. But I did recognize among them the tall seaman now nicely dressed and no tattoos visible. The car drove off.

I suddenly realized whom I must have met in the sauna: King Frederick of Denmark. The newspapers had reported on his visit to Stockholm, but I had paid no attention. Besides, who would expect a king to attend a communal bath house? Surely there were more exclusive facilities available to him. But, I had no doubts. His extensively tattooed body was more-or-less his "trade mark", a "trade mark" well known to people who cared to know. I knew of it, but that knowledge was totally overwhelmed and wiped out by the context – a king in a communal bath house in Sodermalm, at that time the least fashionable part of Stockholm!

Nevertheless, a king I had met, and a king had met me.

Double Occupancy

Well into my academic career and still striving upwards, I had a job interview in Baton Rouge. The arrangements were for two nights in a major downtown hotel not far from the city's government buildings.

The day of arrival was spent, with my guide, exploring potential housing areas. It was an amazing experience. Large houses, large lawns with luxuriant growth of various kinds. But no signs of children. When I remarked on that, Mr. K said, in a matter-of-fact manner, that, as a precaution against snakes, children did not, usually, play outside at this time of the year. This opened the way for us to talk about snakes. I, as a rational, trained economist, admitted to an irrational, unreasonable fear of them. Mr. K assured me there was no need to worry. There were so many ways to guard against them. For instance, he said, swimming pools were usually lined with light colored tiles and surrounded by wide, white painted aprons, to enable the easy spotting of any snakes around, or in, the pool. It was merely a matter of inspecting the pool before jumping in.

Furthermore, he continued, snakes were easy to fend off. Just this morning he had taken a swim in a pond near his house outside town when he spotted an unknown kind of snake in the water. He caught it and put it in a five-gallon paint bucket to bring to the university for identification. "No problem at all", he said. I asked the natural follow-up question, "So, what kind was it?" He did not know because he had not yet been to the university; he had picked me up first. "So", I asked, "Where is it?" To my great horror, he pointed to the back of the station wagon where the tightly closed paint bucket stood. I felt very uneasy with an unknown kind of snake in the back of me, held off only by a thin plastic lid. Indeed, I was on the verge of an attack of hysteria, and was glad when we stopped at a 7-Eleven for coffee. Mr K, who had seemed preoccupied and perturbed since pointing out the bucket in the back, immediately took it out and began to pry open the cover. A smell, foul beyond foul, puffed out of it. The snake was dead and had started to decay. "Just as I thought," said Mr K.

He dumped the brightly colored body in a wire-mesh enclosed waste paper basket just outside the store entrance. It was clearly visible through the wire-mesh. While inside the store, we suddenly heard a frightful, loud shriek followed by sobbing and incoherent speech. A woman had put some trash in the basket, seen the snake and, not knowing its harmless state, had a fit of hysteria, the kind I had barely avoided myself some minutes earlier. Other customers rushed to take care of the lady and took various measures to contain the snake in the basket. We continued our house hunting.

A cluster of town houses appealed to me, but prices were high. Some units backed up on an old graveyard. A humid, dark, gloomy place, the trees covered with Spanish moss and the stones with dark green growth of some kind. An eerie place not conducive to lightheartedness. Like a rational person, I assumed that such an undesirable location, looking at a graveyard from the breakfast nook, would be reflected in a lower price. Not at all. The unit commanded a premium. I was taken aback. Clearly, in this environment I had to re-define the parameters for rationality.

The day over, I returned to the hotel. It was large and modern. The foyer and reception areas were filled with people. There was a busy, comfortably energetic atmosphere about the hotel, and I looked forward to a pleasant stay.

The building was laid out in an "L" shape; my room was on the second floor and located just inside the elbow of the "L". From my window I could see the river straight ahead while, on the left, stretched the hotel's short wing; it seemed empty. At night I could see a brightly lit walkway along the water.

It had been a long day and I went to bed early. There was a swag lamp in the corner of the room; its reach brought it above the bed and, as it had a fluorescent bulb, it would give good reading light. But it did not work. I tried pulling the cord several times to no avail. No light to be had from that lamp; no reading for next day's meetings. Only options were TV or early sleep. I chose the latter. With a six o'clock wake-up call, I slept at ease.

I was awakened by the swag lamp's bright shining light over my head. So, this is how they awaken you in a Southern hotel. Strange, but certainly effective, and not out of line with my experiences of the previous day. While shaving, I reflected on that new, strange custom. It did not seem right. I checked my watch. It showed 2:00 am; clearly the lamp's turning on was not the wake-up call. But, there was no reason to be upset, another couple of hours in bed were welcome. The telephone rang, as expected, at six, and I was off to my business.

I thought much about that lamp during the day and finally came up with a perfectly rational answer: the bulb was fluorescent and I knew these bulbs could take a long time to warm up sufficiently for the light to appear. But it was some eight hours between my trying to turn it on and the light's finally appearing. That was strange.

Back in my room I tried, again, to turn on the swag light. No luck. But, since I now did not know which of my pulls on the cord was "on" or "off", I simply unplugged the lamp. I did not want to be awakened at the silly whim of a malfunctioning lamp.

And so, I again went to bed early. Could not fall asleep although, with the curtains drawn, the room was pitch black. For no reason, I felt uneasy. Surely, opening the curtains would lighten my mood. It was beautiful outside, and, soon, my room looked beautiful as well, as it was flooded with the reflections from the street lights along the water walk amplified by an almost full moon. I felt much better, and went back to bed.

It is a curious phenomenon that, in a lit room, one can, even through closed eyes, literally see if the light fades and the room darkens. This is what happened to me. The room was definitely getting darker. I opened my eyes and froze in the bed. Goose bumps formed and my hair seemed to stand up, especially in the back of my neck. The curtains I had opened wide, as far as they could go, were slowly closing. I did not dare to move, pretended to be fast asleep although my lack of breathing would tell anyone around that I was not. The curtains closed completely, it was again pitch black, but not for long. They began to open, slowly, slowly and stopped their movement when about half open.

I waited a long time to be certain nobody was in the room, then got up to investigate. My rational mind told me this could not be anything but a trick. Was there an extra cord so that the curtains could be operated from elsewhere? Nothing to be found inside the room, or seen outside the window. I could not think of an explanation. This, simply, could not happen. Yet it had happened. The curtains were now only half open whereas I had, earlier, opened them all the way. Apart from my goose bumps and my hair imitating the appearance of a threatened hedgehog, I felt none of the unease I had felt in the dark room. Nevertheless, I spent the rest of the night watching TV, a perfectly rational thing to do.

I checked out next morning without mentioning anything to the desk clerk, partly because I was embarrassed to refer to a "ghostly" experience, and partly because I did not want to be charged for double occupancy.

Upon return to Denver, I felt the story about the closing curtains was a particularly good one to tell. The first to hear it was a psychiatrist friend. He laughed heartily, and told me it was a brief dream that had come to me in the transitory moment between wakefulness and sleep. I told the story to several other people. It was a good conversation piece although it was met with indulgent skepticism. The incident with the swag-lamp faded and became background material only.

I also told the story to the secretaries in the front office. They listened politely, but there was no question about their true beliefs in matters of ghosts; they too were rational people.

There was one exception, though. Born and raised in Baton Rouge, she knew the area where the hotel was located and recalled that in her youth there was another hotel on that site. Named *Anderson's Guest House*, it had a reputation for being haunted. As people avoided staying there, part of the hotel was razed to make room for a new facility. One part left intact, she said, became the wing that constituted the short segment of the "L"-shaped new hotel. As my room had been right in the elbow of the "L", she thought I may have encountered the remains of the old, haunted Anderson place.

She certainly believed my story. And I chose to believe her. After all, a haunted house is a better story than is a dream.

Father Knows Best

It is simple to take care of a flat tire. Or is it? Depends on who is taking care of it. In many cases, there is AAA to help. In my case, I can also draw upon the Road Service that came with the purchase of my car. In neither case, though, can one be sure of when the service will arrive and, in my view, it is imperative that anyone who drives a car should be able to also change a tire.   Recognizing that fact, I waited only for the right moment to teach that skill to my daughters. It came one day when the right rear tire, on the car they used, went flat in our drive way. With the girls standing on the side, I proceeded to instruct them in a methodical manner. "First locate the jack and the spare tire. Both are in the trunk. What you need first is the handle of the jack." Continuing the lesson I pointed out that the handle was very important because it was the wrench to be used to loosen, and tighten, the lug nuts of the wheel. "These", I told them, "should be loosened before the car is jacked up off the driveway. If you forget that, the wheel will turn as you try to loosen the nuts." I showed them. The girls observed closely as I worked hard to illustrate my points.

With the lug nuts loose, I took my time to consider the next, pedagogically right, steps. Rested and sure of what to do, I retrieved the main part of the jack from its hiding place under the spare tire. To get to it, I had to remove that tire which was entirely proper given it was to replace the flat one. Again hard work closely observed by the girls. Taking the stuff out of the trunk, I put it all on the left side of the car, went inside for a glass of water and returned ready for the final tasks.

"It's not easy", I told them, "to know where to put the jack properly. Every car has its own place for this to be done." "See," I said, "here it is. Now it is easy to raise the car." And I proceeded to put the jack to work. I pumped vigorously and the car began to rise. I heard some noises from the girls standing by the other side of the car, but paid no attention. Everything was going so smoothly. I was proud of the skills I was transmitting to my daughters. Pausing for a moment to wipe the sweat from my brow, I saw their astonished looks. "Any questions?" I asked. "Dad", said Sheila, "this is great, but why do you raise the left side of the car if the flat is on the right?" Truly a hard question to answer. But, even without an answer, my daughters are now perfectly capable of changing a flat tire.

The Master Gardener

Eagle Heights, married graduate student housing of the University of Wisconsin at Madison, was an ideal spot from our point of view. The fairly small two-story brick buildings were attractive. There were three entrances, each serving four apartments, two on each floor. Views were open towards the green-belts and, in our case, open fields with woods in the background. Plenty of small children provided a great deal of noise, but it was a relief not to hear the big city's constant honking of horns and the grinding of bus and truck engines.

But, best of all was the large open field across from our building. A large part of it had been set aside for student garden plots. They went fast; it was a popular arrangement. I had never done any gardening but thought the lots, at fifteen by fifteen, were small. Varda agreed. How can anyone live on the yield of such a small area? No wonder most people referred to them as "patches". Fellow students told me there would be ample produce, probably more than enough. I did not believe them and, acting on my beliefs, managed to get two plots. Even that enlarged garden-to-be, fifteen by thirty feet, seemed small, but the manager refused further allotments.

Time for planting arrived. The purchase of implements, a spade, rake, hoe and water hose, was a major financial commitment for a graduate student. So were the various seeds needed; it was, after all, a larger than average garden. We chose several kinds of cucumbers, some lettuce, honeydew melon, and garden peas to start from seeds, and tomatoes from seedlings. There is nothing I like better than garden peas and tomatoes picked from the vine and eaten, preferably, on the spot. The cucumbers, lettuce and melons were Varda's choice. The immediate culinary future looked bright.

Now to prepare for that future. My intention, based on a garden manual, was to use the spade to turn the soil, crumble the chunks finely with the hoe and smooth the surface with the rake. The conceptual process seemed sound, but the implementation presented problems we had not foreseen. First, the sun was HOT and no shade could be found anywhere. Second, it was backbreaking work, much more so than we could have deduced from the manual. None of that happy ease conveyed by those pastoral museum pictures of farmers wielding hoes or scythes. Very soon Varda's advanced stage of pregnancy deafened her to the call of the soil, and I was left to work it all by myself. Third, and most importantly, it was, indeed, a BIG plot.

No matter how hard I worked there was very little impact on the ground. Having tilled perhaps one third of the plot, I found an abundance of weeds had taken over the prepared area. Weeding done, I continued spading, hoeing, and raking but at a much reduced pace because, frequently, I had to go back to weeding. All this, mind you, before any seeds had been put in the ground. It was also very time consuming. Taking care of the garden plot interfered with my studies.

The gardeners around me were finished. Soil prepared and planted, their job was now to water and weed. Also I weeded, but, with no seeds in the ground, there was no need to water. Even so, somehow my weeds grew faster than theirs, and their work, after planting, seemed light. When would I be ready to plant? My garden was not going anywhere no matter all the time spent in the sun with a bent back, or on my knees. It had to stop. I conceded defeat and, without further ado, scattered the seeds haphazardly through the area, left the tomatoes on the side to shift for themselves, and dumped the tools next to them.

The relief was enormous and immediate. I could now spend more time with family, studies, and television, a novelty we had just purchased second hand. A quick stop at the supermarket reassured us that we were not dependent on homegrown produce. The store had plenty of whatever

I had attempted to plant. The farmers' market on the square had even more. We were not to suffer shortages.

The summer progressed with much heat and no rain. The gardeners continued to water and weed their plots. My admiration for their perseverance and gardening skills increased each day. My own plot was by now covered by a rather dense canopy of weeds. The rain stayed away, the drought continued and, no matter how much the gardens were watered, most of the crops withered, and what remained was small and late in ripening.

I did not visit my garden again. Why be reminded of dismal failure? One day, however, one of our neighbors asked if she might be allowed to pick some cucumbers from our garden. Of course she could. Filled with curiosity I went to see how cucumbers could grow in my weed lot.

A wondrous sight greeted me. Among all the dry, brown squares that now constituted the garden area, there was one, fairly large and very green patch: mine. It was totally overgrown with weeds. But, under the weeds I could see a veritable horn of cornucopia brimming with cucumbers and melons. An occasional head of lettuce was also there, but no peas or tomatoes.

What had happened? I had not been to the garden for months, had not watered, weeded or fertilized it. Yet, I had a bumper crop. How to explain this? An agriculturally inclined friend explained that the weeds covering my garden were drought resistant and sun-loving, just the right kind for the hot, dry summer. They had sheltered the seeds from the blistering sun and had retained moisture for them to grow. The weeds had done for my crop what an accomplished gardener may have done with plastic sheets.

Neighbors, however, thought I had done this on purpose. That I knew what I was doing. In their eyes I was a master gardener; they regretted I did not resume gardening the next summer.

The Sinister House

In the early 1980s I had a position as Senior Research Fellow with the Marine Policy and Ocean Management (MPOM) program at Woods Hole Oceanographic Institution. Housing was scarce, but I managed to rent a cottage being vacated by another researcher in the program. It was a convenient house, he said, close to town and the program offices in Woods Hole; and it was furnished, including bedding and other linens. While everything was old fashioned, well worn, and uncomfortable, it was not bad given the rental market. The house was older than the furniture, but not by much, and creaky, and it seemed to amplify all kinds of sounds inherent in old buildings. But, as none of that bothered him, I did not see why it should bother me and so assumed the rental. Later on I wondered if I had misheard him. Did he say "creaky" or "creepy"?

I moved into the house late at night after picking up my car from my daughter, Yael, at Wellesley College. The house was not exactly isolated, but well set away from its neighbors. Across a dirt road was a large cemetery. No street lights and an overcast sky made it somewhat difficult to find the key hidden on the back porch. It is a New England custom, it seems, that one is not supposed to enter a house through the main front door. The back door is, in essence, the front door. I have encountered that custom many times and it certainly held for this house.

The entry led directly into the kitchen, a large square space. I was immediately assaulted by a smell of stale air tinged with an acrid component I thought was sulfur, or a gas leak. Much searching revealed some light switches and opened up the rest of the house for inspection. I was too tired, though, to look it over carefully. But I found my bedroom on the second floor, and the bedding in the dryer in the basement, just as promised.

The bedding looked clean, but did not smell good. Smelled like a mixture of insufficiently rinsed bath towels and damp woolens. I did sleep that night, but not very well.

It was a typical Cape Cod cottage. The main floor held the kitchen, a small living-cum-dining room, a small study, and a full bath used at all times because the second bathroom, up stairs, did not work. The upper floor had two bedrooms separated by a foyer from which the non-working bathroom opened. The basement was messy, full of boxes, broken furniture, and numerous loose pipes to be used for I-don't-know-what. At the very end of a clear path through the mess were the washer and dryer. A huge crucifix hung over each appliance. The lighting was poor, making a flash-light a necessity. However, the basement was so unpleasant I began to use a laundromat in town.

I had the gas pipes in the kitchen checked. The repairman commented on the strange smell but found no leak. He thought the burners may have had some coating giving off the smell when lit. With continued use, he said, the coating would burn off and, with it, the smell would be gone. This did not happen during the eight months I lived there. Indeed, the smell seemed to become more pervasive as time went by.

It was hard to pinpoint what made me feel so uneasy in this house. First I thought the many crucifixes mounted all over the house were the cause; after all, I was not used to these decorations. They were everywhere and of many sizes. On the walls, doorposts, window sashes. The one over my bed was about eighteen inches high. I removed them. The final count was fifty, of which more than half were in the basement. The now empty spaces made me feel somewhat better, but there was still something bothering me. The noises at night were everywhere except in my bedroom. I thought I heard footsteps, heavy breathing, panting followed by eerie scratches and creeks of the floor boards. Finally I admitted, at least to myself, that I did not feel alone, that there was a "presence" in the house. Indeed, trying to introduce more normal sounds around me, I caught myself having one-sided conversations with my unseen company. I did not like to be in the house more than necessary and was grateful for the easy access to my office. Nevertheless, I got used to both noise and unease, that is, until my family came to visit.

First was Nili. She spent a sleepless night in the second bedroom, did not like to go downstairs at night to use the bathroom, and returned to Princeton the next day. Next was Varda.. She, too, felt uneasy, but not strongly so since we stayed in my bedroom, off limits to the sound effects. Yael came with a couple of friends lured by the prospect of spending a few days on Cape Cod, where, in a very general sense, the house was located. They were outright scared. No one would go to the bathroom without one of the others standing guard outside. Indeed, they would not venture alone anywhere in the house. A few days were enough for Cape Cod to lose its luster for them. Sheila came toward the end of my stay and felt just like the others, only more so: bothered by the strange smell, the strange noises and a strong feeling of unwanted company. Like the others, she would not use the bathroom at night or when alone in the house.

There was nothing unusual, or threatening about that bathroom, but the entrance to the basement was next to it. Undoubtedly my visitors felt, even more strongly than did I, the eerie atmosphere in that space, although no one ever went there.

A young family lived about 200 yards away, closer to the cemetery. The wife's early evening walks took her close to my house, and mine close to theirs. Neither of us took the numerous, and quite beautiful, paths through the cemetery. But she wanted to walk there, to cross it and meet her husband who worked on the other side. She asked me to go with her and all three of us would return later in the evening. During one of these walks, they told me that the house I rented belonged to the cemetery care taker and grave digger, or, rather, to the family he had left behind as he died two years earlier.

I am not really superstitious, although I admit to a vivid imagination. Nevertheless, I certainly had a creepier feeling than usual, almost chills along my spine, when I entered the house that evening. Was the care taker visiting his house at night? What to do? Perhaps I should put up the crucifixes again? I didn't. But I talked to whatever might be there, saying it was OK to hang around, but could there, please, be less noise? I imagined the house being much more quiet that night.

It was time for me and Sheila to move to my new job with the U.S. Merchant Marine Academy at Kings Point, Long Island. Varda would follow as soon as our house in Denver was sold. During our house hunting on Long Island, we saw a house in Port Washington, on Avenue B. It was big, old and unappealing, but, since the price was right, I made an offer.

One evening I brought Sheila to see our prospective new home. It was not a dark evening, but still not much light as fog was setting in, swirling among the large elms on the street. Not a soul to be seen. An evening not for the faint hearted because, with very little imagination (and we had a lot), anything could be seen in the twisting fog patches. Actually, Sheila did say she saw something down the street that unsettled her.

The house was locked up and the only way to get a glimpse of the interior was from the large doors opening from the deck in the back. I went there and urged Sheila to join me. She was clearly not enthused by the idea, but, very reluctantly, she came to look. She peeked inside where my flashlight revealed parts of the kitchen, sniffed the air and took off quickly for the car. I followed. With the doors locked, she explained, with horror, that this was the house we had left a short while ago in Falmouth. Did I not see, she asked, that it was the same deck, the same doors and kitchen, AND the same SMELL.

Nothing in the world could make her move into that house. Varda agreed with her. I rescinded the offer and made an enemy of the real estate agent. That was not too high a price to pay for avoiding another sinister house.

Brothers

My brother Lennart was the true free spirit of the family. He was ten years older than I. At age sixteen he left home, involuntarily, as father banished him for some religious infraction. He was not part of my life until one day in 1948 he visited me aboard my ship in Gothenburg.

I was awestruck by my long lost brother. He was everything I was not. Light-hearted, sociable, self-assured, well dressed, witty and funny; and a ladies' man as became evident that evening. Over the years we became close. After Varda and I married, he visited us many times in the US as part of his gambling itinerary which included horse and dog racing as well as casinos.

Once, in Denver, I went with him to the horse track. He knew a great deal about the sport since, at that time in his life, he owned a horse in Sweden. Lennart did not speak much English, so in response to his questions, I translated whatever data I found in the program. He also took a good look at the horses, and advised me to bet as he did. I followed his advise and both of us came out ahead, he substantially so because he bet large sums. It was so easy: read the statistics, look at the horses, bet and collect, in my case, $20 for the day's efforts. What a deal!

Lennart left for Las Vegas. Came back with ample winnings and returned to Stockholm. Now it was my turn to replicate the winning streak at the horse track. There I was reading statistics, looking at horses and betting. A poor performance – by the horses. I lost every race and left never to return. However, I could not free myself from the nagging thought that the program may have listed the wrong statistics, or that I may have looked at the wrong horses. Or could it be that Lennart, indeed, knew what he was doing?

Lennart had a stormy life. Entirely self-taught he was an expert in electronics as well as in some chemical processes. Most of his business attempts failed, but ultimately, in his late forties, he started a small jewelry factory that prospered. Generously he gave Varda and the girls many beautiful items of all kinds including pearls.

He was married twice. His first wife, whom he had known since their early teens, left him because, she said, he was irresponsible, unreliable and unpredictable. His second wife said the same but stayed with him. He admitted to some short-comings but felt, in general, that they asked too much of him, that they were unfair. The daughter from the first marriage agreed with her mother but thought her father, with all his faults, was too lovable and funny to be judged harshly.

Early one summer morning, Lennart was out of cigarettes and without the newspaper, both needed to make his morning coffee enjoyable. He told his wife he would pick up these necessities from the nearby store, about half a block away. Nice weather, warm and pleasant, he took off in his shirt-sleeves and slippers. Two weeks later he returned, sun tanned, nicely dressed with the cigarettes and the current morning paper.

On the way to the store, Lennart had run into a friend waiting for a taxi to take him to the airport. He was worried and upset. His wife, with whom he was to vacation in Spain, had at the last moment cancelled her trip. There was now an extra ticket the reimbursement of which was uncertain. A thought occurred to him: could Lennart use it? Lennart saw no problems, only an opportunity to see a foreign country and, without hesitation, entered the taxi that had just arrived.

Lennart's wife waited. A few telephone calls from, and to, various friends established what had happened so she did not worry about his safety. But she was upset and knew exactly what to tell her husband when he returned. She used harsh words. Lennart said that for emphasis she even went after him with a hammer. He did not understand, he said. After all, he had returned with the promised cigarettes and the paper. Why was she so upset? He was at a loss. His visit to Spain opened a wide fissure in their marriage. However, after the inevitable divorce, they remained very good friends.

On Lennart's desk, prominently placed, was a nicely framed picture of Field Marshall Montgomery watching something through a pair of binoculars. On his right is Lennart, his left hand on the Field Marshall's shoulder and the right arm pointing in the direction of the binoculars.

My brother insisted it was not a doctored photo in the sense of cutting and pasting. Nor was it, on the other hand, the result of a friendly encounter with the famous soldier. Here is the story as he told it.

Lennart was at a resort in Switzerland where also Montgomery was staying. Seeing an opportunity to be seen around a world famous celebrity, my brother instructed a photographer to follow him and snap pictures whenever he was close to the Field Marshall. He got many pictures but none was particularly noteworthy.

One day Montgomery was watching a slalom race through his binoculars. He seemed totally unaware of his surroundings. Lennart saw his chance and, followed by the photographer, quietly stepped up to the soldier, quickly raised his right arm to point, and very briefly cupped his left hand, without touching, so it looked as if it rested on Montgomery's shoulder. The camera snapped, the Field Marshall was unaware, and the picture found its place on my brother's desk.

Among Lennart's friends were two brothers, Tore and Zacke. I only met the latter who was as poor as his brother was wealthy. Since Tore was very, very rich, one can imagine how very, very poor was Zacke.

He was rather fat, always wore a vested suit, a once-upon-a- time white shirt and multicolored tie enhanced by food stains. A big cigar was his constant companion. When lit, the ashes were generously deposited on his clothes brought within reach by his protruding stomach. His overcoat was grey, had once been elegant, but now merely acted as cover for his equally well worn suit. Same with his hat, now too worn to be anything but meager coverage for his straggly grey hair. He also wore rimless glasses with thick lenses. In all, his was a strange appearance.

Once he invited me and my brothers to a party in his small apartment. It was shabbily furnished but had a small refrigerator, a true luxury feature at that time. I was impressed. It was a joyous gathering. Plenty of good whiskey, no ice or mixers but great, expensive food, rarely served to company like ours. Among other delicacies was smoked "hamburger", that is, smoked horse meat much appreciated by all. Its being on the table, with more in the refrigerator, testified to the no-expense-spared high quality event. There were even cigars of some well known brand. We drank. We ate. We smoked. We had a superb time.

I could not fathom how Zacke with his poor resources could throw such a party. What had happened? What was the reason?

Zacke, on a chair happily puffing on his cigar, was keen to expand on his good fortune. His brother had, for whatever reason, bestowed upon him a cash gift of a couple of hundred crowns, a substantial amount at the time. Stunned by this enormous windfall he had to decide on wise spending. He felt rich, but even so thought carefully. To spend on clothing would be foolish; he clearly did not need any. But good food and drink had suddenly come within reach. For Zacke that was irresistible, and so was to share it with friends. Hence the party.

In this atmosphere of sharing and good will someone asked Zacke, "How come you're not a millionaire like your brother? If you were, you could have parties like this all the time." Zacke surveyed the room, took a slice of hamburger, a puff on the cigar, flipped some ashes to add to the discoloration of his vest, and answered with great certainty and feeling: "He may *be* a millionaire, but has he ever *felt* like a millionaire?" After a few moments he added dreamily "I have!"

On one of his trips to Denver, Lennart boarded the plane in New York. He was seated next to a lady who seemed friendly and talkative. Lennart felt sociable and exerted his charm, consisting, at the beginning, of much smiling and a debonair demeanor. After awhile it was time for actual conversation. By necessity it was limited because Lennart did not know much English. But he persisted and thought he was making headway both with the language and the lady's esteem of him.

Sometime into the flight the pace of the conversation began to slow. Lennart, intent on pursuing his perceived advantages, did not realize the strain his incessant talking imposed on her. She appeared increasingly bewildered by his, mostly, unintelligible prattling. Finally she asked him where on earth he had learnt to speak English the way he did.

Lennart was as unaware of the American educational system as he was of that in Sweden. The only thing he knew was that his nieces attended Wellesley College and Princeton University. Since he could not pronounce Wellesley, he chose to claim Princeton as the source of his language skills. The lady looked at him in amazement, probably trying to absorb the implications of this example of a great university's failure. Shortly thereafter she excused herself, left her seat and did not return. Judging from this, Lennart concluded that Princeton was not as good a school as he had been led to believe.

My other brother, Herman, was entirely different. While married three times, he was not a philanderer or unreliable man. But, like Lennart, he was charming and outgoing; every casual acquaintance was considered a true friend and enjoyed his loyalty and generosity. He bore malice to none.

He had a marvelous sense of humor seen particularly in his play on words, and often manifested in harmless practical jokes. Often when going to some events requiring a fee, he would walk ahead and simply point to me when the cashier asked for payment. Once through the gate he disappeared and I had no choice but to pay for both. It did not bother me as I tried to do the same to him, usually without success. We similarly competed to stick each other with the bills in restaurants or cafes.

As simple an event as going to a coffee shop with him could be an unpredictable experience. Herman liked doughy yeast cakes but they had to be soft and moist. He achieved that consistency by dunking big chunks of cake into his coffee. One dunk usually sufficed to drain the cup. Certainly, it was a harmless habit. The problem was that it required more coffee than was commonly served. Coffee was expensive and the "bottomless cup" had not yet arrived. Each customer usually received a little pot holding enough for two small cups.

Once, having been deep in conversation with someone around the table, I turned to take a sip from my cup. As I lifted it, Herman said, "Thank you", and quickly drained it by dunking his cake. He again thanked me profusely for my generosity, refilled his own cup from my pot and sat back to enjoy the continuing conversation. Unpredictable, harmless, and, in my view, funny. I could not pay him back in kind since my preference was crème cakes, and he was well aware of that.

He did not drink but smoked heavily; did not gamble and enjoyed the outdoors. He visited us once in Denver but found the altitude too stressful, particularly since it hampered his habit of talking rapidly and incessantly.

We began to drift apart after I had gone to sea. For a few years we saw each other only briefly and at long intervals as each went his own way. We drew closer again in early1949 when he returned from having served with the *Machal*, the volunteers, in the Israeli army.

Sometime in1947, before the state was a fact, Herman volunteered for the nascent Israeli army. Later that year he was sent to a training camp outside Marseilles and, after the State of Israel was declared early 1948, saw service almost immediately upon his arrival there. A year later he returned. He spoke rarely about his time in the military, but it was clear the experience had affected him in some ways I could not fathom.

His sense of Jewishness was strengthened; he was more thoughtful and introspective than I had ever seen him. He studied the religion; became knowledgeable beyond anyone else in the family, but was not observant. As to family backgrounds and relationships, he knew it all. Yet he did not seem to have found peace of mind. That came when a couple of years later he emigrated to Israel, stayed for two years and then returned.

Both of us shared a room in our parents' home during my years at the Ships Officers' School; and his mandatory military service in the Army coincided with mine in the Navy. We became very close again although our lives did not overlap. I did not know of, nor did I meet, most of his friends. Similarly, my social circle did not include him. This had been the case also in our early ages but became more pronounced as the years passed.

While each of my siblings was somewhat of a mystery to me, Herman was more so than the others. My memory of him is endearing and his death in 1994 widened immeasurably the void left when Lennart died in 1989.

Hand-me-downs

Who, having siblings, does not remember wearing hand-me-downs in childhood? In our family, as probably in most families, it was a matter of necessity, not choice.

The youngest of my sisters was Maj. Thus it was that she inherited dresses from Nanny, the middle one, who, in turn, was the beneficiary of Lilly's, the oldest's, discards.

Maj tells the story of a dress handed over to her at about age ten. It was a very nice dress; hence each previous owner had worn it happily and often. Maj had waited a long time to get this wonderful garment, and it became her favorite dress. She wore it as often as Mother allowed her, and so, because there were few alternatives, the dress was worn almost every day.

This intensive use left its marks. Sleeves began to fray, seams loosened up, and the material itself became thin and faded. The day did arrive when Mother admitted it was no longer fit for her daughter to wear such a well worn item notwithstanding Maj's assertions to the contrary.

Mother stayed firm, but, to quiet Maj, she mused aloud: "I don't understand why you're so hard on clothes", she said, "Here you had such a nice dress and now its gone. After all, Lilly wore it for four years. Nanny, for two, but one year with you and it is totally worn out. What is wrong with you?"

Maj felt guilty for a long time. But one day she suddenly saw clearly the fault in Mother's logic. With righteous indignation she told Mother that she, Maj, was not the reason for the decay of the dress. Age and wear had done it. At this, Mother smiled, hugged her and said, simply, "You certainly are growing up. Even getting smart."

Maj also tells a story about my vanity at an early age, an event of which I have no recollection although there is a photo verifying it. As was the custom and fashion at that time, boys wore golf pants, those pants that were tied closed just under the knees letting the upper part of the pants fall in a generous fold over the tie.

For some reason, I, at the age of three, wanted more than anything to have pants just as those my brother wore. When would they be mine? Crying did not seem to help, but I kept at it until one day I got such pants of my own. A bit big and not really a good fit, but beautiful because they had some kind of pattern that my brother's pants did not have. And they folded very nicely and abundantly over my knees.

Maj tells of my happiness and pride as I wore those pants, my Mother's discarded bloomers.

Herman was a big boy even at an early age but Mother succeeded in making his clothes fit me. His shoes, though, could not be altered. Those I had to wear as they were, at least two sizes too big. While I did put newspapers inside to make them feel smaller, I still felt I had to take two steps before they moved. This was a bit awkward but as time passed I became used to wearing roomy shoes and adept at making them move as if they fit.

When, in due time, Herman's shoes were too large to serve me as hand-me-downs, I continued to wear shoes at least one size above what

I needed. Little did I think there would be any benefits from this habit; I was merely comfortable with it.

But, the time came when I had to pass the physical for my naval service. Everything was routine until my feet were examined. The doctor was puzzled. There were none of the usual signs of someone having worn shoes. I had no tweaked toes, no calluses, no corns. The toes were nicely spread out as if I had walked barefoot most of my life. But that was clearly not the case because that would also have left some traces, at least some calluses under the feet.

The doctor was fascinated and called a few of his colleagues to marvel at me. There I stood on a table while they pointed and poked at my feet. What, they asked, had I done to have such well formed feet? I did not know the answer but told them of my too large shoes. That explanation seemed to satisfy their curiosity.

Time Goes Fast

In 1980 I spent a sabbatical year at Dalhousie University in Halifax, Nova Scotia. The city, a major seaport, had prepared a new container port thus freeing the old port facilities for re-development. Like so many other ports in similar circumstances, the city decided to preserve its maritime heritage by creating the Maritime Historical Properties. There were shops and restaurants with maritime themes, and good views of the waterways. Harbor tour boats were docked along the old piers as was a replica of the old, famous, fishing schooner *Bluenose* which offered cruises under sail.

We enjoyed strolling around this area, and when some restaurant offered evenings of sea shanties and music from the Maritimes we were sure to be there. For me this was a real tie to my youth. Among the many attractions was a ship chandler's store. It was not a shop, but rather an exhibit of how such a store used to look. Inside were shelves and tables with whatever merchandise and supplies a ship or a seaman might require.

The shelves displayed coils of ropes and wires of various dimensions. Splices in several stages of completion were shown with marlin spikes stuck into them, and mallets lying at the side, to show how it was done. There were rolls of canvas and sail trimmings. Next to these, on a working table, were sail makers' palms and needles. Throughout the store were paint cans, rust chippers, tar buckets, rain gear made of tarred canvas, sea bags, rough denim working clothes, rubber boots and heavy shoes with rag socks as well as anything else a seaman might need. The smell of tar hung in the air, life at sea was palpable.

I loved the store. Nostalgia swept over me like the swell of the ocean over stones on the beach. This was, after all, an integral part of my life. Not only had I worked as errand boy in such a store, but this was the venue of my youthful "shopping". All the things I saw existed in real time for me. If I had a ship-board job to do today, these were the things I would use even if it was a long time since I had last done so. I went to the store often.

One day I was the only visitor. I went through it slowly, abandoning myself totally to nostalgic reverie. I thought, with a sense of achievement, of my mastering the proper way to splice rope and wire. I lingered in front of such mundane things as an angled paint brush, and other old-fashioned equipment, thinking of how they had been used, with skill, by me.

My self-adulation was interrupted by a noisy group of children, perhaps second graders, who stormed into the store, rushed through it with ill concealed disappointment. There was nothing to see, they said, except old ropes and other, unmitigated, junk. No interesting displays, nothing inviting to touch. Why were they here? That question was directed to their teacher, a young woman, who entered somewhat late. With one glance around the store, she had the answer, she could explain the visit. "This is part of the Maritime Museum," she said, "this is the kind of stuff they used on ships a long, long time ago." "What for?" asked a child. "I don't know," answered the teacher, "nowadays no one knows what these things are for, or how to use them. But, now that you have seen it, let's go on." And so, after ten minutes perusal of their maritime heritage, they left. I was again alone with my thoughts.

And they were confused. What was to me very real and current, was to a new generation incomprehensible and uninteresting. The environment of my youth, so close to me, had become a very distant past for the children, suitable only for display in a museum. Could I, by implication, also be seen as a museum piece? Ought I to be replicated in wax and displayed as one of those who, in olden times, used all this "junk" for some unknown purpose? Was it possible that my seafaring, so vivid and recent in my mind, had lost its contemporary relevance? That time had passed so fast that my experiences were now the subject, and contents, of a museum exhibit?

Although I was only fifty, time had, indeed, flown.

The Centipede

I am not fond of pets. Yet, there are occasions when I derive comfort from having a small animal about. As a child I once found a baby hedgehog in the woods not far from our apartment. My mother allowed me to keep it in a box close to my bed. I checked on it every evening and morning, as well as in between. We fed it milk and it thrived.

The hedgehog grew and soon managed to leave the box for the pleasure of staying under my bed. Of course, this was not a cuddly pet, but it was nice to have it around. It was part of my daily routine. Finding it every day where it was supposed to be assured me that everything was as it should be, and that was a comforting feeling. One day it was gone. Mother had brought it back to the general area where I had found it. I missed it only in the sense that there was an empty space where before there had been a hedgehog. While it had been part of my daily life, its absence did not leave a hole in it. I adjusted in no time at all.

I thought about that event when, in 1974, I had an assignment in Guyana. It was with a company under contract to the United Nations Development Program (UNDP). I stayed in an old-fashioned wooden hotel in Georgetown, the capital. The name, I think, was Park Hotel.

My room was large. The bed was well raised above the floor and amply covered with mosquito netting. The bathroom's toilet seat was similarly placed on a raised platform substantially higher than that of the bed. The water tank was of the old fashioned type sitting way up toward the ceiling with the pipe connecting it to the seat running along the wall. Pulling on a long, thick chain released the water. Several weeks into my stay, I was told that raising the bed, the seat and the water tank served to discourage insects and other pests from taking up residence in those places. It sounded like a good rationale, but I refused to accept it for the simple reason that, if it was true, I would be too afraid to either sleep or go to the bathroom. That is the way I feel about creepy-crawlers.

A few days into my stay I was in my bed reading. My eyes caught something in a corner of the ceiling. Closer inspection revealed a critter about five inches long, perhaps half an inch thick. It was a centipede, dark red with some black and yellow and not very hairy. Much less cuddly than my childhood's hedgehog, it nevertheless was not an unpleasant room mate. There it sat, still and immobile. I got used to it as I checked every morning and evening that it was still there. As with the hedgehog, the centipede became part of the daily routine which was far from pleasant.

It was a miserable assignment lasting six weeks. The city was hot, humid, insect-ridden and crime-ridden, the latter far exceeding the former. Most houses, residences and businesses, were fenced in and barricaded and had armed guards. An American engineer staying at the hotel told stories about the ruthless behavior of the criminals and their prey, the latter as they tried to avoid becoming victims. In a common ploy, one person would lie down in the road hoping that a car would stop to help in which case the stage was set for the intended robbery. He, the engineer, would not stop for anything, but evidenced his humaneness by trying to avoid running over the prostate person. Should that not be possible, he aimed for the legs. He claimed to have run over a number of people, but not to have killed anyone.

It was a nightmare. Whatever social life there was took place on the hotel's large veranda where meals and drinks were served. The first night I went for a walk. People told me not to do so, it was too dangerous. But what could be so bad? The US embassy was next door. The hotel guard let me out from the backdoor. A few yards into the lane I was persuaded by a man with a straight razor to part with my watch and available cash.

Three days later I moved to another hotel just across the street. It was more modern, had no raised platforms for bed and toilet, and gave the impression of being safe as it was surrounded by larger open areas. Many westerners stayed there, among them a Dutchman working on the development of potable water supplies. He wore a thick gold chain around the neck and several rings on both hands. Most of his work was done in the open fields where he was accompanied by soldiers to keep his equipment safe from thieves. He thought my robbery was an unusual event and felt it should not prevent me from going out at night. To prove his point he suggested we go to a movie theater nearby. It was an open structure, dirty with wooden benches; thoroughly unappealing. The movie did not start on time. After a long wait, we decided to forego the performance and started our walk back to the hotel.

The streets were empty. Not a soul around. But, half way to the hotel, a group of three men overtook us at a fast pace leaving us behind. Some fifty feet ahead of us they turned around and walked towards us, one with a drawn machete. Of course, like the man with the straight razor, they wanted our watches and cash, but they also demanded whatever rings we wore. The Dutchman, still thinking robbery the unusual event, and not reflecting on the fact that we were alone on the street, refused. I, being an experienced coward and having no more watch to lose, had already begun to comply by putting some cash on the ground. The man with the machete approached stretching the weapon in front of him. The Dutchman grabbed at the blade and held him off. At that point a car driven by some engineering consultants drove up on the sidewalk and saved us by trying to run down the robbers who quickly disappeared. I got back to the hotel; my friend was taken to a doctor as he lost the top joint of his left little finger by holding on to the machete.

The hotel was very noisy that night. Yelling and screaming and what may well have been gunshots seemed too close for comfort. The next day I moved back to the first hotel where comfort awaited me in the sight of my centipede room mate. It was exactly where I had last seen it.

A young man from the Ministry of Development had been assigned to help me to find my ways around the bureaucracy and the city. He was keenly aware of the dangers around us and steered me away from what would be natural behavior in most other places. Once we were caught in a terrible rainfall; that kind of deluge only the tropics can provide. We were in the middle of a street in the port area. People who had taken shelter in doorways and shops were waving, inviting us to shelter. I thought it was a kind gesture and would certainly have accepted if on my own. He, however, refused and we walked in the middle, not on the side, of the street. The raindrops fell fast and hard, they hurt.

At other times cabs would drive alongside offering us rides. He would not even stay close to them. As they drove up, he would push me out of the way and drag me along at a run. He insisted that I either take a taxi, a secure one registered with the hotel, or walk with him to the office. I was not to walk alone. When walking we tried to vary the route as much as possible to thwart potential plans of robbery.

The city had absolutely nothing worth seeing or doing, apart from trying to avoid thieves. I did my work, sat on the hotel veranda, spoke to interesting people and slept in my room admiring in the morning the bright colors of the centipede. It never moved, just sat there. Nevertheless, like the hedgehog, it added a sense of steadiness to my days.

I asked my guardian from the Ministry if he could suggest anything to relieve the boredom of the place. Was there no museum to explore? Yes, there was a recently opened Museum of Natural History. It was small. The entire collection was housed in one mid-sized room. There were some artifacts of the native Indians, but most exhibits were of various insects, birds, and snakes. Not much to see. But, there I saw it. A bigger version of my room mate, bright red and not so pretty when seen up-close, was pinned in the middle of a display case as if it was the pride of the collection. And it was. The plaque identified it as the most poisonous centipede in the area, on par with venomous vipers and mambas. My friend told me that if I ever saw one, I better be guided by three Bs – Big, Bad, Beware.

That evening when I arrived in my room I checked, as usual, on my room mate, but with a new sense of respect and fear. My breath quickened.

It was not in its usual place. The immobile object had moved. But to where? I began searching the whole ceiling, then the walls, every corner of the room. Not there! Next, a search of the bed, the sheets, the pillows, the netting. Every minute detail of the bed was examined, even the mattress was turned and inspected. Now I was frightened. The dubious comfort I had derived from the centipede's presence was gone. I desperately wanted to find it. Next, look in the bathroom. If it was not in the bed, it must be there. Again, I examined every corner. Nothing! Very gingerly I lifted the lid of the toilet seat. It was not there. My neck prickled. Perhaps it was on top of, or behind, the water tank? Or sitting on the water releasing chain? I could not reach high enough to inspect those places properly.

I was close to panic and hysteria. What to do? I rushed to the concierge, laid out the situation, and asked if somebody could, please, help me to inspect the room and ensure my safety? The young man looked at me with amazement, and amusement. He then calmly explained that the maid had that very morning discovered centipedes in my room, not only the one on the ceiling, but also a few more in the bathroom; they had all been removed and the room fumigated. I could sleep peacefully, he said, but, should I find any more, the staff would be happy to take care of them.

Thus ensured I did not sleep very well during the remainder of my stay, and I entered the bathroom with great trepidation.

The turtle and the chameleon

Once I had a turtle. Very small, easily held and hidden in one hand. Easy to take care of it posed no demands on my time. It just sat in a small box on a shelf in my cabin on the ship. A perfect pet. But the time was ripe for it to travel.

I was going from Gothenburg to Stockholm by train and took the turtle along. My luggage was sparse, merely a cloth bag with a few necessities. The turtle needed nothing, not even a ticket as I put it into my jacket pocket. And so the trip began.

The second class compartment had two nicely checkered upholstered benches facing each other. Between the window seats was a small table useful for food, drinks, and for restful support of the arms, or head for a nap. It provided a small measure of privacy. These seats were, of course, the most desirable ones. I secured one, the other was taken by an elderly man. Soon the compartment was filled with people and, as was customary in a Swedish crowd of strangers, deep silence. A young girl sat next to me.

The turtle needed air and exercise so I placed it on the table. But it had difficulties walking on the glossy surface. The girl was fascinated by such an unfamiliar animal, and felt compassion for its slippery struggle on the table. Breaking the silence she suggested it would be easier for the turtle to move if placed on the cloth upholstered bench. It was sound advice but, before following it, I was moved by her good looks and my natural sense of chivalry to offer her my window seat. She sensed my lack of ulterior motive and accepted. The turtle was now on the bench in the space between us. I held my hand lightly on its back to keep it from falling off onto the floor. As it moved, so did my hand, if I relaxed it properly.

I must have relaxed more than I intended because, when I again became aware of my surroundings, the turtle had found refuge in the girl's lap. In the process of getting there it had brought my hand along. I was delighted, but this wonderful situation did not last. With a smile she moved my hand, still clutching the turtle, to the space between us.

Again I closed my eyes, relaxed my arm and fervently hoped for the turtle to resume its explorations. But I dreamt in vain.

The turtle was replaced, in due time, with a chameleon. It was much larger and more strange looking than the turtle. It was also a much more successful conversation piece giving me many opportunities to show off.

It stayed in my ship's cabin where it took on the pattern of whatever material I placed it on. As with the turtle, I brought it with me, in a cardboard box, on my train trips to and from Stockholm. I would bring it out to show fellow travelers, particularly girls, its amazing ability to change color and pattern. On a red background, it became red; on yellow, it became yellow, and so on.

Once, just after I had shown its color changing scheme to a very sympathetic and approachable girl, I put it on a grey striped scarf. Of course, the chameleon became grey with several black lines along its body. Amazing! I then turned it ninety degrees so it lay cross-wise over the scarf's lines. In no time the animal appeared with the lines circling its body. What a spectacle.

It was time to let the performer rest a bit. I took the chameleon off the scarf and put it next to me on the upholstered bench. Suddenly there was a popping sound. The chameleon had split into several pieces. It was an unpalatable sight. What had happened? I suddenly understood. The upholstery was checkered. While the animal could adapt to horizontal and length-wise lines, it obviously could not show both patterns simultaneously. Trying to do so, it went from cross-wise to length-wise and back again many times until it simply broke apart.

The girl cried, bemoaned my heartlessness and left for another compartment.

When I told these two stories to Varda, she was amused by the turtle, but very saddened by the chameleon's fate. So sad that I finally admitted that, while I indeed had a turtle, did take it on the train, and showed it off, the story about the girl was essentially wishful dreaming.

The chameleon, though, is entirely a figment of my imagination – but it does sound reasonable. Doesn't it?

Parental duty

Sheila wanted an after school job. She wanted challenge, responsibility, independence. After all, she was almost sixteen, a junior in high school and most of her friends had work of one form or another. A short search landed her an offer from a formal wear rental shop in a mall not far from our house. The mall was fairly new, but not yet, in 1983, a busy place.

The hours were not good: from around dinner time until closing at nine. Varda and I did not like the idea of her working in a store located in a sparsely attended, open mall where the most isolated area of the parking lot was reserved for employees. In addition, it was winter so she would leave the store after dark and, when her boss, the only other employee, left early, she would close the store which entailed many responsible tasks not usually given to an inexperienced part-time worker. The good part was that she would work week-ends and only two or three afternoons during the week.

Varda and I were in a quandary. We did not want her to work. We preferred her to focus on her studies. On the other hand, we wanted her to be self-confident, to be unafraid but careful, and to feel independent. For this we wanted to give her our support. But how to reconcile that with our very deep concerns for her safety? What to do? We discussed back and forth. Then in a flash of absolutely brilliant insight I came upon the solution; a solution so simple it amazed us both. It only depended on Sheila's being totally unaware of it

Sheila would accept the job. She would arrive at the store in day light when the walk from the parking lot seemed safe and easy. The return, when it was dark, was our concern. That was where my solution was put into operation. I would arrive in my car about twenty minutes before her leaving the store. This would give me time to check the area for any suspicious characters. That done, I would park somewhere mid-way between the store and Sheila's car so I could keep an eye on both while not being seen by her. A beautiful solution. Sheila would get what she wanted and Varda and I could set our fears aside.

The plan worked well. As soon as I saw Sheila safely in her car, I took off -- fast. I wanted to be home before her so that there would be a semblance of normalcy in the house, that we were not in any way worried about her. At times she arrived before me, but I could always claim I had been to the office for whatever reason.

This went on for a long time. I would arrive on time, take my drive around the parking lot, driving slowly scrutinizing both cars and stores before finding my own observation spot at the dark edge of the lot. After a while it became routine and I tended to park more or less in the same spot away from the lamp posts. Also I became very adept at leaving the parking lot at high speed, sometimes even with squealing tires. Varda was proud of me, my solution and my implementation of it. Even I admitted to some pride.

Everything worked so well it was bound to change. One day Sheila asked me, with concern in her voice, if I could possibly meet her at the store in the evening and escort her to the car. All stores had received a message from the mall's security office. It pertained to a suspicious car that had been seen on many occasions driving past the stores at low speed, apparently "casing" them. The car had then parked for a while in a dark area before taking off at high speed. The police had not yet been alerted but employees were urged to be cautious.

I listened with embarrassment but said nothing that could implicate me in this worrisome situation. That evening I parked far away on the street, walked Sheila to her car, came home late, and gave up future guard duty. From then on, Varda and I worried in silence.

In one respect the plan worked exceedingly well. Sheila never caught on to the truth about the stalker. When asked, she always maintained it was a good experience working at that store except for that scary time when a man, undoubtedly deranged, stalked the mall frightening all who worked there. That fearful time, she will not forget.

Some twenty years after the event, I finally told her the truth.

The Shortcut

It was a bad day full of unexpected meetings and long known deadlines. But the schedule had finally fallen into place. Some meetings had been re-scheduled, some deadlines were postponed until the evening, and by late afternoon I was breathing with relief. But not for long. Arranging the pile of papers on my desk to reflect the new schedule, an official looking, blue colored slip told me the real estate taxes were due that very day. No reason to worry, though. I could take care of it in person before closing time of the City Clerk's office in the Court House of the City of Superior.

There were an unusual number of cars around the Court House forcing me to park in the back and at a considerable distance away. It was a long walk to the front door, and, given that it was late, I reasoned that using a back entrance to the building would save a great deal of time. But, where was that entrance? There were several wide, rather steep, stone stairs to choose from. And, considering security issues, would this entrance be open this late in the afternoon?

Luck was at my side. I could see a small cleaning crew starting to mount one of the stairs. I walked fast, then ran to make it before the door might close. As I caught up with the cleaning crew, I slowed down so as to walk with them. Surely they knew which door to use and where to go. And, should I get lost in the huge building, there, walking with us, were two police officers whom I could ask for directions.

I was very happy that I had found this shortcut and felt good about my resourcefulness. It reminded me of a childhood experience when I and a friend, at summer camp, had gotten lost in the northern woods of Sweden. We were totally lost and the woods were scary. Would we ever be found? After a terrifying hour, or so, we stumbled upon a couple of cows grazing on the meager grass among the trees. One of them had a bell around her neck. Clearly, sooner or later, the farmer would come to get them guided by the bell. It was a matter of staying close to the cows, and we would be found and returned to the summer camp. It worked. We were lauded for having been so clever staying with the "herd".

Now, being with the cleaning crew, I felt much the same way as with the cows. I was achieving my goal by following the "herd". I felt I was, once again, very clever. That feeling, however, did not last long. Once inside the building, a strange procedure took place. There were several police officers meeting the crew and checking them off against a roster. Each one was then leg-cuffed. What on earth was going on? Before I could ask, an officer turned to me asking whom I represented. Could I, please, show him my court credentials.

I now understood. The orange jump suits were not the uniforms of the cleaning crew. My explanations of how, and why, I got there, took up much time, were received first with disbelief, then with amusement, and, finally, with undisguised laughter.

I had to go out the same way I had come in; had to take the long walk around to the front door and arrived at the city clerk's office just after closing time. It was an expensive shortcut.

Finding Myself

I need, from time to time, respite from everyday frictions, noises and tensions. I need solitude and silence to soothe my nerves, renew my senses, and allow me to look at life from a new perspective; in essence, "to find myself". Maybe a religious retreat is the answer. I found, though, that those organized by Jewish congregations usually required intensive study focused on specific themes. They involved much preparatory reading, and the ensuing group discussions were, too often, tendentious, argumentative and noisy. I returned home more agitated and tense than when I had left. I needed silence. While I had some success attending a few Catholic silent retreats, I became more and more dependent on my own resources to find what I wanted.

And so I set out "to find myself" in long, solitary walks in the municipal forest in Superior. The woods were large, dense, and wild. There was beauty, there was silence, there was wild life, and there I found serenity. Yet the pleasure was not totally unmitigated. I could not free myself from the thought that, perhaps, the bears in the area might also be trying to find me. That thought interfered with my peace of mind, it caused me to see dangerous animals where there were none; my walks became shorter and shorter. Peace and serenity left me. But relief came when I bought a pontoon boat. I would now seek, and find, myself on the water. There I would be safe. No more fears that the bears would find me before I did.

The boat came with an old engine possessed by some strange mechanical deficiencies, not unlike those of my very first car. That did not bother me; I fancied myself adept at fixing such things. That delusion made me persist in not buying a new engine. The old motor and I were at war. Ultimately the motor won, but, for the time being we got along.

It took many attempts, and, therefore, a long time to start the motor. Once started, it had to be kept going because it was uncertain if it would restart if stopped. But, stop it did as soon as I tried to put it into reverse. That being the case, it could only be used in forward and idle, and that determined where the boat could go. No excursions into narrow inlets and coves because, without using reverse, a big expanse of water was required to turn the boat around to return to my landing.

And so I set out to find the silence of the river. That objective was thwarted by the noise of the engine. It could not be turned off if I wanted to return to shore. As a compromise, I would forego silence and find my solitude and peace by enjoying the scenery and abundant wild life along the banks of the river.

The St. Louis River was beautiful. Wide enough, before it entered Lake Superior, to give the feeling of space and openness. Where it narrowed, up-river, were some islands with plenty of berries and flowers descended from old, abandoned gardens. The river banks were eroded and, mostly, steep. Heavy forests covered the crests and, where the ground allowed, trees and bushes crept to the water's edge where narrow ledges of hard clay outlined the course of the river.

Our house was located at the very end of an inlet which gave us immediate access, by boat, to the east side of the river where the wilderness of the Superior Municipal Forest bounded it. There was all the reason to expect serenity and balm from the beautiful surroundings. While there were no sandy beaches, and silt from the eroding banks gave the water a dark brown color, there was swimming and water play from boats anchored on the many shallow sandbars that seemed to shift location daily.

I began my exploring and search for myself. I saw a lot. Down that narrow bay, where I could not take the boat, I saw a bear hanging on to a half submerged tree trunk, just off the shore. There, at the bottom of the steep promontory, I saw a majestic blue heron sitting absolutely still waiting for its fish dinner to appear. I also saw some beavers leisurely floating in the water, and several deer wandering along the river's edge.

This was enough for a day of finding myself and I returned home where I told my girls of all the things I had seen from the boat. Would they, please, come with me later in the evening to see all these wonders?

After dinner we set out. I took the same route as before; there was little choice given the motor's mode of operation. Wonderful! The bear was still there, in the same spot. Same with the blue heron. How could they be so patient, to stay in the same place and position for several hours? And, what do you know? The beavers were also floating in the same spot. This was remarkable. It was as if the animals had waited for me to bring visitors.

The girls looked bewildered. Did I not see, they asked, that the bear was merely another log stuck on the first one; the blue heron was just a couple of wind blown sticks; and the beavers were tufts of grass from somewhere up river? The deer were probably the only real animals I had seen, because they were now gone.

Well, we can all make mistakes. Nevertheless, I enjoyed my outings and continued to see much animal life, some of it real, I am sure.

The boat gave me much pleasure. I finally had the motor repaired, but it reverted to its old habits as soon as I brought it home. I got used to it and did not hesitate to go out on the river.

Friends from Denver, Gil and Jane, came to visit and, what was more natural than to invite them to see the river's beauty from my boat? This time also Varda would go with us; usually she did not like to be on the water dependent on the, mostly, malfunctioning motor. But everything went well as I took the now very familiar route.

On the way back, I showed off by racing the engine as fast as it could go. How fast can three horse powers push a 2000 lbs pontoon boat? Not very fast, but enough to perceptively raise the bow, thus lowering the stern. That was sufficient for us not to clear a shallow sand bar and, suddenly, we were at a stand still no matter how I revved and manipulated the motor. Putting it in idle, I went over the side and pushed the boat off the bar. The water reached just above the knees.

The gear was put into forward again, but we stayed where we were. It took a while before I realized that we had lost the propeller. With the motor turned off, it was silent and pleasant, but that bliss was marred by our having to paddle back, a strenuous job, not for older people. Varda and Jane settled comfortably on the boat's padded benches. No one, not even I, appreciated the silence and peace that had descended on us. Our boat trip was not, so far, what I had expected.

"How far is it", asked Gil straining at his paddle. "Oh", I said, "Just around that spit of land to the right." We turned the point, but there was no dock in sight. "Sorry, it must be the other spit a bit further ahead", I explained. "There, where the erosion has left a large, brown spot on the bank."

More paddling, more groaning, more disappointment; the dock was not around that spit either. Gil was getting frustrated. His scientific mind questioned my river navigation; surely there must be more to it than guesswork. I, wisely, refrained from averring that our destination was around the next land spit; after all, that landmark looked exactly like those we had already explored. We passed the point. I was prepared for another disappointment, but, behold, there, far at the distant end of the inlet, was the dock. I didn't think the outing had been an unmitigated success.

Gil and Jane left before I managed to put on a new propeller, and Varda reverted to her staying away from river excursions. The true joy of boat ownership was mine alone to enjoy.

However, the craft did provide the solitude I craved mainly because no one wanted to go with me once my many mishaps became known. As to silence, it happened only when the motor was off and that happened only when, twice more, I lost the propeller. With hindsight, I really should have bought a new engine.

Have I found myself? I certainly have. I know I am here, and I have good memories of my walks in the woods, outwitting the bears, and of observing them from a safe distance aboard my boat.

Worthwhile Leisure

Northern Wisconsin must have been created for outdoor life. Fishing, hunting, hiking and boating, that's what makes life in the North worthwhile, be it summer or winter, spring or fall. For me, berry picking in the early fall was the best; hunting was totally out, fishing half in, and boating yet to be explored.

Our neighbor was into berry picking, fishing, boating and helping with my yard's upkeep. He was a huge man, energetic and enormously strong. He had served in the Navy towards the end of WWII and for a few years thereafter. How he lost a lung was never clear; he did not talk about it except to say it was gone. He always wore a baseball cap, usually a checkered flannel shirt, and jeans inserted in heavy, insulated boots worn regardless of weather and temperatures. His face was rectangular, the forehead heavily creased, hair grey but full, and the nose enhanced by a bushy mustache. His speech pattern was colloquial and, at times, incomprehensible to me. He used expressions I was not used to. A "picture" was a "pitcher" and "youse" meant, "you", I think.

A native of the area he had done well financially by investing in a bar and some land. Now he was retired and determined to make the most of it. We rarely saw his wife. She preferred to stay indoors where she practiced organ playing, rather successfully, in my view. Her speech pattern matched that of her husband's and I think she was uncomfortable with the big words I tended to use.

I liked my neighbors, notwithstanding our limited conversations. Both were very kind and helpful. If I began to mow my lawn, he, invariably, brought out his riding mower to help, and ended up doing most of the job. It was the same in winter when he enjoyed his snow-blower on my paths. I reciprocated by being available when he wanted to fish on Lake Superior. The more people with fishing licenses aboard the boat, the more fish he could keep. Since he was in it for quantity, he often asked me and another neighbor, a doctor, to come along.

He had two boats: a big one for lake fishing, a small one for the river. We would go out about five miles, on the lake, before setting the lines. It was pleasant to move towards the fishing ground; the wind generated by the speed was cool and refreshing. But when the lines were set and fishing begun, things changed.

Fishing would not be good, I was told, unless the water was very still and placid. Therefore, he only went out during warm and windless days, and that caused some problems. Once on the fishing spot, there was no wind to mitigate the hot sun. No wind to keep bugs away. Even five miles off shore, there were more gnats and flies than most barns could house. No real movement of the boat, just enough to bring us forward to keep the lines taut. Nothing to do but wait, wait, and wait .... As the doctor said, "watching paint dry would be more exciting". It was boring beyond belief. To keep the tedium at bay, we drank beer and told stories, one more dirty and incomprehensible than the other. After several trips of this kind, none of which yielded any fish, I stopped going out on the lake. The fish store by the docks became a good substitute.

River fishing was more enjoyable. First, we went out in the cool air of the early evening when some bugs were on break. There were still many insects to cope with, but there was, at least, a few minutes respite every time we shifted from one fishing spot to another at high speed. Secondly, we cast our lines, heaved them in, checked the bait, and cast again. No waiting for the fish to come to us; we were going after them. Admittedly, not with much success, but with enthusiasm.

Winter brought ice fishing. Also quite eventless but, given proper clothing, relaxing and peaceful. I enjoyed hiking on the frozen river, to talk to the fishermen widely separated, appearing like dark spots, across the snowy, white expanse, much like floaters in my eyes.

I tried fishing a few times but did not have the right equipment to drill through the ice. Consequently I looked for an existing opening that, while being unused, had not yet frozen over. However, each time, as I was ready to start luring the fish, someone claimed to be the owner of the hole, and I had to move on. That is how I became, and enjoyed being, a river ice hiker.

Berry picking was something else entirely. Like so many others, my neighbor had discovered his own berry patches. While he was willing to share the berry harvest with me, he was not willing to share its location. He, like other berry fans, kept his picking grounds a secret. Along the roads, usually hanging in the trees, one could see all kinds of signs that indicated, to the initiated, where berries were to be found.

Going to his patch, he would drive around for ever, it seemed. I saw clearly that he passed the same landmark several times and so concluded that we were going in circles. Finally we were there. An empty coffee can hoisted up a tree, just off the dirt road, was his sign for the treasure patch.

The place looked like a large bog, but it was dry. No people around, and we started the picking.

It was a wonderful place with a lot of blueberry bushes. From time to time, I stood up to straighten my back. Looked around; still no one to see. But as I was about to bend again, someone, a bit further into the area, stood up to stretch. I realized people were there, they were just not visible when bending down to pick. Somewhat later, another stretch was due and, again, I saw someone, this time at the far end of the field. I felt I should acknowledge a fellow berry picker with a friendly wave, and did so. Much to my surprise, the fellow disappeared taking off with a jump that became a loping run. I could only assume it was a bear. My companion confirmed that; he, too, had seen it.

I was in berry picking heaven. Blueberries, raspberries, blackberries, and berries I did not know the name of, grew wild. I found my own patches and, like everyone else, tried to keep them secret. But I knew from all the cans, jars and cloth strips hanging in the trees, that my secrets were shared, and enjoyed, by many.

Boating Skills

How beautiful is a canoe gliding gracefully over the water propelled by the seemingly effortless, and leisurely, strokes of the paddler. And how impressive and exciting to see it, forcefully controlled by the same paddler, making its way down a rapidly moving river. In my mind's eye I can see myself in either situation.

For a long time I harbored thoughts of taking a canoe trip in northern Minnesota, in the Boundary Waters between the USA and Canada. I could see myself, with minimal effort, traversing open, tranquil waters and, occasionally, with more effort, navigating some narrow passages where the water might be more turbulent. Even though it seemed easy, I felt I should have some exposure to canoeing before setting out.

In 1992 Yael and I decided to gain experience by taking a short canoe trip down the Brule River not too far from our house in Superior. The agent at the boat rental office asked which run we wanted: two miles, five, eight, or twelve? I saw little point in skimping on the experience and suggested eight miles. Seeing the agent's questioning look, clearly doubting our athletic abilities, I admitted this was our first time taking a canoe down a river. He immediately suggested the two mile run; indeed, he would not rent us a canoe for any longer trip. We did accept his ruling and were transported to the proper launch site.

Everything was ready for us, canoe, paddles and life vests. Our starting point was at a square, wooden landing jutting out over the water. The water flowed gently past and disappeared beyond a bend in the river. How to proceed was clear: climb into the canoe, push off and float slowly down stream until we reached the end point. How much simpler and easier could it be? If we completed this run quickly, and there was no reason why we shouldn't, there might even be time to try the next level, five miles.

Into the canoe we went. Not without difficulty because we tended to rock it too much. Finally, sitting with the knees bent in an unnatural angle, we pushed off. All went according to expectations until we reached the bend, about twenty yards from the landing. Beyond the bend, the river abandoned its tranquility.

Suddenly the water rushed fast bringing us along to a rather narrow passage between two rocks. It would not be a problem for a strong, experienced paddler, who could point and hold the canoe in the right direction. Not so for us. We approached the passage broadwise and got stuck. The water was fast, but shallow. We got out and straightened the canoe, lost our grip and it took off on its own through the passage. Luckily it got stuck again at the next bend where we managed to climb aboard.

The whole trip, the two interminable miles of it, proceeded in this fashion. Where the river was reasonably straight, we were aboard, not enjoying it. Where it bent and flowed faster, we were in the water, not enjoying it. Several times the canoe filled with water and had to be emptied by overturning. The canoe was light, but the water was not; it was heavy and hard work to empty it. I am sure we spent more time in the water than on it.

Added to our tribulations was the vivid image we had from Larry McMurtry's *Lonesome Dove* where he describes a river crossing through the bottom nest of cottonmouth moccasins. I had heard that Wisconsin did not have such snakes, but the unease of tramping along the river bottom was close to panic.

We finally made it to the end landing and were brought to our car, wet and miserable. The driver, wisely, refrained from making any comments. There was time for the five mile run, but the two miles we had just traversed sufficed.

My thoughts of a canoe trip in the Boundary Waters had taken a blow, but its placid waters still held my imagination. I needed more training, though. In a rented canoe I began practicing, at our dock, the fundamental skills of getting in and out.

There was no difficulty getting in; I had learnt that on the river run. Now, sitting in the stern I paddled out into the river. It was exhilarating. I could see myself gliding over the water in that beautiful, serene fashion I had always imagined. Reluctantly, I returned to my pier. That was when the trouble started. I could not get out.

My knees had locked. They hurt when I moved. I also had leg cramps. The canoe was too rickety, the space too constrained, to unfold my limbs. The longer I sat there, the more did I hurt. I could not stand up, and to remain on the stern seat was not a solution. I was stuck. What to do? I tried to massage the legs-- to no avail. In desperation I tipped the canoe over and slid into the water. With much spluttering and thrashing I escaped drowning by getting hold of the pier. After a while I was able to move my knees and legs, the cramps subsided and I could move out of the water.

That experience finally brought me to reality: leave canoeing to the young or those who know what they are doing, groups to which I do not belong.

PHOTO GALLERY

"Verna" – in the Baltic coal trade (1945–46). The ship was about 80 years old at the time, and its equipment matched its age.

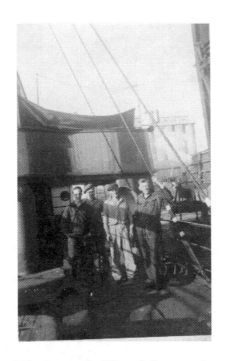

Part of the deck crew on the "Verna". I am on the extreme left.

I, washing my work clothes on the "Verna".

"Rudolf" was newly built. It carried mostly coal from English and Baltic ports.

"Bifrost" traded to north European ports.

"Lillohus", a tanker, traded from Sweden to Curacao, Aruba and Maracaibo.

"Virginia" traded from Sweden and north European ports to western Mediterraen.

"Industria" engaged in the Mediterranean trade. Here seen in southern France. She and "Virginia" belonged to the Swedish Lloyd Co.

"Seattle" was large and modern at the time. It traded from Sweden to the US West coast and belonged to the Johnson Line.

Israeli ship "Etrog". Built in Sweden and seen here prior to delivery. Note the Swedish flag at the stern. It and the "Tappuz" and "Tamar" were sister ships.

Bovine passengers on the "Tappuz" from Norfolk to Israel via Prince Edward Island.

I, on the "Tappuz", with the ship's cat on top of the stalls housing the cows.

The Master Mariners' Class of 1953.
I am at the extreme right in the first row.

Reserve Officers' Class of 1954. Again, I am at extreme right.

One of my fellow cadets at the Naval War College was an able cartoonist and a keen observer of the humorous, and often absurd, aspects of our life. I was at times the subject of his drawings. Here are some of them.

The caption says: "Attention I said!" During a Phys. Ed class I was climbing the ropes when a higher officer entered. As protocol required, the officer in charge called out "Attention". There was little I could do except to try to look as straight and immobile as possible in my hanging position. The high officer lingered; my arms were getting tired and I simply had to move a bit. That movement elicited the call directed at me: "Attention, I said!!" The visiting officer stayed, and stayed, and …. I think he wanted to see my next action to deal with the situation. My arms grew increasingly tired. Finally the choice was to move or to fall. The choice was not hard. With everyone's watching me intently, I moved along the rope to the wall where, high above the floor, I made my best imitation of being at attention. The officer left. I, unlike the others, did not think of it as a particularly funny incident.

ABRAHAM CICERONEN.

... DET DÄR ÄR EN GÖBBE, SOM EN ANNAN GÖBBE MÅLADE NÅGON GÅNG EFTER NÅRA ÅR EFTER EN ANNAN GÖBBES DÖD...

I was appointed to lead tours of the historical castle that was the College. As I was the only one so assigned, the others made much fun of me and my recently acquired knowledge. The art collection did pose some problems given the intricate relationships of kings and noblemen depicted in the paintings The caption is "Abraham the guide" and the text is "... this is a fellow whom another fellow painted some time a few years after another fellow died..."

DEN "BUBBLAN" SPRACK!

This refers to my waking the admiral instead of the ship's commander.
The caption is: "That bubble burst", (which sounds better in
Swedish than in English).

I had on some occasions made fun of the very dry formulaic language used in the filing of formal reports. I suggested they would be more readable if a more personal, perhaps chatty, approach was used. The artist very generously gave me lieutenant's rank. The text reads, "Listen to this air defense report: 'We have wonderful weather here on the islands outside Karlskrona and I just said to Sergeant Jansson that we will not see any airplanes here before Easter. But, what do you know, just then something showed up on the horizon and we all wondered what it could be. Pvt Eriksson guessed they were sailboats but he was wrong. Instead there were many, many airplanes. Best regards from us all'". (Karlskrona is the main naval base in southern Sweden.)

Destroyer #8 "Karlskrona" on which I served my active duty.

Destroyer #9 "Norrkoping" – sister ship to "Karlskrona".

I, awaiting some ceremony alongside the "Karlskrona".

The King, Gustav VI Adolf, inspecting the fleet from a mine sweeper.
The King is on the extreme left. (The person in white, on the right, is carrying
the King's coat.)

*Ball at the Naval War College. Princess Desiree is in the middle of the picture.
I am, in profile, with my escort at the right edge of the picture.*

I as a newly commissioned reserve officer.

Printed in the United States
By Bookmasters